TURN ME ON GUV

'Tails' from the Racecourse

Marcus Armytage

Illustrated by Mark Huskinson

RACING POST

Copyright © Marcus Armytage 2009

The right of Marcus Armytage to be identified as the author of this work has been asserted by him in accordance with the Copyright, Designs and Patents Act 1988.

This edition first published in Great Britain in 2009 by
Racing Post Books
Raceform Ltd, High Street, Compton, Newbury, Berkshire, RG20 6NL

Material reproduced with the kind permission of Telegraph Media Group Ltd

1 3 5 7 9 10 8 6 4 2

A catalogue record for this book is available from the British Library.

ISBN 978-1-905156-62-7

Designed by Fiona Pike
Printed in the UK by CPI William Clowes Beccles NR34 7TL

www.racingpost.com/shop

Contents

ACKNOWLEDGEMENTS

It is a sign of the times that what was a long list of sub-editors on the racing desk at the *Daily Telegraph* is now much smaller. But without Kevin Perry, the racing editor, and his wingmen Steve Dillon and, occasionally, Hugh Bateson knocking my ramblings into shape, the Racing Diary's reputation would not be for light breakfast entertainment. It would be best known as a misspelt strangulation of the English language, invariably truncated at the three quarter point because I invariably write more words than there is space. Adrian Hunt and Mike Roberts undoubtedly did their bit too before they sought pastures new.

The biggest thank-you has to be to all those people who feature in *Turn Me On Guv*, often for telling stories against themselves (and their best friends) and for allowing us to have a bit of fun at their expense. When I spoke to Andrew Thornton, the first story in *Turn Me On Guv*, he was only just out of hospital and was facing the prospect of a long spell on the sidelines with his dislocated shoulder and yet, with great humour, he told me in great detail of his epic journey to hospital in the back of an ambulance.

Maybe it is something to do with working with or around horses but, for sure, no other sport or industry has the capacity to do this in the same way. When did you last read a similar book about multi-millionaire Premiership footballers?

For *Hot Cherry* I was lucky enough to have the great Irish artist Peter Curling as illustrator in residence to not just compliment but improve the stories. This time, in the same role, is Mark Huskinson. I knew he would be a good man to work with when I was given his ink and wash cartoon 'A father's advice' to his son on the birth of my son, Arthur Armytage.

'There are three things you should never do, dear boy,' it reads. 'Never hunt south of Thames, never drink port after champagne and never have your wife in the morning ... lest something better turn up in the afternoon.' I immediately warmed to his sense of humour and I am very glad, albeit briefly, to have collaborated with him.

Introduction

It would have been inappropriate to call this book 'schadenfreude'. Had we done so we might have sold a couple of copies in Germany at best. Alas, the thought of an unattended book signing in Dusseldorf did not quite hold the appeal of one man and a dog attending a similar function at Cheltenham or Newbury so we went with *Turn Me On Guv*, something more traditionally English.

But the German word sums up much of the essence of this collection of anecdotes – the derivation of pleasure from the misfortune of others. I don't feel too bad about that because I like to think I practise a bit of self-schadenfreude – if there is such a thing.

Since I joined the *Daily Telegraph* back in 1993, I have produced a weekly column, the 'racing diary' which, I hope, provides a little light entertainment for those (close relations) who read it at breakfast. That is certainly the idea. Like *Hot Cherry*, this book's predecessor, it is the best (least worst), most recent stories to have appeared in that column which I hope raised a smile at the time and that they continue to do so.

So why 'Turn Me On Guv'? *Hot Cherry* was so called because Hot Cherry, an inflatable doll used to break in a difficult horse, was one of the stars of that book. For continuity we were quite keen on *Hot Cherry Rides Again* but, after suffering a couple of unfortunately terminal puncture wounds on her epic gallop through a Kent village, there was no way she'd ride anything again.

Turn Me On Guv is the punchline to one of the stories involving the Derby winning trainer Mike Bell and the highly successful but also extremely attractive female jockey Hayley Turner but beyond that I will not spoil it for you.

I hope that one of the attractions of the column and, therefore, the book is that it does not require of the reader an intimate knowledge of racing or horses but just a passing interest. It should suit the expert just as well as the man in the street who only really wants to get in front of the television to watch a race once or twice a year, usually to for the National or Derby.

Chapter One

INJURED JOCKEYS' FUN?

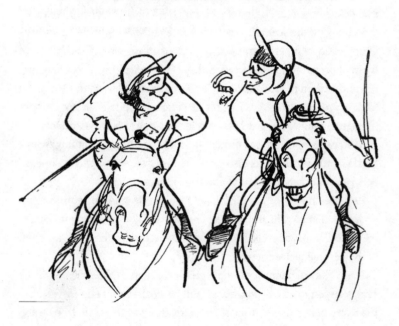

ANDREW THORNTON has had a bit of a tough time of it lately. As I'm sure you're aware, he dislocated his shoulder ten days ago and it will keep him out of Cheltenham and Aintree, where he was due to ride one of the Grand National favourites, Simon. He's taken it all very stoically.

The key to a dislocated shoulder, according to Doc Pritchard (trainer, jockey, GP, racecourse doctor, personal physician to AP McCoy and medical adviser to this column), is getting the ball back in its socket joint as quick as possible. The longer it is out, the longer the recovery period.

So imagine the scene. Thornton, whose fall was in the fifth race, was wrapped in blankets, strapped to one of those stretchers that have hydraulic legs on wheels, was breathing an intoxicating mix of laughing gas and oxygen to ease the agony and was hurtling down the M3 in the back of an ambulance heading for St Peter's Hospital, Chertsey, where the jigsaw puzzle that was his shoulder was due to be reassembled.

Now, remember, he was pretty high and breathing something from a bottle in a mask that was also covering his nose, so you might suppose he was somewhat oblivious to external odours ... but no.

He's not known as the 'Blindman' by his colleagues for nothing and, as you well know, the other senses of the visually impaired are usually enhanced. "Can you smell something funny ... like burning?" he inquired of the paramedic leaning over him.

The paramedic tapped on the window through to the driver. "Oi," he said, "can you smell burning, mate?" But inside the cockpit the driver, from the instrument panel in front of him, already knew he was in trouble and was indicating to pull over on to the hard shoulder. The turbo had gone.

On health and safety grounds – presumably it is better to be squashed by a 20-tonne articulated lorry, into whose path Thornton had now been perilously placed, rather than burned (but the ambulance wasn't actually on fire) – Thornton, his arm somewhere beside him but not quite attached under the blanket, was wheeled out on to the hard shoulder and there he was parked for 20 minutes while a new ambulance and the AA were summoned.

Meanwhile a steady stream of Thornton's colleagues, who had ridden in the seventh race, were now passing him on their way home – and, on seeing a pair of boots sticking out from the end of the stretcher, hooting.

The new ambulance eventually arrived but the all-singing, all-stationary hydraulic stretcher didn't fit – it wasn't quite the right 'spec'. So where you'd usually expect to see wheels being changed, it was instead the patient – by this stage losing the will to live – who was being changed, from one stretcher to another.

Meanwhile, in true Carry On style, the first ambulance driver, who was going nowhere fast, started moaning. "Bloody 'ell," he said. "I'm supposed to be knocking off in half an hour."

"Shit," said Thornton, who had by this stage lost most things including his Grand National winner but not his humour. "You've had a bad day then!" MARCH 4, 2008

LAST WEEK a car-load of jump jockeys including Jason Maguire, Mark Bradburne, Jimmy McCarthy and Timmy Murphy got as far as Carlisle before Musselburgh was abandoned and, as the snow-capped mountains of the Lake District were all about them, there followed a collective decision to go skiing. But where?

The geographically challenged McCarthy suggested Glenshee, a further four hours north, quite apart from the fact that it was only accessible to those with snow ploughs, helicopters or reindeer.

Having dismissed this idea, they decided to head back south to the Tamworth Snowdome, where a certain level of experience is one of the prerequisites for a day pass.

That was fine for Bradburne, brought up on the usually muddy slopes of Aviemore, and for Murphy, who claimed to have skied once before. But while McCarthy, still smarting over his geographic faux-pas, at last demonstrated a degree of wisdom by sitting it out as a spectator, Maguire, a man in terrific form at the moment, decided to bluff it. "Sure, grand, not a bother," he replied to the question, "have you ever skied before?"

As soon as he hit the snow at the top of the lift he turned his first somersault. This was not so much falling at the first as being unseated in the paddock. After being picked up by a sympathetic snowboarder, he pointed his skis in a downhill direction and proceeded, rapidly.

But while scientists have made great strides in the steering of modern-day smart bombs, which can go round street corners and stop at traffic lights, this was more like the good old-fashioned torpedo, unable to deviate from the course it had been set.

So much so, in fact, that when he came to an area dolled off for novice skiers under instruction, he quickly found himself wrapped round a plastic bollard at the feet of an instructor.

His colleagues – I hesitate to call them 'friends' – who by this stage were finding their skiing impaired by tears of laughter, made no effort at mounting a rescue. So Maguire attempted to get back upright and, apologising profusely to the instructor, now found his skis pointing perfectly parallel, but up the slope. Soon gravity was doing its thing, taking him backwards downhill at a gathering gallop.

Now I can testify to the fact that there's nothing worse than riding a runaway horse towards an impenetrable obstacle but even I can't imagine how it feels if, as it were, you're on that horse backwards.

Somehow, though, he managed to pull up half an inch from the barrier at the bottom and, for the benefit of other skiers and more particularly his own safety, he was escorted off the snow and described, probably not for the first time in his life, as a 'liability'. FEBRUARY 17, 2009

SATURDAY will be some sort of anniversary for John Francome, though not one he will particularly want to celebrate. It was in the Grand National, riding Golden Rapper, that he took one of the worst falls of his career. The gelding fell at Becher's second time and broke the Greatest Jockey's wrist.

"I think of him every time I look at the lump on the back of my hand,"

he says fondly. "He'd gone a circuit and a half right down the inner and never put a foot wrong or left a twig out of place. Then he jumped Becher's and forgot to put his legs down. I've got a picture of him landing, his nose is on the ground, his front legs are still neatly tucked up underneath him and, of course, my eyes are shut."

This week, however, the Channel 4 Racing pundit and bestselling author is back in the wars. He's off games, golf in particular, with a wing up. He broke his collarbone playing football but it was not, as you might expect, in the rough and tumble of a game. It was in his backyard by himself – making witnesses somewhat hard to find.

"I was kicking a ball around and tried to do a Ronaldo-style step-over, trod on the ball and tipped upside down," he says. "The first thought that occurred to me was 'what a silly ****er'."

Of course a broken collarbone may be normal for jockeys but it is fairly detrimental to the swing of a golfer. So, until this latest hiccup, what was the Francome handicap? "As it's always been – myself," he says. APRIL 5, 2005

AGEING jump jockey Warren Marston, who has just returned from a month-long ban, was moaning to trainer Richard Phillips about his dislike of dentists and his impending visit to one. "Why don't you just send them in the post?" suggested Phillips, not unreasonably. MAY 2, 2005

MARTIN DWYER arrived at Ascot on Friday to be informed that his name had been selected out of the hat for the jockeys' random dope test. The news was imparted to him by the clerk of the scales, Caroline Carr, who is much appreciated for her sense of humour.

"That's fine," said a slightly resigned Dwyer, "but you should know this is the third time my name's been selected in the last fortnight."

"Well," she replied, "perhaps it's time you stopped cycling to the races." JULY 31, 2007 – SHORTLY AFTER ANOTHER TOUR DE FRANCE DOPING SCANDAL.

WITH the recent passing of George MacDonald Fraser you might have thought we'd finally heard the last of Harry Flashman. But the spirit of the great Victorian soldier and anti-hero lives on – in jockey Warren Marston.

We've lost count of the would-be amateur jockeys from Richard Phillips' yard who have tipped up, on Marston's earnest advice, at the saddlers, Mangan & Webb, in Stow-on-the-Wold, asking for left-handed whips.

His most recent victim is Adam Wedge, who has had a couple of rides in bumpers and, according to the trainer, can "actually ride a bit". From Phillips that's high praise indeed.

But Mr Wedge (7lb) made the mistake while riding out recently of telling Marston, wind-up merchant extraordinaire, that the chimney in his cottage was smoking and that he needed to find a sweep.

"I'll tell you what," said the stable sage, "you want to get hold of a bloke called Twist. He's the best around here."

Picking up on the conversation in front of him, Phillips' assistant, Gordon Clarkson, chipped in. "Yeah," he said. "I can't remember his first name but it begins with 'O'; it's Oliver or something. Go and see the secretary at breakfast and she'll get his number from directory inquiries."

At breakfast the trainer was just exiting the office when the amateur barged past him in a rush. "Where you off to in such a hurry?" he inquired.

"I need a number for a chimney sweep," he replied.

"Ah," said Phillips, "you need Eddie, that's who we use."

"No," said the amateur. "Warren says Mr O Twist is the man for the job and that Joline will be able to find his number."

Out of the corner of his eye Phillips, shaking his head in disbelief, could see Marston smiling – it's not his own smile, obviously, because the teeth are false – across the yard.

"How did you get on with that number?" asked Marston, senior lecturer at Adlestrop's university of life, later.

"They wouldn't look it up for me," replied the amateur. "They're mental in that office, both the trainer and the secretary were shaking their heads and almost in tears." His search for a sweep continues. JANUARY 22, 2008

IT IS reassuring to know that there is still the semblance of a pecking order in the weighing room and that young up-and-coming conditional jockeys still have some respect for those colleagues old enough to be their fathers.

There is a big meeting coming up at Newbury but cast your mind back to the last meeting about ten days ago. In the first race, a two-mile hurdle, a loose horse was running about erratically and interfering with the other runners down the back straight.

It knocked into Willie McCarthy on the eventual third – a horse close to my heart because it is named after my favourite fashion item, Tank Top. He in turn squeezed up Warren Marston, riding Storm Surge.

It is a good rule of thumb that the older a jockey the more vocal he is and, unable to see that the root cause of the problem was the loose horse, Marston started swearing at McCarthy.

"Oi you ****, give me some ****ing ... " he said, his sentence coming to an abrupt end before he could complete it, presumably with the word 'daylight'. His gumshield and false teeth had flown the nest, as it were.

On their return to the weighing room McCarthy went to apologise to Marston. "Oh don't worry about that," mumbled Marston, much in the manner of Lester Piggott. "It's not a problem but I've lost my teeth and that is. I'm in the next, do us a favour and go and find them. They're between the second and third flights down the back straight, three hurdles out from the inside."

When Marston returned from his next ride he found his teeth in a glass of water beside his peg. McCarthy may not go to heaven for it but he rode a winner, Ballyfoy, later in the day. FEBRUARY 4, 2008

EVERY jockey riding remembers his first ride over the Aintree fences. In fact so memorable is that first taste of The Chair and Becher's Brook that most jockeys take the recollection of it to the grave.

John Maxse, 38, the Jockey Club's PR director, waited a long time to have his first ride at Aintree and, in his mount, Gielgud, he appeared to have the perfect conveyance in Thursday's Fox Hunters. Alas, the horse fell heavily at the eighth, knocking him unconscious. He was back racing yesterday to watch Senorita Rumbalita, a horse in whom he has a share.

So, in a sort of tribute, the rest of this Aintree Diary for 2006 is John's entire memory of his first ride over the big fences: APRIL 6, 2008

SEAN QUINLAN, a conditional jockey attached to Richard Phillips' yard, won the Jockeys' Jumping at Finmere Show on Sunday, a prize that used to be prestigious until the advent of Sunday racing. Having never showjumped before, instead of looking for a stride, he went flat out down to the 5ft 4in obstacle in the final – on the basis that the horse might knock it down but it wouldn't be possible for it to refuse. "He's a very brave rider," confirms his trainer. "I think it's because his IQ is a negative number." AUGUST 8, 2006

IF THE Coral-Eclipse is anything to go by considerable attention to detail is being given to tactics in the ops room at Ballydoyle before their multiple challenges on the Group 1 races. Though it failed to work for George Washington on Saturday, a 1-2-3 in the St James's Palace Stakes and Irish Derby suggests they get it right more often than not.

Just before the Derby Aidan O'Brien gathered round his six jockeys, all of whom were fellow countrymen but several of whom weren't regular Ballydoyle riders, to give them their instructions.

"Mick you do this," he whispered, half under his breath as he does. "Seamie, I want you to do that." And so it went on. Eventually he got to the last of them. "And I want you," he said, "to take it up at the t'ree."

Not wanting there to be any confusion over his instructions and what with the top side of Epsom being quite a wooded place, the Ballydoyle new recruit replied earnestly: "And which tree would that be, boss?" JULY 10, 2007

BEING a jockey and a trainer means that Carl Llewellyn has more than his fair share of riding colleagues pitching up to ride out. In the last few weeks alone he's had AP McCoy, Seamus Durack, Timmy Murphy, Andrew Tinkler, Will Kennedy, Robert Lucey-Butler and, obviously, himself riding out.

Of course, there's nothing more likely to put stable girls in a spin than the presence of a few top-ranking jockeys but the opportunity to look attractive with a muck-sack on your back is, we're all agreed, limited. I think even Kate Moss would struggle there but, apparently, at Weathercock House there's no lack of trying. A neighbouring trainer's wife recently described Llewellyn's first lot as "death by mascara". OCTOBER 10, 2006

ONEWAY, who is unbeaten in four outings, is just beginning to repay Mark Rimell – one of the few trainers who also holds a licence to ride – for their first outing in a point-to-point together.

In fact, having spent his youth behaving like he was a first cousin once removed of Oliver Reed, it is even beginning to look like Mark, now 34, settled, married and training at Leafield near Witney, is a chip off the old Rimell block. Grandfather Fred trained four Grand National winners while grandmother Mercy won the Champion Hurdle.

Last week he paid £330 to enter Oneway in the Champion Chase "just in case" he wins his next engagement, the Victor Chandler Chase, handsomely. It's all a long way from that first point-to-point, however.

Mark and Oneway were striding on down the back at Barbury Castle when Oneway, who at the time had the "attention span of a gnat", took his eye off the fence to take a look at the fence judge and turned a somersault. The trainer came round believing the horse had killed them both.

Having ridden Oneway all last season, when the summit of his achievement was a minor amateur race, Mark gave up the ride at Worcester in October when he had too little weight. Needless to say, racing's television pundits put the improvement in form down to the change of jockey. In fact the reason was pin-firing during the summer to cure sore shins, from which he had suffered throughout last season.

Now that he is beginning to be taken seriously as a trainer Mark, who picked Oneway as an unbroken store, is employing someone else other than himself to ride. Last season, his first as a trainer, it was handy to gauge the fitness of his horses. Now he puts up other jockeys when the horse belongs to an outside owner. "If you cock up," says Mark, "you're liable to get two bollockings; one for giving it a duff ride and the other for putting up the jockey." JANUARY 11, 2005

JOHN FRANCOME and Steve Smith Eccles were leaving the stewards' room one day after Francome had been awarded a race and Smith Eccles demoted to second. "He must be ****ing blind," said Smith Eccles in a stage whisper to Francome, in reference to the head steward who had made the decision.

"What did you say, Smith Eccles?" challenged the steward, who had heard perfectly well.

Smith Eccles, still in a stage whisper, turned to Francome again. "What's more," he said, "he must be ****ing deaf as well." APRIL 11, 2006

SEVERAL jockeys use a gumshield but, hitherto, the champion AP McCoy is not among them. When he slipped up on the bend in the Robin Cook Memorial – he won't forget Robin Cook in a hurry after this – on Risk Accessor one of his front teeth was shunted backwards and three others had their angle of orientation altered.

When a call was put out over the public address to see if there was a dentist in the house the authorities were pleasantly surprised when five came forward. They were, however, unanimous in their diagnosis. He needed to see a maxilo-facial surgeon. Having had such success with their dentists, the authorities weren't going to push their luck asking for one of them. DECEMBER 13, 2005

JIM CULLOTY was over from Ireland at the weekend to receive a tribute at Cheltenham's Open Dinner. Richard Pitman, in an on-course interview, put it to Jim, now training point-to-pointers in Ireland, that he would now be running horses round fields with a course marked out by big bales – which is how some deeply rural courses in Ireland operate.

This prompted Jim to recall how one of Ireland's crack amateur riders Michael O'Connor happened upon the sobriquet 'Mick the Bale'.

Mick was riding a fancied horse in one of these point-to-points and, despite travelling well enough to go round the outside of the horse in front, he tried to sneak up the inner on the last bend. The consequence of this action was that the rider of the horse in front squeezed him up, forcing his mount to run into the big bale that they were supposed to race round rather than through.

The big bale, being pretty much the same size and weight as a horse, up-ended Mick's mount. After a couple of somersaults the jockey eventually rolled down the track to a halt. There, none the worse physically for his fall, he sat up with head held in hands in disgust at himself for attempting the manoeuvre, which had cost him a certain winner, and with contempt for the rival who had put him into the straw.

However, he had dislodged the bale enough to turn it on its side and set it in motion and as he sat there, contemplating life as you do after a fall, the bale gathered momentum, rolled down the track, rolled straight over the top of him and knocked him out. To this day he's known as Mick the Bale. NOVEMBER 15, 2005

RICHARD JOHNSON was unable to fulfil an engagement to tip a few horses to a corporate box at Cheltenham so sent up young Tom Scudamore as a replacement. It was Tom's first such 'brown envelope' job and all he had to remember was the box number. Recently married (to Boo Scu), he has, you'd imagine, become more organised and arrived bang on time.

Anyway he delivered his tips and, slightly more nervous than you might be before going out to ride Redemption in a chase, did not question why the guests in the box initially looked puzzled.

It turned out, however, that he was talking to the wrong box. The tips, it turned out, weren't much good either so it saved the original box a fortune on two counts: they didn't have to pay him and they didn't follow his suggestions. He's adamant a Cheltenham official pointed him in the wrong direction. NOVEMBER 15, 2005

BARRY FENTON, the jump jockey who broke a leg for the third time in January, has not been idle during his enforced layoff – though the trainer Emma Lavelle wishes he had.

To amuse himself and help out the Andover-based trainer, who wanted to re-lay an existing sand gallop and install a four-furlong trotting ring, he hopped on a digger and set to work. He reckoned he'd accomplished the removal of sand from the gallop with some aplomb, a debatable description of his work and the untidy dunescape beside the gallop as it turns out. He moved on to digging out the trotting ring, crucially upsides another jockey and fellow Irishman Liam Cummins, whose calling came when he heard the old Village People number 'In the Navy' and mistook it for 'In the Navvy'.

As any trainer will tell you it is unwise to let two jockeys gallop horses together because a competitive edge often takes over and, though hindsight is a wonderful thing, letting two loose in a pair of JCBs was equally unwise. Having completed about 40 yards of the four-furlong track the pair had not only excavated off course – it was like an oil pipeline heading for Salisbury – but they had dug to different specifications; one to three feet, the other to 18 inches. Their groundwork, to put it mildly, was undulating in a ridge and furrow sort of way.

Having seen their morning's handiwork, Emma confiscated both sets of digger keys and sought professional help from Malcolm Cox, a digger driver lent to her for a fortnight by Newbury racecourse.

He arrived to be met by the trainer and her slightly sheepish jockey, and cast his professional eye over the mess in front of him. "Oh my God," he exclaimed. "What sort of idiot cowboy have you let loose on a digger round here?"

A blushing Fenton, not wanting to dwell on the cowboy's identity, could only concur with him that the man had, indeed, been an 'eejit' of the highest order. August 16, 2005

THE following story will have resonance with all those who go hunting on a regular basis and are familiar with the terminology. Hunting regulars, therefore, are advised to skip the next introductory paragraph.

For the uninitiated it is worth knowing that on any given day a hunt usually appoints a couple of subscribers to ride along at the back, armed with lengths of bailer-twine, on gate-shutting duty making sure all gates are closed, demolished fences patched up and that no stock gets out. So while everyone else is having a terrific time crossing the country with carefree abandon up front, they're up to their knees in mud struggling to put a rusty gate back on its hinges three-quarters of a mile behind.

Tom Doyle, who has just returned to Ireland to ride for Jim Culloty's burgeoning yard, was recently booked to ride a horse who was terminally slow, although the trainer did not wish to convey that news to the jockey in quite such blunt terms.

"Have you been hunting lately?" he asked the jockey when he came into the paddock.

"Why's that?" replied Tom, thinking it a slightly obscure question.

"Well," said the trainer, "you're on gates today." OCTOBER 16, 2007

ONE of AP McCoy's more devoted female fans has opened up a website dedicated to the great man. It is full of photos and there's a forum where similarly like-minded girls (mainly, I think) use words like 'hunk' to describe the 10st male waif.

Now, as you probably know, Seamus Durack, with a broken leg, has had time on his hands and, much to his glee, he discovered this site and thought he'd have some fun at his colleague's expense. He wrote an email to the gushing forum purporting to be from a certain Mike Hunt. The gist of it was that not only is McCoy vastly overrated but "let's face it, not that good-looking either".

The following day Durack checked the forum to see if his email had been 'pinned up'. It hadn't. Instead there was a curt new instruction on the forum. "Any abusive post will be deleted and reported," it read. Mission accomplished. OCTOBER 18, 2005

THE Australian jump jockeys team of Paul Hamblin, Brad McLean, Brett Scott and the injured Craig Durden slipped quietly into the country from Ireland for a one-race competition against the British at Plumpton on Sunday. They won the competition too – unlike some Australian tourists this summer. Plumpton, however, did not let them forget the Ashes. At lunch the three tables at which they sat were titled 'Edgbaston', 'Trent

Bridge' and 'The Oval'. SEPTEMBER 20, 2005 FOLLOWING ENGLAND'S EPIC
ASHES WIN.

WE GET plenty of letters here from grateful punters wishing to pass on
their thanks to AP McCoy – any in respect of Kia Kaha at Cheltenham
on Saturday should include a percentage of your winnings – but we had
one with a difference last week.

Andrew Chilton pointed out that the great Victorian jockey Tom
Cannon had two sons, the first named 'Mornington' after a horse Cannon
rode on the day of his son's birth and the other named 'Kempton' after the
racecourse where he rode a winner on the day of the second's birth. "What
a good thing," Andrew concludes, "AP gave up his rides at Huntingdon."
It should also be pointed out that the winner he missed, Sunnyhillboy,
would hardly have been ideal for his daughter either. NOVEMBER 20, 2007
– SHE IS CALLED EVE.

YOU HAVE TO hand it to Hennessy. While many sponsors are here today
and gone tomorrow they have stood the test of time. This weekend their
Hennessy Cognac Gold Cup is run for the 50th time and it is believed to be
not just the oldest continually sponsored race but the oldest commercially
sponsored sporting event in Europe and probably the world.

That first race, run at Cheltenham for two years until Hennessy realised
the racecourse didn't sell their brandy, was worth £5,272. On Saturday it
will be worth £150,000 while the cup itself, 9ct gold, is valued at £30,000.

You may have read elsewhere that to celebrate this anniversary
Hennessy have decided to give the winning jockey his weight in Cognac.
They toyed with the idea of doing the same for the trainer but they saw
Charlie Egerton had Montgermont in the race, looked at their cash flows
and realised they couldn't take the hit.

Needless to say the idea of giving the winning jockey his weight in brandy
has caused a few raised eyebrows for several reasons. A number of jockeys,
like AP McCoy, are teetotal. At the other end of the scale is Timmy Murphy,

a former alcoholic, to whom it also wouldn't be much use. And in between, if it's anything like my day, there are several borderline cases.

A 10st jockey would win 45 bottles or 567 pints of brandy which, if misused, makes it the first all-in-one DIY suicide and self-embalming kit ever given out for winning a race. Sadly Hennessy have slightly had to back-track to appease the pc police by saying that they could give the money equivalent instead. I hope they don't.

But, alas, it's worse than that. Despite the fact that pubs are now open all hours, because Hennessy have responsibly signed up to the nanny state's sensible drinking initiative, should the winning jockey accept the cognac, Hennessy will only be allowed to deliver it at a maximum two bottles a week. If, for example, they were unlucky and jockey Peter Buchanan were to win it they will have to make 23 separate deliveries to Fife. NOVEMBER 21, 2006

ONE of the revelations of this season has been jump jockey Peter Buchanan. Last season he kicked home a miserly three winners, this time it's 36 and rising. His two wins on Forest Gunner have comprised a victory round Aintree and Saturday's Red Square Vodka Gold Cup and he has ridden 24 of Lucinda Russell's 25 winners. He was at the dentist for the 25th.

What's more, if he wasn't claimed to ride the fancied Strong Resolve by Russell in the National he'd be agonising between that horse and Forest Gunner.

Despite having the next most Scottish name after MacDonald and living there, Peter is from Northern Ireland, so he is. His father runs a menswear shop near Belfast but a life in tailoring was never going to suit him. Before Saturday the height of his achievement was representing Northern Ireland in the junior European three-day-event championships at Blair in Scotland. Whatever he does, it seems, takes him back to Scotland.

Aged 26, he is also something of a late starter but his early years were put to good use. He spent a year at Trinity College, Dublin studying science but even there splitting the atom was always going to come off second best to riding. After a year he swapped to the University of Dublin and read accounting.

Last year, seeking to turn professional, he moved to Howard Johnson and spent one season there. In the summer he rode Catch The Perk for Russell. Horse and jockey have since reeled off six wins together and so often was he riding for the Scottish trainer that he moved further north.

He has now taken over as the jockey who travels the furthest. In fact the only time he has disappointed Russell was in his choice of new car. "He used to have a beaten-up old Rover," says the trainer whose own education was at St Trinian's – on an overnighter to Haydock she organised sleeping bag races in the lads' accommodation. "With all his winning percentages I was expecting him to buy a Lexus or something sporty. Instead he went for a boring Renault Laguna." That, Lucinda, is form working out. He did study accountancy, didn't he?

She is also ambitious for him to get his HGV driver's licence so he can also drive the horses to the races. "I've given him the forms but they haven't got beyond his 'pending' tray," she says. The Laguna, positively sporting compared to the lorry, did 2,000 miles in the first eight days that he had it. FEBRUARY 22, 2005

IT WAS just like the old days when 11 'jumping greats' and field-shelter salesman Simon Sherwood lined up for the Cortaflex Charity Flat Race at Kempton on Sunday. The race, appropriately given that most of them will be on the stuff before long, was sponsored by Cortaflex, the herbal joint remedy, and was run in aid of Sparks, Spinal Research and Racing Welfare.

All the riders could be in trouble for breaking the law on assisted suicide – the race was partly run to publicise Richard Dunwoody's next polar trip, a two-month, 650-mile trek across Antarctica following a route that foiled Shackleton early on in the last century. And the auction beforehand was notable for the fact that both John Francome and Hywel Davies made bids – albeit unsuccessful. But it's a start.

When Francome opened his racing bag, he discovered a *Sporting Life* from the last time he rode in a geriatric jockeys' race – back in 1992. It was to mark the occasion of the first Sunday jump meeting at Cheltenham. Among the jockeys riding that day were a Mr D Pipe while a little-known trainer in his first season, Paul Nicholls, had a runner.

"Dunwoody could remember that he won Ride of the Day that day," said Francome afterwards. "How sad is that? A few weeks in the cold ought to do him some good."

Describing the event, he added: "It was like an apprentice race. The one amateur, Simon Sherwood, was all over the place, even though he won it. If it had been a proper race he'd have been given enough time off to go with Dunwoody – and walk there."

Dunwoody has been trotting round Richmond Park scaring the deer by dragging a tyre behind him as he trains for his unsupported trip with James Fox and a guide, Doug Stoup. It will involve starting from the Filchner Ice Shelf and take in a 3,000m climb to the South Pole. Part of his training involves bulking up and, even set to carry 12st, he was, for the first time in his life, a pound overweight. "I didn't bother trying to cheat with the weight," he said. That is probably because I still have his original pair of cheating boots. OCTOBER 22, 2007

BEN HITCHCOTT, the shortest jump jockey, has retired with the stirring quote: "I've ridden for some nice people and some bloody idiots, and the idiots know who they are." It has set a number of trainers looking in the mirror.

Ben, 25, who managed to squeeze in just the 47 days with the Old Surrey & Burstow Hunt last season, gets more kicks jumping a five-bar gate out hunting than "wrestling a bear round a racecourse".

He is to say goodbye to delicate and clean hands to become a farrier. "It's City money in the countryside," he says, a pronouncement he probably won't repeat once qualified in five years but with which anyone who pays a blacksmith's bill will concur. JUNE 23, 2006

TWO CHAPS were at the bar in a Cotswold pub when in walked a young man who they'd never seen before. "All right, mate?" they asked. "What'ya been up to?"

"Just been schooling horses," he replied. "Nothing beats the thrill of jumping horses at a fast pace."

"What, you a jockey, are you?" they asked as one.

"Yep," he said.

"How do you do? I'm Dan and this is Warren," said one of the two. "You must tell us what it's like to be a jockey."

"Well," he said, "you probably wouldn't understand, it's hard to explain to people who've never done it before. But, you know, enormous highs, crushing lows. Great thrills."

"Don't you ever hurt yourself?" asked Dan.

"No. No fear in me. I just attack every fence."

"You wouldn't catch me doing anything as daft as that," pointed out Dan.

"Yeah," he replied. "That's what everyone says. But I'm an adrenalin junkie. It's the only thing that would keep me occupied."

After carrying on for some time like this the jockey went over to the mates he had arranged to meet in the pub. "Just been talking to those two lads over there," he said. "Who are they?"

"Well," replied one of his mates, "one's Dan Forte who won the Hennessy on Cogent and the other's Warren Marston, and where do you want to start on the winners he's ridden?"

The young man who, it turns out, had had just three rides in races, put his head in his hands and left the pub shortly afterwards. Soon he turned up working for Richard Phillips. "I did smile at him the first time I went in to ride out afterwards," says Warren, who hopes to be back from his broken ankle in ten days' time. "He's actually not a bad bloke."

JANUARY 24, 2006

NOW that he has been fitted with a new hip, Adlestrop trainer Richard

Phillips is back riding out again. He has always regarded himself as one of the greatest jockeys never to be offered a ride and last week he rode a bit of 'swift' upsides Timmy Murphy "There was nothing between them," said impartial spectator Choc Thornton, "except seven and a half stone." SEPTEMBER 25, 2007

JOCKEYS occasionally get hurt in schooling accidents. Limbs are broken and bruised, brains concussed and, in Jenny Pitman's day, compound fractures to the ego a not uncommon occurrence. However, news comes from Lambourn of a doubly unique schooling injury.

I say 'doubly' because, for starters, it involved the trainer or, more correctly, her husband who wasn't on a horse and, secondly, it involved a lost finger and that must be a first. And by 'lost' I don't mean like a mutt that strays and might well turn up at a dog pound later in the day. There is, it seems for John Taylor, no coming back for the top inch and a half of his tickling finger.

Having chronicled in previous editions of this diary how John managed to get an ocean-going racing yacht stuck in Uplands Lane and how he managed, one Punchestown meeting, to wedge his horsebox under an arch at Rathsallagh Hotel, this accident may not altogether come as a surprise.

I also stood back once and admired him felling a large elm tree. A man of great practicality, he had, by means of Pythagoras, worked out where it would fall and cleared the space accordingly.

However, when the moment came it pivoted round vindictively, narrowly missed him and chose for its landing site a hen house. The consequence of this miscalculation was a lot of clucking, enough stuffing for several feather duvets and scrambled eggs for breakfast.

John designed his schooling fences himself; by means of hydraulics, they would swing on and off the all-weather gallop at the press of a button, along the same principles as the fences at Clairefontaine. That this is not an altogether trustworthy system was evident at the Normandy course recently when the hydraulics failed, on the last circuit, to remove

the fence just before the winning post from the course. Heads down, in a terrific drive for the finish, the leading three horses turned somersaults upon meeting this unexpected obstacle just short of the line.

John's hydraulics also failed with equally drastic consequences. When they jammed he sought to un-jam them manually, a manoeuvre, it seems, he achieved with partial success. The steel frame of the fence landed on a steel block and, crucially, the Taylor digit. He had an Aron Ralston moment. Ralston, you'll remember, sawed off his arm with a blunt knife after a climbing accident in Colorado. John didn't wait five days to be rescued though. He tied some baler-twine round his arm as a tourniquet, pulled what remained of his finger out, recovered a few bits of flesh and drove home in the tractor. The stump is now mending, one presumes, under a rather filthy-looking plaster. "If one is stupid enough to stick your finger in an unsafe place there's a good chance you might lose it," says John, seeking no sympathy, with the moral of the story. OCTOBER 26, 2004

RICHARD JOHNSON'S wedding to Fiona Chance, daughter of Gold Cup-winning trainer Noel, went off smoothly at Belmont Abbey in Herefordshire at the weekend.

While it is traditionally the father of the bride who takes the biggest hit financially on a wedding, Johnson chipped in with the wine and while the jockey is not tight – in fact he's really quite generous – he's very well known in his circles for knowing the price of everything.

A few months back, after a wine-tasting session to select a suitable vintage, one of his trainers, Richard Phillips, knowing Johnson would be absolutely clueless about what he'd been tasting, asked him what red they'd be drinking at the wedding.

"I'm not sure," said Johnson, "but it begins with an 'F'."

"Oh," said Phillips, "you mean a Fleurie, do you?"

"No, I remember what it is now," replied Johnson. "Five pounds, 23 pence."

It was very good by all accounts. SEPTEMBER 28, 2007

IT MAY never have been safe to be a jump jockey but now more than ever; the spoof phone call is all the rage.

During the winter Dominic Elsworth rang Felix de Giles, a day after he had ridden a winner for the Queen, pretending to be Prince William.

After congratulating him at length – with de Giles replying 'yes, your royal highness' occasionally – Elsworth invited him and 'Adrian' (getting a first name so wrong makes it more plausible – it's Andrew) Tinkler ("he looks like jolly good fun") up to Boujis for an evening's nightclubbing.

More recently, to kill time between Lambourn and Wetherby, Kevin Tobin, in one car full of jockeys, rang Sam Jones, in another packed car. After massaging Jones's ego ("you're the only conditional jockey people want to speak to these days") he asked him if he could go through the card for the public on his arrival.

Jones accepted and spent the next two and a half hours going through the form. The jockeys in the first car even won their bet that, before leaving the weighing room for the non-existent interview, he would vainly glance in the mirror and straighten his hair.

In the first car with Tobin, enduring a 'wasted' journey, was David

Crosse who had been going up to Wetherby for one ride which, soon after setting off, he'd been informed was a non-runner. "I can't believe Sam's so gullible," he said. "The thick ****."

But one member of the car had already texted Nicky Henderson's assistant, Jamie Snowden, as they had left Lambourn telling him to ring Crosse, pretending to be the trainer of his one ride, and inform him that the horse was a non-runner. It wasn't until his valet gave him his silks and insisted that he get changed that Crosse realised he, too, had been had. APRIL 8, 2008

BEST wishes to Charlie Egerton's secretary Lucy Cowan who is recovering in the Ridgeway Hospital, Wroughton. Riding East Lawyer, she was going for her third win of the point-to-point season when her mount pitched her head first into Kingston Blount's turf ten days ago.

She fractured her T1 vertebra, bust ribs, collapsed a lung, lost a tooth, and, probably worse than the others put together, she 'de-gloved' her bottom lip, the medical term for tearing it from the gum, something that is, she confirms, as painful as it sounds.

The irony is that her father, Alastair, broke his neck at precisely the same fence 35 years ago. "The only good thing was he went back a year later and won the race," she said. "I hope to do the same."

Initially she was taken to Stoke Mandeville, it being the local hospital. The medical team surveying the wreck thought, on top of the catalogue of broken bits, that she was having a fit. A fit? Not quite ... she was furious. Having seen them cut her father's silks off her body, they were about to take the knife to her racing boots. "You can't do that," she screamed, "they're Jimmy McCarthy's." APRIL 29, 2008

TOM DOYLE recently got married in Ireland. Among the congregation, sitting next to each other, were AP McCoy and Jim Culloty.

McCoy: "Fair play to her for turning up."

Culloty: "Fair play to him for turning up – after all we've told him about marriage."

McCoy: "Ah – why should he be happy?" JULY 15, 2008

IT IS hardly a toy poodle, the slightly – if I might be so bold – effeminate choice of breed for French champion jockeys. But if as it is often said, an owner comes to look like his dog or vice versa then it would appear our rather more macho champion jockey Seb Sanders still has some way to go before he gets mistaken for his French mastiff.

She is a dog so big you could put a saddle on her according to his former colleague Kevin Darley. Otherwise known as the Dogue de Bordeaux, the French mastiff, which is about the same size as a Shetland pony, was historically used for flock protection and as a dog of war. Going back to Roman times it was used to fight against bulls, bears and other dogs.

However passive she may look, somewhere beneath that thick skull and behind the rolls of chin, nose and skin so loose its face looks like a badly upholstered cushion, those old instincts must lurk – so Darley is convinced anyway.

He once – he never again accepted the offer – went to stay with Sanders for a Newmarket meeting and, as the former champion saw it through the dog's eyes, she could (and probably would) have him in the time it takes to run the July Cup. But having won over the bitch, it was his suit that met the sticky end – death by drool and slobber.

The following morning a builder wandered into the kitchen where Darley happened to be. The cumbersome dog jumped up, putting a paw on either of the new arrival's shoulders. In that interminable moment when he wasn't sure whether he'd be greeted by tongue or dispatched by teeth, he squeaked, somewhat panic-stricken, to Darley: "What do I do now?"

The jockey, who has clearly seen too many cop movies, replied slowly and deliberately: "Put ... the drill ... down."

Bad news for visitors Chez Sanders, the bitch has gone and had eight puppies and she's on the SAS side of protective about them. "I won't go near the place," says the jockey's driver, Keith. "Bravery is not part of my job description." JULY 22, 2008

ABLE to ride at 7st 7lb, William Buick probably doesn't cast a very big shadow at the best of times but David Probert, 19, another apprentice with Andrew Balding at Kingsclere, is rapidly emerging from it. Last week he rode his first double and the week before he won a valuable £100,000 handicap at Newmarket's July meeting for his boss.

If he's not well known to the British racing public yet, he is at least well known to the Basingstoke constabulary. He may be 19 but he looks about 12 and, quite apart from the fact that the only painkiller they'd sell him over the counter in a chemist is Calpol, his child-like looks are proving a hassle whenever he goes shopping in the town.

On a recent trip he stopped in his Peugeot 106 to ask an elderly lady for directions. Instead of giving them she demanded to know if he was old enough to drive, took down his number plate and rang Crimewatch. When the local bobby arrived he took one look at the jockey and, before departing empty handed, raised his eyebrows skywards, and said: "Oh God, not you again." JULY 22, 2008

DAVID PROBERT, last season's joint-champion apprentice, has been inadvertently keeping officers and troops alike entertained at Andrew Balding's Kingsclere yard. He was recently called into the office where he was required to fill in a form. One of the questions it asked was for him to name the doctor to whom he is registered and, without hesitation, he wrote down: Dr Fong.

Subsequent research by the trainer has come up with four two-year-olds in the yard by the stallion Dr Fong but, as yet, no doctor practising in the locality under that name. JUNE 9, 2009

THE WEIGHING-ROOM wind-up, as we have alluded to already this jump season, is alive and kicking. The latest jockey to be 'had' is young Hadden Frost, a conditional attached to David Pipe.

He was sitting in the changing room at Taunton recently when one of his more senior colleagues, Mattie Batchelor, wandered back in from weighing out. "Hadden," he said earnestly (I imagine he finds this hard to do with his cheeky chappie man-about-Brighton sense of humour). "There are a couple just outside the weighing room called Rod and Annette who'd like to see you. They say they knew you when you were little and taught you to fish."

Frost went out to find them and even came back to ask Batchelor what they looked like because he couldn't locate them. Eventually he was so intrigued as to the identity of the couple he rang his father, Jimmy, to ask if he could recall a couple called Rod and Annette who taught him to fish. "Someone's pulling your leg," replied Jimmy instantly. "You've been had."

Another jockey on the receiving end was the impressive young Rhys Flint. He gave Tom Scudamore a lift to the races recently and proudly announced as they set off that he had just had a talking satnav installed to help him find his way to the races.

"They're very good," said Scu, "but they stop talking to you eventually if you don't say 'thankyou' to them."

The rest of the journey was spent with Flint saying "thankyou very much" in his Welsh accent every time the good lady opened her mouth to tell him where and when to turn left or right. MARCH 24, 2009

Chapter Two
THERE MUST
BE A BETTER WAY

A FEMALE racegoer, not in the first flush of youth, walked into the racecourse office at Royal Ascot after racing on Friday, wearing nothing but a tailcoat. "I'm terribly sorry," she said, "but I've lost my dress." It makes a change from losing a shirt. JUNE 26, 2007

IRISH trainer Henry de Bromhead will, all being well, have two or three horses to bring over for the Festival in March. The Spoonplayer, Sizing America and Whatareyouhaving will all be entered in a bid to emulate his father Harry's Fissure Seal, who won there in the early '90s.

On Sunday he took delivery of a half-sister to Racing Demon who should be interesting but it was not her imminent arrival that was bothering him last Friday. The bank manager from whom Henry was organising a loan to tart up Knockeen, his yard just outside Waterford, wanted to pay a visit.

That morning Henry had had jeep trouble and that, when the bank manager arrived, was also playing on his mind. The jeep had boiled over – so when he was reversing it out of the yard in order to take your man on a guided tour of the farm and gallops, he was concentrating on the temperature gauge and not where he was driving. He promptly reversed straight into the bank manager's car.

Having taken that remarkably well, certainly better than Henry anticipated, the bank manager then asked whether he would need boots for the tour of the farm instead of the smartly polished loafers he was wearing. "Not at all," replied Henry. "You'll be fine in the jeep."

Naturally he was, as the way things were going, at the furthest point of the farm when the jeep boiled over again and conked out, forcing the occupants to trudge back across several muddy fields. They are apparently a hardy sort, Irish bank managers. Despite having had both his car and shoes ruined by de Bromhead he still granted the loan. FEBRUARY 7, 2006

THERE was a time when Alice Plunkett featured so often in this column that she earned the sobriquet 'the mistress of mishap'. Incidents and accidents included a head-on car crash on the drive down to her parents' farm – the other driver was her father – and the occasion when a horse fell over some poles and, in the ensuing melee, her ear came off. The healing process included the fitting of leeches.

Now married to Captain Sensible, William Fox-Pitt, who clearly keeps one hand on the tiller, and with Ollie and Thomas, her two small children, as her personal assistants, things have been going smoothly for the Channel 4 presenter.

But, I'm glad to say, not that smoothly and all it took to rekindle that old spark was a trip home to her parents, David and Celia, for the normal hectic, flying-about, working weekend. She was doing Channel 4 on the Saturday and had a runner at the nearby point-to-point course at Chipping Norton on the Sunday.

After a frosty night Alice borrowed a car from her mum to nip up to the course to check it was safe to run. The boys (William, he's quite thin you know, Ollie and Tom) all stayed at home with granny because it was so cold; the pointer ran without great distinction, and after a somewhat frenetic day divided, as usual, between horses and small children, the Fox-Pitts finally got back home to Dorset.

Fast forward about three weeks. Christmas has been and gone. Alice, by now banned from driving for speeding, gets a call from her ma. "You won't believe what happened over Christmas, Alice," she said. "The car was stolen. Just checking you haven't borrowed it at all, have you?"

"No, Mum," replied Alice. "Not since the point-to-point three weeks ago." And then there was a brief silence before that tinkling sound of a penny dropping. Celia Plunkett promptly drove the short trip to what is a point-to-point course three days a year and a working farm for the other 362 to find, randomly parked among a field of sheep, the Plunkett second-string vehicle, a white, battered Subaru – with the keys still in the ignition. You can sort of see where Alice gets it from. January 29, 2008

THERE are many ways of arriving stylishly at the races but late, on the back of a low-loader, probably isn't one of them. That is how Fife trainer Sue Bradburne and one of her runners, Almire Du Lia, turned up at Newcastle last Wednesday for the 3.50. "Not a day I wish to repeat," she says.

Things were going swimmingly as she sailed down the A1, a clear road in front of her, the border in her sights and safe in the knowledge that, even with a hurricane behind her, the old wagon wasn't quite fast enough to trigger the speed cameras that line that part of the road. This was, thought Susan to herself, trucking at its very best and what's more Almire Du Lia and Chief Scout were travelling like lords in the rear of the lorry.

Even when pulled over for a routine lorry check, she had no reason to fear that her journey would be held up for anything other than a moment, the vehicle having recently passed its MOT.

But the mechanical lads from the ministry had other ideas. "'Ere, what's this oil dripping?" they asked before adding, unequivocally: "Sorry, love, this lorry goes no further."

As luck would have it another Fife trainer, Lucinda Russell, was taking the same route and was not far behind. She stopped and picked up Chief Scout – a runner in the 2.20 – but she did not have room for Almire Du Lia.

his first jump of the day.

So the next problem was, short of riding him there, how to get the horse to the races. Susan rang other trainers whose lorries might be passing. She rang other horse transport companies. She rang the breakdown people. She rang the racecourse and, ultimately, she rang her mobile phone battery dry.

Eventually a mechanic arrived and summoned back-up in the shape of a low-loader. With an inch to spare either side her horsebox was slowly but surely winched on board for a piggy-back south until, three-quarters of the way through the loading process, it became stuck at an angle of about 45 degrees when the tail-gate became wedged against the ground.

Unlike the lorry Almire Du Lia was unmoved by the experience, but he was still passing through Morpeth on the back of the low-loader when, under normal circumstances, he should have been stepping into the pre-parade ring. He arrived just in time to be saddled but not in time for the Bradburne lorry to be disembarked from the low-loader – the big horse's first jump of the day was 4ft down off the back.

Having run moderately all season he proceeded to run his best race by far when finishing fourth while the Good Samaritan, Lucinda Russell, not only booked her place in the kingdom of heaven but had a more immediate dividend, a Newcastle double. JANUARY 5, 2009

THE BLOODSTOCK agent James Delahooke, who bought the great Dancing Brave many moons ago, was recently asked by Doncaster Bloodstock Sales if one of their interns (student placements) could, for the benefit of her experience, trail him during their yearling sale and see how he selected young stock for his clients.

Delahooke agreed and, with one thing and another, ended up getting a lift to the sales in the student's car. As soon as they arrived in the car park the valet parking team sprung into action and asked the intern for her keys. Having never experienced the delights of this American import, at first she was unsure whether she should just hand over her keys to someone she had never met before (especially at Doncaster, where horseboxes have a habit of going missing in the middle of the night).

Delahooke reassured her that this was valet parking and that when, later in the day, she emerged from the sales she would merely have to snap her fingers and her car would immediately be brought to her.

But she still hadn't quite grasped the concept of valet parking. Half an hour into the sale, having clearly given it some thought, she brought up the subject again. "Mr Delahooke," she asked excitedly, "do you think they'll clean the inside of my car as well as the outside?" NOVEMBER 3, 2008

THE NIGHTMARE of last-minute Christmas shopping is upon us – I have the added crisis that Christmas Day is also my wife's birthday – so hopefully the following story of an elderly, old-school, slightly fey lady owner in Ireland will cheer you up.

At a recent Christmas she was given a lovely box of smellies by one of her houseguests. "Oh look, how delightful darling, Jo Malone!" she exclaimed on unwrapping the present. There was then a momentary pause before she added: "Isn't he Dermot Weld's head lad?" DECEMBER 23, 2008

IT CAN now be revealed. Ascot's new chief executive Charles Barnett did have sleepless nights in the run-up to the royal meeting, not because of the innumerable things that could possibly go wrong but because the beds in his temporary residence (the stewards' house) were too hard.

Mrs Barnett had to ship some beds down from their home near Wrexham, a job at one stage she was about to undertake herself in the horsebox. They arrived safely at the chief executive's tied accommodation but, according to one prominent guest – closely linked to Barnett's last job at Aintree – they had not been accompanied by any bed linen.

Ascot's new boss knew the royal enclosure lodge had not been included in the racecourse's £210m redevelopment on his first night there when he opened a window and it promptly fell out. JUNE 19, 2007

ONE of the golden rules of being a bloodstock agent is to get in with trainers but this can be taken too far. Bear this in mind while you recall that Tuesday was coloured with traffic jams. So getting in to the course was a slow process with a maximum speed of about two miles an hour. Hard, therefore, to imagine too many shunts.

Gerard Butler, the trainer, was in one lane in his Volvo, a car designed to withstand all sorts of high impacts, when the car on his inside smacked into his side at walking pace denting both near-side doors. When he looked to see who the driver was he discovered the man at the wheel was none other than bloodstock agent Oliver Gaisford St Lawrence.

"The two of us were both in the wrong," says Gerard of the slow-mo accident. "But he was wronger. It was only really a fender bender and there was no blood lost. I don't know about Oliver buying horses for me, I should think he'll be washing my car for a while." JUNE 18, 2005

EVE JOHNSON HOUGHTON, who officially takes over the reins from her father Fulke on February 1, had her first owners' open day on Sunday and, apart from writing off a car and a marquee, in the absence of any human fatalities I think we can say the event was an unqualified success.

The car belonged to her brother Gordon, another member of the family to have trained, albeit briefly. He was involved in a prang on the M25 en route to the Blewbury yard on Saturday night. He was shunted from behind and let's just say he now drives a two-seater.

With a slight disregard for predictions or rather warnings that the country might be in for some weather on Saturday night, a marquee was put up on the, and I quote, "sheltered" front lawn for the following morning's post-parade drinks.

As my own garden shed, bolted to a concrete base, was uprooted during the night it seemed pertinent to ring on Sunday morning and find out which of Didcot power station's cooling towers the tentage was wrapped around. "Remarkably it is still in the garden," she replied, "but it's upside down with several broken legs." DECEMBER 5, 2006

FROM SMALL ACORNS … it's one of Epsom's 'new traditions' – an oxymoron if ever there was one – that in these green times in which we live, when our every move is measured not in miles or furlongs but by our carbon footprint, the authorities present the winning Vodafone Oaks connections with an oak sapling and a plaque to plant next to it explaining the tree's significance.

For some reason this presentation takes place not on the winner's podium nor at the local garden centre but in the post-race press conference – much to the astonishment of hacks and connections alike. The first one was given to friends of Imagine in 2001 and Aidan O'Brien has parked his by the forward machine-gun post at the front gates of Ballydoyle.

On Friday the lucky recipients associated with Light Shift were Maria Niarchos, who no doubt has a man, or several, to do her gardening, the green-fingered Henry Cecil and Ted Durcan about whom we have zero gardening form.

Transporting a sapling taller than most Flat jockeys in the immediate aftermath of Classic glory, however, presents a problem that would have been unforeseen by all three recipients when they were going through the day's potential pitfalls at Friday breakfast.

THE OAK

Ted's wouldn't fit in his car and he forgot to organise a horsebox to transport it to his Newmarket home. But, in time, he intends to retrieve it – at the next Epsom meeting, he said, but as that's next Oaks day because of the building work I think he'll have to do it sooner – and plant it at the bottom of his lawn, then "bore everyone senseless with the story of the tree".

It is the Niarchos sapling that has proved to be a thorn in the side of the Epsom authorities, however. An unnamed member of staff was appointed to ensure it was loaded on the Niarchos helicopter for the short hop back to France. Unfortunately, I guess because there was more than one helicopter to choose from, the now much-travelled tree was stuck on a helicopter bound for Kent.

Not such bad news for the tree to be off to the Garden of England instead of France but bad news for Epsom, which spent a not inconsiderable amount of time on the phone to the nation's helicopter charter companies on Friday night trying to track it down. It's small wonder, though, that no-one on the Kent flight ever questioned why they were giving the stowaway foliage a freebie lift – that's possibly the short-term consequence of hospitality for you. It has now been retrieved and is being DHL-ed to the Niarchos stud, Haras de Fresnay-Le-Buffard. JUNE 5, 2007

FOR much of the winter – in fact until last week – Kim Bailey had an unintentionally amusing answerphone message for a trainer on his mobile phone. Sadly, since it was pointed out to him, he has wiped it off and re-recorded it. It is now just the bog-standard "leave your number and message and I'll get back to you".

Without the 'noises off' it doesn't quite give the same insight into the job of a trainer that the last one did. The original was recorded when Kim was in a hurry and, as is so often the case with trainers, trying to do several things at one time. In the background you can hear the clip-clop of a horse being trotted up and, while it is difficult to hear whether the animal was actually level or not, the trainer's groan as he signed off from his message suggested that the horse was very much in possession of three good legs and one bad one.

It was not as bad as all that, however. The horse in question was Very Special One, who recovered to win next time out at Huntingdon on Boxing Day, the first leg of a treble the yard sent out that day. APRIL 3, 2007

THE HIGHLIGHT, no question, of last week's Punchestown Festival was the victory of 13-year-old Moscow Flyer in a charity race to raise money for kidney donation in Ireland (not specifically for those in attendance at the festival, but Ireland more generally). He was a first ride for 17-year-old Kate Harrington, daughter of his trainer Jessica.

They were clapped round the paddock, roared to the start, cheered again when he moved smoothly into second on the last bend and screamed home by a crowd of more than 30,000. And you should have heard them when he got back to the winner's enclosure.

Nina, I mean Kate, gave him a very cool ride, pushing him out with hands and heels and, like Barry Geraghty, indulged in a bit of looking round in the closing stages. I believe she even had time to admire herself on the big screen. The smoothness of the operation prompted one former trainer to ask Geraghty how he had managed to make it look so difficult when he used to ride the champion chaser.

However, favourite backers might not have been so keen to lump on to Moscow had they witnessed Kate's first attempt at her driving test a day earlier. Having been "attacked" by a motorbike in a housing estate, which she had to swerve to avoid, she completely lost her stride. At the next T-junction the examiner asked her to turn left whereupon she went right.

Nothing was said until they reached the next junction. "I think we'll go to my left this time if you don't mind," said the quite obviously charming instructor.

"I suppose," surmised Kate correctly, "that I've failed?"

It is believed the last instruction from the trainer on getting the leg-up was to remember that as far as Kate was concerned Punchestown's a left-handed track. MAY 2, 2007

PLAYING golf, the well-fed bloodstock agent David Minton once got a hole in one. You might recall the great event being recorded in this diary. Getting a ball to roll into a hole is one thing but getting himself into a suit is a completely different story and not, it appears, quite so easy.

Following the death of David Nicholson, his widow Dinah decided that the Duke's last three suits, all beautifully cut tweed, should not go to Help The Aged in Stow but should be donated to the friend whose frame most closely resembled the Duke's in his latter years. Step forward Minty. And while, after the first fitting, the jackets are a perfect fit around the shoulders it is across the stomach region that the buttons fail to meet in the middle to the tune of two to three inches.

However, although Dinah does not mind the trousers being taken up a few inches, she does not want the jackets altered, so she has come to a deal with Minty and his inheritance – he can only have them if he fits them (rather than them fitting him) by the Cheltenham Festival in March. "The food and drink will go after Christmas," says Minton. "Actually make that just the food." NOVEMBER 21, 2006

THERE'S a week to go but the first result is already in from Cheltenham and the 'winner's all right' as they say in Ireland. The prize-money's been distributed, although a few bets are yet to be settled.

Just to recap, in a modern-day take on Great Expectations, that larger-than-life bloodstock agent David Minton, a man of very few sharp edges, would only qualify to 'inherit' a blazer and two tweed suits from the late David Nicholson on one condition – that he lost so much weight before the tapes go up for the Supreme Novices' Hurdle a week today that he actually fits the suits rather than the other way round, which would require a tailor. It's body sculpture really – isn't it?

To give him an added incentive generous owner Andy Stewart chipped in by saying he would give £5,000 to the charity of Dinah Nicholson's choice should the big man slim down the required amount (knowing Andy he'd have given it anyway).

On top of this several friends of the bloodstock agent took the view that having lived off the see-food diet for his entire life he would fail, hopelessly, and they bet accordingly, also for charity. So it looks like the 'penalty value' of this particular contest might top about £5,500.

Well, way ahead of schedule, I'm delighted to announce that the suits fit. Stewart was so impressed he's already coughed up and Minton's tweed hacking jacket – you still wouldn't want, God forbid, to be a horse who Minty wanted to take hacking – was looking positively double-breasted at Newbury on Saturday such was the over-lap round his (nevertheless still formidable) girth.

Having lost two stone comfortably, he intends to lose another stone and a half but not an ounce more and for very good reason. If he loses any more weight than that the suits won't fit – they'd all be too big.

So – Atkins, cabbage soup, WeightWatchers, high-fibre, the Scarsdale, Rosemary Conlon's hip and thigh, low-carb (favoured, of course, by Jennifer Aniston), the Beverly Hills (I presume that's champagne and sex) or the AP McCoy (crisps and Kit Kats) – which diet plan worked for him? Well, it's the 'Edgy' diet, although it seems to have singularly failed the man who invented it, trainer and fellow all-rounder Charlie Egerton.

"I've allowed myself red wine and vodka with soda," says the svelte Minton, beginning with his treats. "Edgy told me he cut out all root vegetables when he was in training for the London Marathon, so none of them, no dairy and no wheat."

He has, however, been getting his oats. "I've had porridge for breakfast every day," he says.

You can see him bucking and kicking in his new suit next week and having, with his business partner Anthony Bromley, a total monopoly on purchases from France, it looks like the Duke's suits will return to their old haunt, the winner's enclosure, on a monotonously regular basis. One place you won't see them is in the also-rans unsaddling area – it's a no-go zone for bloodstock agents. MARCH 6, 2007

AS BEFITTING a gallery owner in Motcomb Street, London, Geoffrey Hughes drives a smart new BMW but it hasn't always been thus. His penchant previously had been for stylish third-hand cars bordering on the antique, and many an artist has waved goodbye to Hughes and a year's worth of work wondering if it will ever make the garden gate let alone the framer or the gallery.

So worried was Hubert de Watrigant, the French artist whose exhibition of 60 works goes on show at the Osborne Studio Gallery from midday today, that he rang Hughes five times after he had collected the paintings from near Paris in the summer.

The last call went unanswered for very good reason – the alternator had gone on Hughes's old mode of transport. He and de Watrigant's 60 works of art were being towed 600 miles home by the French AA. Even worse, Hughes was forced to shack up in a grotty Calais hotel waiting for the following day's ferry. Hughes's night was fairly disturbed as the car park was out of sight from his hotel room and, every half-hour, he felt it necessary to check up on his car (scrap value £120) and its contents worth, precisely, £250,000. NOVEMBER 6, 2007

TOR STURGIS, at 28 one of the country's youngest female trainers, has made an impressive start to her career in Kingston Lisle this season. From her first four runners she sent out three winners. There has been a certain amount of speculation in the press about her first name, a shortened version of Victoria. Peter Scudamore surmised she was a Norwegian import and the Racing Post referred to her as a 'him'. But after a headline in the *Horse & Hound* that beautifully combined name with start – 'Tor-nado' – a racegoer at Fontwell was overheard: "I can't believe anyone would really christen their daughter Tornado." DECEMBER 6, 2005

THE RESURGENCE of Doncaster as a popular racecourse is one of the feel-good stories in racing at the moment. Urban racecourses, however, present the management with certain problems that, one imagines, wouldn't affect rural idylls like Ludlow or Fakenham.

The first lesson for the clerk of the course, David Williams, at Doncaster was: if it isn't tied down it's likely to go walkabout. Only last Friday, as he was assembling the wings to the second hurdle in the straight, kids were dismantling the wing at the first in the straight.

But Doncaster sets the standard for the theft or rather the long-term borrowing of racecourse property. A whole flight of hurdles once went missing.

The authorities could see from footprints in the frost that the missing hurdles had been carried to a nearby wood. There they were in use as the walls of a primitive house for an extended family of Lithuanian refugees living rough in a ramshackle hamlet.

Quite apart from the commentary on this return to the dark ages in the social history of Donny, no doubt the local buildings inspector would have had something less than complimentary to say about the insulation properties of birch twigs. The roof had been made from a frost-protection sheet that had also been half-inched from the course.

"When we saw that that they'd cut down trees with machetes, we said they could have the hurdles for a bit," recalls Williams – not nominated for a VC on this occasion. "Structurally what they'd done was magnificent."

Recalling the incident Adam Waterworth, Doncaster's MD – whom you wouldn't fancy in a wrestling competition with an 18st Lithuanian – said that they waited until the larger of their eastern European cousins had gone off for the day before moving in to fetch their hurdles.
FEBRUARY 4, 2008

ED JAMES, the East Garston trainer, has retired. His last runner was Selberry at Newton Abbot recently. Although he never had any world-beaters in his six and a half years at the job he had some decent horses like Falmouth Bay, Country Star and Big Bradford, a useful performer on the Flat.

After his first winner he stopped at a fast-food drive-in in Bracknell to celebrate with a Chicken Zinger Burger. Engrossed in his meal, he carved someone up on the first roundabout he came to. Two roundabouts later, the same, but by now rather agitated, driver swerved to stop in front of Ed and citizens' arrested him for eating a burger at the wheel. Alas, all the evidence had been eaten and charges couldn't be brought. Because the other driver, by this time apoplectic to the point of carrying out his next arrest – a cardiac arrest on himself – had technically bumped into Ed he also ended up having to pay for the repair to Ed's bumper. JUNE 8, 2004

WHEN Doncaster reopened, you'll remember, the point was made that the man in charge of signage had an old-fashioned sense of humour and, unlike anyone else these days, was prepared to take the mickey out of the local stewards. Underneath the sign outside their room, he had repeated the same information in Braille.

Well now the poor man has, unfortunately, completely lost the plot with a classic misuse of a post-nominal honorific unless, of course, he's just trying to ensure all angles are covered. Outside the weighing room on Saturday, for the finale to a wonderful jockeys' championship, was a list of acting stewards. They were: Captain P.M.L.Hibbert-Foy, J.E.Rose Esq, Mrs S York Esq and Mrs D Powles Esq. Like all esquires Sarah and Didi may be of 'gentle birth' but they are most definitely female. NOVEMBER 13, 2007

SATURDAY was a memorable day for the Nicholls team but for Donna Blake, his second travelling head lad, it was not for their treble at Cheltenham. She was taking Just For Men to Uttoxeter.

Driving through Bristol she was flashed, not as you'd expect and as Nicholls assumed, by a speed camera, but by a male in a mac who jumped out in front of a set of traffic lights and 'revealed' himself.

She had only just caught her breath after that when she pulled in for fuel on the M5. While she was filling it the engine spontaneously combusted. She and Just For Men were saved from any further punishment and rescued by the Nicholls horsebox already at Cheltenham. NOVEMBER 14, 2006

MUCH has been made of the problems faced by those, like jockey Martin Dwyer, trying to reach America towards the end of last week, in his case, to ride in the Arlington Million.

For similar reasons there were mixed emotions among Richard Phillips' staff at Adlestrop Stables last Thursday but to understand why you need some background.

Richard may be progressive in his use of a sports psychologist and a riding coach for his staff but in some aspects he's positively Victorian. For example when it comes to holidays he likes to wear the hairshirt and claims that his annual family holiday as a child, if he was lucky, was a day trip to Littlehampton for a round of crazy golf and a gritty sandwich before catching the bus home.

This austerity was reinforced when his first job in racing was for Graham Thorner, another man who thinks more than one holiday every decade is a waste of time and money. Frankly it baffles Richard that stable staff now have the wherewithal to take off to Majorca and Tenerife for a fortnight when a few hours at Butlins should suffice.

So when it was announced in the yard earlier this summer that he had decided to take up an invitation from his childhood hero, Michael Dickinson, and some owners to come and stay in America – for the first time – there was cause for much celebration as it meant he'd be away for ten days.

The American holiday was given a big build-up by trainer and staff alike as the day approached. The lads lined the drive to see him off (and to make sure he'd gone) and then came the news that among the first casualties of the airport security clampdown was Richard's flight to Philadelphia.

This was a bittersweet moment for his lads, bitter in that the holiday might now be abandoned, sweet in that the boss was among the thousands being inconvenienced at the airport. Their worst fears, however, were realised when he returned to Adlestrop. One lad even texted the secretary saying he'd pay her to book him on the next available flight out and another said he felt sorry for all the thousands having to queue outside Heathrow – except the boss.

As for the trainer, who had to endure the real hardship of waiting six hours without the use of his mobile phone, which had been packed in the hold of his re-booked flight on Friday, he has the last word. "I can't believe it," he says. "The one day in 43 years I decide to go to America for the first time ... " AUGUST 15, 2006

ONE wonders which Derby-winning trainer should be most bothered by racing's latest case of mistaken identity. At Windsor last week a young racegoer approached Paul Cole. "Can I have your autograph please, Mr Cumani?" he asked. MAY 16, 2006

NICKY HENDERSON was being pursued round Aintree by former fellow trainer John Edwards, a man who, a bit like Paul Nicholls with Silver Birch, managed to sell Little Polveir months before he won the National.

Henderson recently turned up to stay with Edwards, now based in Ireland, to combine the Irish National at Fairyhouse with looking at some young horses. After going upstairs to change for the races, Henderson appeared at the foot of the stairs with a towel round his waist requesting Edwards' 'help' in his bedroom.

Now 'wifeless', as it were, he has to pack his own bag and instead of a more recently tailored suit, he had packed one he had last worn at Eton circa 1975. It did not, according to witnesses, come within ten inches of doing up. He couldn't even be forced into it.

The only solution was for Edwards, a not dissimilar shape to Henderson these days, to lend one of his Savile Row suits to the trainer for Fairyhouse. Presuming it to have been sent to the dry cleaners before the Master of Seven Barrows returned it, Edwards was slightly surprised to see Henderson wearing it again at Aintree last week. The chances of its return look slimmer than either man. APRIL 17, 2007

WE ALL have our favourite racecourses – for various reasons. Lester Piggott's was Newmarket, because it cost him less in petrol to get there than anywhere else. Paul Cole's is Deauville due to the availability of fresh fish while Andrew Balding's is – it was revealed by his best man at his wedding on Friday – Sandown.

During Andrew's two years as assistant to Lynda Ramsden, he was often the grateful recipient of Jack Ramsden's chuck-out clothes. Indeed, it was one of the attractions of the job especially as Jack's idea of second-hand is nearly new to the rest of us. Sandown is Andrew's favourite – because of its proximity to a second-hand shop in Esher. JULY 19, 2005

TRAINERS and jockeys are always in trouble for driving too fast but, without having it verified by the Guinness Book, you have to hand it to Chaddleworth trainer Charlie Egerton. He appears to have set a new world record for points amassed for speeding on one licence at one time.

Starting off with a healthy nine points, a spate of speeding tickets in the weeks after his 12th point had triggered an invitation to Devizes Magistrates Court meant he had collected a staggering 26 (I'll spell that out just in case you think it's a typo – twenty-six) points in all before his appearance in said courthouse. Put it this way, had England's batsmen collectively averaged the same number of runs in the Ashes so far it might be 0-3 as opposed to 3-0.

But the story, as you'd expect with Edgy, doesn't quite end there. Obviously he has now become quite camera shy and if, when you next pass one of those yellow-backed boxes beside a main road, the car in front slows to almost a standstill, it would, were he not banned, almost certainly be Edgy.

And on his way to Devizes – this was not a case of over-confidence as he was meeting a driver there to bring him back – to hear his fate (six months off the road) he slowed to such an extent on the A4 that a following police car pulled him over.

The irony of being pulled over for driving too slowly on his way to court to explain why he had 26 points for driving too fast was not entirely lost on the trainer (his solicitor, presumably, used it in court as mitigating evidence).

But the irritation of being stopped mid-morning had a hackle-raising effect on the normally placid Edgy. "Haven't you got better things to do with your time?" he demanded. "Shouldn't you be out catching robbers?"

I don't know if you've ever heard Edgy speak but even under normal circumstances one syllable tends to, for want of a better word, 'slur' slowly but surely into the next. "No need to be like that, Sir," said the policeman. "Been drinking, 'av we?"

After further warm discussion he was allowed to continue his journey, the last for some time at the wheel, and the cop, one presumes, went back to the more regular business of catching robbers. DECEMBER 19, 2006

YOU can tell autumn's here. Every jump trainer in the country with half an eye for PR is holding an open day to amuse owners and attract new clients. Last Sunday alone Hen and Terry opened up at Lockinge, Richard Phillips held one at Adlestrop and Paul Webber held his at Cropredy. For trainers, though, they represent perhaps their greatest challenge.

I arrived, slightly late, at Richard's to be met by a loose horse galloping down the road with its reins between its legs followed, at a respectable interval, by the screeching wheels of two 4x4s full of expectant horse catchers. Goes well on the firm was the overriding impression the horse gave.

It seems the Phillips parade coincided, in an unfortunate accident of timing, with a vintage motorbike rally passing through the picturesque village. The phut-phut-cough of two-dozen ancient BMWs the other side of the hedge doesn't go down well with a lot of fresh racehorses with the wind up their tails.

The good news according to the trainer, who had heard from someone who had come on from Cropredy, was that Webber had had eight loose ones though, granted, none of his had got as far as Kingham Station before being caught.

"One of them was a horse we hadn't cantered for a year and a half so I was particularly pleased at how well he was moving," explained Paul yesterday. "Another, a young filly, was very pleased with herself. I had visions of her sliding under the paddock rails, taking out seven octogenarian spectators, plastic chairs being splintered in all directions and the vet having to put down local stalwart David Stoddart – all the while pretending we were in complete control." SEPTEMBER 21, 2004

CHRIS BONNER, who remains the last amateur rider to be placed in a Grand National – he partnered Sir Peter Lely into fourth in 1996 – is now Andrew Balding's trusted right-hand man at Kingsclere.

Just recently Balding and Bonner were invited by racing PR consultant Johnno Spence to a poker evening in London, which he had arranged for some of his clients. Obviously, in these situations if a trainer has a runner in the north of England the same day it's a no-brainer – he sends his assistant to the far-off race meeting, which in this case was York, with the instruction: "See you later, alligator."

It being Bonner, however, who is hardly Michael Palin when it comes to travelling the length or, indeed, the breadth of the country, the trainer suggested that his assistant make his way after the race to York station, get himself to Liverpool Street and thence to the poker evening at the Palm Beach Casino in Mayfair. Simple, really and Bonner followed the instructions pretty much to the letter.

Early in the evening Balding was just about to arrive for the card school when he received a call from his trusted sidekick. "Mate, mate," said Bonner, "I screwed up. I did as you said and jumped on the first train to Liverpool Street but I thought it was a bit odd when I got out and everyone was speaking fluent Scouse – I'm at Liverpool Lime Street."

The next problem for Bonner, who had used up his cash reserves on the trip from York to Liverpool, was how to raise funds for the rest of his onward journey. Cashless, he successfully blagged his way on to a train to London and arrived well into the evening having completed two sides of a rather large triangle. The Bonner family motto has been hastily revised to 'better late than never'. SEPTEMBER 26, 2006

IT IS the vogue for jump trainers to take a short skiing break in the middle of February these days but Henry Daly's was shorter than he anticipated. Due to fly out from Coventry, he turned up at East Midlands, which geographically sounds like it could be an identical grid reference, but is not quite the same thing by about 40 miles.

Consequently he missed his flight and when he should have been turning up at some beautifully appointed alpine chalet he was sitting down for dinner in the somewhat less attractive local Travelodge. We're just hoping that when he finally made it his suitcase wasn't packed with swimwear for the beach. FEBRUARY 8, 2008

EVE JOHNSON HOUGHTON sent out her first foreign winner last week when Judd Street won a six-furlong handicap, worth the equivalent of three Listed races here, at Nad Al Sheba. She missed the race because she had just come out of hospital after having pins and plates removed from her ankle, the shrapnel of an old skiing accident.

The owner, her father, was not there either. "There's no way he can go eight hours without a fag," she said, explaining his refusal to fly to Dubai. FEBRUARY 24, 2009

IF YOU saw the work Simon Claisse recently put into the new point-to-point authority, quite apart from running the racecourse side of things at Cheltenham, you'd realise he is a thorough man.

The same applies to his holidays and if he goes for a week, as he recently did to Egypt's Red Sea, he needs to put aside at least a day for packing his suitcase, an exercise, some might say, in fastidiousness; everything laid out, neatly folded and pressed and packed. It's nothing like the laundry-basket style of packing preferred by a journalist closely connected with this column.

However, he was lucky, he now concedes, not to spend the majority of the week at Her Majesty's Pleasure after inadvertently packing his Swiss army penknife – to peel oranges on the beach – in his hand luggage.

Neatly hidden in a deck-shoe, his knife had been packed away in his suitcase bound for the aircraft's hold until he had substituted the shoes for his sponge bag – he'd remembered, at least, you couldn't take liquids in hand luggage – at 6am on the morning of the flight, a time when the brain wasn't functioning as it might, say, at 2pm on day one of the Festival.

The first he knew about it was when a policeman took his passport and boarding card and began reading him his rights. He then announced with some confidence that while his girlfriend, Annabel, and her two children might be going to Egypt, Claisse's likely holiday destination was a less sunny place called Custody. JULY 1, 2008

CURTAIN CALL'S owners are having a picnic for friends in the old Derby Stables before racing at Epsom on Saturday. (This isn't Facebook and that isn't an open invitation to the youth of Epsom, by the way.)

One notable absentee, however, will be the horse's former trainer Jessica Harrington, who campaigned the colt so successfully before he joined Luca Cumani.

However, she is not staying away on the basis that it would be like going to an ex-boyfriend's wedding – she is nursing a broken arm and will be rooting for her former pupil from an armchair.

"It's a right pain," she says. "It's my right arm and bust above the elbow so I can't do anything with it. I'll be cheering him on like a good 'un from home."

So did Jessica, who broke her neck on a riding safari when her horse put its foot down an aardvark's hole, bust her arm by falling off? "Of course," she says.

But she was a bit sheepish when asked to give more detail. "I forgot to tighten my girths," she explained and, before there was time to ask her to estimate how many thousands of saddles she has put on a horse, she added: "I know. I know. I know. There's no-one else to blame." JUNE 3, 2008

Chapter Three

YOU DON'T HAVE TO BE MAD TO WORK IN RACING ... BUT IT HELPS

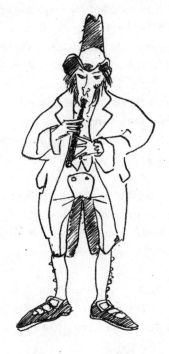

(WARNING: THIS CHAPTER MAY CONTAIN NUTS)

A SMALL scruffy Irishman with long dreadlocked hair and a knotted beard was playing the tin whistle for the entertainment of racegoers leaving the course at Cheltenham. "If that's not a leprechaun," said one of his audience, "I don't know what is." MARCH 21, 2006

THE IRISH point-to-point's autumn season is now in full swing. No names, no pack-drill on this one I'm afraid. A solicitor with ambitions to get onwards and upwards socially in the world of racing was acting clerk of the scales at a point-to-point in the sticks recently and, in his tent before racing, was perusing the card.

He noticed that the jockey engaged to ride one prominent trainer's runner in the third race was called TG James and he mused out loud to the secretary: "I think I was at school with his father."

Now the secretary, a wise old stalwart of the point-to-point scene, knew slightly different. "Hmm, interesting," she replied under her breath for she knew that TG James's roots, if you could call them that, were in the mobile population that, for want of pinning them down to any particular place, inhabit Limerick's outer ring road.

Between the second and third races the jockey, quite rough-looking and sporting a spiky haircut, plonked himself down on the scales in front of the solicitor whose original opinion was clearly unaffected by appearances. By way of polite introduction to his 'friend's son' he began by saying: "I think I know your father."

"If you do you're a better man than me," replied the jockey, "because I've no idea who the **** my father is." NOVEMBER 3, 2008

THIS MAY or may not be good news for London, its citizens, its position as the world's most cultural capital or Ken Livingstone's much-talked-about traffic flow. Indeed, in a round-about way, it could have implications for our Olympic bid.

Peter Walwyn, the retired trainer, has been recognised for his services to racing – and not before time – by being elected a yeoman of the

Worshipful Company of Saddlers, one of the oldest trade guilds.

The guild was given a charter in 1391 during the reign of Richard II but traces back to 1160 when it was the Guild of Saddlers, and Big Pete was 'inaugurated' at a sumptuous lunch in the shadow of St Paul's at Saddlers Hall in Gutter Lane last week. He is among the first people to be elected for 21 years and joins, among others, the Princess Royal and Lord Oaksey. Another racing great accorded the same honour was the late Fred Winter.

At lunch he had to place his hands on, according to Pete, 'an old book' – could be a Bible, I suppose, rather than any old book – and swear to obey the rules of the company – motto: hold fast, sit sure.

As a yeoman, Pete automatically becomes a Freeman of the City of London and upon him that confers certain ancient privileges, which he intends to put to good use. For example he is now allowed to drive a flock of sheep over London Bridge.

"I've a good mind to take them up on that one," says Pete, who has been helping the Labour party out lately by canvassing for the Tories. "And one of the things I'll likely have stencilled on the sheep's backsides will be hunting's mantra 'Bollocks to Blair!' If I need a crook to help me guide the sheep, well, there's no shortage of them in racing."

If this stunt goes spectacularly wrong, as it seems destined to, and he is done for treason, failure to pay the congestion charge or aggravated shepherding there is another privilege that he may care to take up. Should they hang him he can choose to be strung up by a silk rope which, apparently, is altogether more comfortable, classy and less prone to burning the skin than hemp. Some people have all the luck. APRIL 26, 2005

IT'S A BATTLEGROUND out there and, very much like the Balkan War, it appears to be dividing families. Although the *Evening Standard* 'London Final' pretty much has the place to itself after racing, those arriving at Ascot in the morning have the choice of the 20-year-old *Racing Post* or its kid rival, the *Sportsman*.

Due to the no-show of one of its salesmen in the prime spot, just outside the main entrance, on both Tuesday and Wednesday, it's been all hands on deck for the new sports-betting paper.

Ed Pownall, recently promoted from plain PR to Director of Communication due to a front-line casualty among the paper's ranks of senior officers, took the place of his missing salesman, flogging his paper but – as you'd expect at Ascot where we like a bit of respect – minus the vocal bullying of a market trader in Covent Garden. On Tuesday he sold eight in his first hour but the Sportsman's circulation figures? That's a different story.

Anyway, when contacted as to why he hadn't shown up at his designated spot the salesman said that it was because he had not wanted to compete with his sister, who was selling the Racing Post there. When told he could move to a different position, outside the royal enclosure entrance, he replied that that too was also an impossibility – there he'd be competing with his mum. "Un****ing believable," commented Pownall. JUNE 20, 2006

IF YOU happened to be driving down Mossop Street, SW3, on New Year's Eve and saw a largish man outside the Admiral Codrington looking like he was in an apparent state of collapse, fear not.

It was Johnno Spence staggering to his feet, having been down on one knee after proposing to his girlfriend Tor Arbuthnot. Apologies for casting the younger female readers of this column into melancholy so early in 2009, but Tor, a speech therapist, said "yes" – without so much as a stutter.

The romance has been a 'whirlwind' one – that is to say very quick rather than destructive of everything in its way. The lovebirds met on holiday in France four months ago. Johnno, who runs his own PR consultancy, will now be furiously consulting wedding magazines as the nuptials are due for September.

Tor works in Ascot at the Heatherwood Hospital, though obviously when she tells Johnno's racing friends that she works at Ascot the rest of the conversation – until she puts them out of their misery – is usually at cross-purposes. JANUARY 5, 2009

AFTER a month of being coupled to John Maxse, the Jockey Club's new head of public relations Paul Struthers went it alone on Sunday. As might be expected his arrival was heralded by a lengthy misquote in the *News of the World*.

As jobs go it is something of a hospital pass but, having given him a desk on the fifth floor at 151 Shaftesbury Avenue, they must reckon he's mentally stable. History doesn't relate how many applicants there were for the job but had a WWI general sought volunteers for a poppy-picking mission to no-man's land one assumes there would have been more takers.

There are some pleasing signs of character about the new man. For example the first time his parents let him out, aged 17, with mates to celebrate a New Year's Eve he woke up the next morning with two front teeth missing. He still, 14 years on, has no recollection of how he lost them.

Sunday wasn't entirely smooth for him though less damaging to his dentistry. He forgot his razor where he was staying, cut himself to ribbons on a borrowed one, forgot his belt so his trousers were at half-mast and then the bottom of his car fell off on the way to Newmarket. Finally he chucked out his winning exacta ticket in the Pretty Polly and spent several minutes upside down in a bin trying to retrieve the piece of paper worth £85.

He is resourceful, however, having subsidised his degree at Trent University by working two days a week in a Ladbrokes betting shop – unlike most of the Jockey Club, who subsidised Ladbrokes during their Eton careers by spending two days a week in the bookie's Windsor branch.

But if you thought dapper John with his Kenzo suits, wide ties and imitation crocodile shoes was riding off into the sunset after eight years you'd be wrong. He's moved within the same building to Racecourse Holdings Trust. After so long in the job he's only considered safe for a desk on the ground floor now. JUNE 3, 2006

ANYONE visiting Newmarket between now and the end of the Flat season with half an interest in fine art should visit the National Horseracing Museum on the High Street. It is holding an exhibition of the 'Life and Works of Sir Alfred Munnings' featuring more than 80 of his paintings, studies and sketches as well as photographs and a mock-up of his old studio.

He died in 1959 but he is still recalled as something of a character in Newmarket. One person who remembers him is Joyce Neville, who now coincidentally works part-time at the museum.

Joyce used to work in Foggetts, the old family chemist shop in Newmarket, to which Lady Munnings was a regular visitor. The Munnings' passion for their dogs is well recorded. One day she arrived carrying one of them, 'The Black Knight', under her arm. Joyce went to stroke the little fella only to find him stiff, cold and particularly unresponsive to her attentiveness. After he had died Lady Munnings had had him stuffed but continued to keep his company – even on shopping trips in Newmarket. Dot, dot or what?

The Black Knight is still going strong – kenneled in the more permanent Sir Alfred Munnings Museum in Dedham – despite the NHR Museum curator's best efforts to organise a summer-long reunion for Joyce. JUNE 2, 2007

Lady Munnings .

THIS COULD be a big week for the Newmarket trainer Michael Bell. On Saturday he runs Motivator, the favourite, in the Vodafone Derby. Obviously you need a few distractions to keep your mind off such an important event and the arrival in his yard last winter of a two-year-old colt called Turn Me On has opened up a world of opportunity for the very happily married father of three.

The stable's apprentice Hayley Turner would, in any sphere, be considered attractive. But in the world of spotty, scrawny, teenage boys that are the would-be champion jockeys of tomorrow, she is drop-dead gorgeous. And every now and again Mike puts her on the two-year-old who made a pleasing debut at Lingfield last week.

After the horses have worked he rides his hack along the string. "How did that work?" he'll ask each lad in turn until he comes to Hayley. Instead of asking her how the horse worked, he feigns a memory lapse and asks her what she's riding. He is hoping, of course, for Hayley to answer: "Turn Me On, guv'nor."

"So far," says Mike, "she has failed miserably to fall into the trap." MAY 31, 2005

Too big for his wallet.

OVER the years Peter Walwyn, the former champion trainer who, in retirement, casts a benevolent eye on the inhabitants of Lambourn, has been a major source of entertainment for this column and, to be frank, it would be rude not to lead off the new year with the latest instalment from Windsor House.

Now, with Harry Dunlop paying what you'd imagine is a small fortune in rent for his yard, you'd think Big Pete's credit rating would be pretty good, especially in the Lambourn area.

After entertaining a group of loyal friends at The Pheasant Inn for a slap-up pre-Christmas lunch, he did the gentlemanly thing of offering to pay. However, he was somewhat disturbed when Johnny the Fish, the landlord and not unknown to regulars of the Diary, took him aside for a quiet word so as not to embarrass the great man. His credit card, he informed him, had been refused by the pub's chip and pin machine.

After some discussion, it became clear why. In order to get his credit card in his faithful old pre-card wallet he had taken the scissors to the oblong piece of plastic and trimmed it up accordingly, snipping off a few edges here and there which he didn't think were of any great importance but rendering the card about as useful as a chocolate teapot.

"It was too big for my wallet," says Big Pete before admitting that he had given his card a short back and sides. "I won't be doing that again in a hurry." JANUARY 2, 2007

KITTENKAT, trained by Nick Mitchell, always used to be ridden by his daughter Sophie Mitchell, a fact of which I am sure you are well aware. Since Sophie retired the ride on the old mare has gone to a number of different but normally male jockeys and, at Chepstow recently, it was the turn of Sean Curran.

Watching from the stands was an old boy who was slightly behind the times vis a vis Sophie's retirement of about 18 months ago. Turning to his subsequently rather embarrassed mate as the runners set off for the second circuit he passed the following judgement: "Ooh ah," he said, "that Sophie Mitchell, she's still got a lovely arse." FEBRUARY 7, 2006

JAMIE DOUGLAS-HOME, who trained in Oxfordshire until 1989 and is now racing correspondent of Country Life, has put together a collection of the late Johnny Henderson's war-time memoirs in a book just out called *Watching Monty*. Johnny, after whom the Grand Annual at the Cheltenham Festival is now named, was ADC to General Montgomery during the war.

Watching Monty is the coming together of two great racing men. Johnny Henderson sired trainer Nicky, but probably a greater legacy was the lending of his financial expertise to the sport and the creation of Racecourse Holdings Trust.

Jamie was Peter Walwyn's right-hand man for five years during the Grundy era. In particular he was there the morning the BBC came down to film the horse just prior to Epsom in 1975. With the race just days away tempers were frayed and Big Pete was in filthy form.

Nevertheless, he bent over backwards to accommodate the cameras and sent his string up a steep bank behind the yard. As they pulled up the director had the temerity to suggest there would be better shots if the string were to canter back down the slope. The prospect of 35 horses, including the Derby favourite, with sore shins proved the straw that broke the camel's already weakened back and the director, we believe, still has tinnitus resulting from the ensuing explosion. JUNE 7, 2005

NOW that former trainer Ed James is back from his honeymoon we can recount the occasion of his marriage to Harriet Montague-Douglas-Scott. After 14 days of heatwave and with another eight days forecast, Ed took the not unreasonable decision to have just a couple of gazebos and a small marquee – to provide shade for the olds – but, otherwise, go al fresco with his reception.

It was the perfect setting, small church, sun shining, drink flowing, happy couple and happy crowd. Then, suddenly, a black cloud appeared on the horizon, the heavens opened, a wind of tornado strength swept down the Pewsey Vale and all hell was let loose.

One of the gazebos imploded on the trio of musicians with the canvas enveloping the double bassist and his instrument. Not unlike the band on the Titanic who were still playing 'Nearer, My God, to Thee' as the ship went under, so they were playing the equally appropriate 'Singing in the Rain' at the time.

The second gazebo parked itself on top of the marquee which, itself, was pinging loose from its pegs and looking a likely danger to air traffic in the area until 40 guests took it upon themselves to wrestle it back down to the ground and sit on it until the storm abated. Even the outdoor seating, straw bales, was turned to mush.

While the bride was kept dry as if in an advert for anti-perspirant, the groom looked like he'd jumped in a pool and the mother-in-law looked like she'd been hosed down. Freddie Tulloch, Ed's business partner, was clearly wearing blue boxers because his white cotton suit had become see-through. Fifteen other guests hid under a table and the bridesmaids, tearfully, under another.

"It would seem to have been a slight misjudgement having it outside," says Ed. "In 21 days of heatwave we picked the five hours that it rained. Looking on the bright side it was a great ice-breaker because you suddenly had rather a lot in common with the person pinning the tent down next to you. It showed great English spirit and made the occasion."

Even so there was one bigger surprise. Trainer Mark Bradstock, most of whose clothes appear to have been pressed by his lurcher (in its basket), was the only man to turn up in tails and won best turned out. "I bet that hasn't happened very often," says Ed. August 8, 2006

NOW we know why it's called Chester. One very buxom but slightly tight young woman wanted a bet on Titus Maximus in the last race on Wednesday, the Cheshire Regiment Maiden Stakes.

Obviously in juvenile contests at this time of year there's not much in the way of form to go on so one can only imagine that the good lady drew inspiration from what she saw in front of her. "A tenner each-way on Tittus Maximus," she demanded rather loudly of a bookmaker. The horse raced up front for half a mile before a bit of a wobble and then flopping. May 10, 2005

SOFT sensitive southerners be warned. This is the sort of homespun Yorkshire philosophy we'll all have to get used to when Ascot goes north next summer. Harvey Smith was talking to a former trainer at the sales recently. They were mid conversation when round the corner appeared larger-than-life bloodstock agent David Minton and his pencil-thin wife Juliet.

"When you see fat shepherd and skinny dog," commented Harvey in a stage whisper plenty loud enough for the objects of his philosophy to hear, "you can always tell who does all 'effing work." AUGUST 10, 2004

A LIFE-SIZE bronze of Persian Punch by Philip Blacker will be unveiled at Newmarket on Saturday. The structure was unceremoniously hoisted into position with slings and a crane yesterday.

There are a couple of things you should know about Persian Punch, the statue. A year ago Philip was enjoying a day's racing at Newmarket. Having gone completely unannounced he was slightly taken aback to hear his name, along with a request to report to the weighing room, over the Tannoy.

When he arrived there he was frogmarched into a back room full of racing's great and good. Five minutes later he emerged with the commission for Persian Punch. One wonders what they'd have done if he hadn't been there. Do you think they'd have put out a second message on the Tannoy, for any old sculptor, to report to the weighing room?

So used lately to doing colts, Blacker's original model for Persian Punch was complete with balls. "I woke up in the middle of the night and thought 'that's not right, he was a gelding'," recalls the artist. "I had great pleasure castrating him the next morning." OCTOBER 11, 2005

THE ICEMAN cometh ... sixth after he tried to runneth out. On Sunday the centenary celebrations of the first races run on the frozen lake at St Moritz will come to an end with the 66th running of the Grand Prix. Banbury trainer Milton Harris will be represented in the race by Salinas and Sargentos.

When anyone ever tells you a horse is versatile then he should be measured against the eight-year-old Salinas. He's a not very good two-mile chaser but he's unique having won over fences, hurdles, on the Flat turf and on the white turf (two years ago).

These last two Sundays, however, he's been warming up for the GP in a couple of skijoring races, an event best described as waterskiing on ice where the horse is the boat and the 'jockey' on skis is towed along by a rope attached to a harness.

"It's a proper, true, amateur nutters' sport," says Milton of the skiers. He is the first British trainer to ever attempt to earn his 'jockey' the revered title King of the Engadine, which is given to the most successful man over three races.

In his first outing nine days ago Salinas finished third but on Sunday he finished sixth. All set for third again he decided to head for the exit gate up the straight and, although he found it shut when he got to that side of the course, it cost him several hundred yards.

"I can't remember the 'jockey's' name," says our would-be kingmaker. His name I'm sure will be on the service sheet at the memorial service – these guys must be hell-bent on self-harm.

This year, after a century of chaotic starts when it has been almost impossible to get all the runners facing the same way at the same time, the White Turf authorities have decided to start the races using starting stalls.

Now there was method in the madness of the founding fathers of this mad sport because, by the time the runners reached the first bend, three of them would be a long way in front. There would be a long gap back to three more and, as the other three would be halfway to Val D'Isere, there was plenty of room.

Now, of course, ten runners get to the first bend at the same time and it's like the nursery slopes in Meribel at half-term – busy. However careful a horse is, it's quite spectacular when he puts a foot on the ski of the 'jockey' in front. Three jockeys were de-ski-ed there last weekend.

But before that there is a new obstacle for the jockey – he's got to ski through the stalls and the result is like Franz Klammer in his downhill finery being evicted in a hurry from a wild west saloon bar smashing through two sets of swing doors – to the power of ten or however many runners there are. "Ow, it's my ribs," were the famous last words of the first skier to miss the swing bit before he was carted off to hospital on the blood-wagon. FEBRUARY 13, 2007

THE thoroughbred racehorse population works on a pyramid system – that's to say there are a few fast ones at the top of the pile and lots of slow ones at the bottom. However, the business is entirely founded by the human belief that this pyramid is inverted.

Of course, it is how we deal with the slowcoaches that counts and the struggle to convert slowness into an admirable trait, like stamina, has been taxing the racehorse trainer and owner for centuries.

The owner of one such horse who keeps getting lapped in Ireland was clutching at straws recently. "I've heard," he said to his trainer, "of a horse whisperer who is very good."

"A horse whisperer?" replied the trainer somewhat indignantly. "What's whispering going to do? I've been shouting at him for ages." OCTOBER 16, 2007

THE twinning of racecourses is good news for the members of each who can have reciprocal arrangements. Newmarket members, especially those who list swimming as their hobby, will be overjoyed that the Rowley Mile is now twinned with what at the moment is a large expanse of Swiss water. Headquarters has twinned with St Moritz.

In February St Moritz holds racing on ice – White Turf – on three consecutive Sundays. Last Friday Barbara Keller, a committee member, was in Newmarket to celebrate the new connection with a race in honour of the new link. Swiss commentator Michael Luxemburger commentated on the replay in three different languages, Italian, German and English. As he did the first few furlongs in German one of Newmarket's older members was seen, standing in front of the big screen, frantically twiddling his deaf-aid in the belief he had begun picking up German long-wave radio.

So is global warming likely to make this a bit of a bum deal for those

Newmarket members who can afford a weekend at 5,500ft in the famously expensive Alpine resort? Unlike any of his British counterparts the main consideration for the clerk of the course at St Moritz is whether the ice is thick enough. In January when the ice is strong he inspects it for bubbles. If he finds one he sticks a crowbar into it letting the air out and water in. What at first sight might appear to be wanton vandalism is in fact a trick to strengthen it.

Two years ago one of the machines that prepares the course fell through a hole. It went so quickly that although the 'gallopman' had time to abandon tractor, the floats to stop it sinking failed to work.

"The crowd of 12,000 is not the problem, static weight is," says Barbara. "There is 5,000 square metres of tentage and it is always the smallest, the kitchen, that is the biggest problem. Last winter for the polo a couple of Argentinian players got cold and switched a heater on in a marquee. It didn't sink but they needed Wellington boots in there the next day."

This could be the start of a trend. Cheltenham could twin with a productive salmon pool on the Dee and, on a sliding scale, Plumpton with a village pond in the Czech Republic. OCTOBER 18, 2005

THE Golden Buttons Ride is being organised by local stud owner and bloodstock agent David Redvers, who is also a Master of the Ledbury Hunt.

Short of a children's entertainer at a recent meet, Redvers filled the breach by splitting his smart hunting coat asunder. He hit a gate, then the deck and as his horse was getting up, it stood on the tail of the jacket ripping it from bottom to top. The damage, if reparable, is likely to test the local seamstress to her limits.

And while the Bible advises us to take the plank out of our own eye before taking the spec out of someone else's – it would be disingenuous of me not to admit to having fallen asleep on occasion at dinner parties – Redvers is one of racing's most entertaining narcoleptics, a man given to occasional bouts of falling into a very deep sleep or, in racing parlance, a man who sometimes fails to see out the trip.

Recently he and two others, both Irish, from the bloodstock world bought a house in Newmarket, a logical investment to save on hotel bills as they spend a not inconsiderable amount of time in the town between July and December.

The trio, Joe Foley, Peter Maloney and Redvers, and their wives except for Mrs Redvers who is currently heavy with child, recently decided, with the end of the hectic sales season in sight, to host a house-warming party during the last week of the Tattersalls December sale of mares and foals.

At the end of the night – and it is here, a bit like the Fallon trial, that the various witness statements don't quite tally; Redvers said he took himself off to bed, his co-owners maintain he just passed out – Messrs Foley and Maloney decided that they should carry the deeply sleeping Redvers out of the house on a mattress and lay him and the mattress down for the night on a big flat tomb in the neighbouring church yard.

However, they were carrying him on his double mattress, which, even neatly folded with him snoring in the middle, wouldn't quite pass through the door. Eventually they gave up on the prank and left him propped up vertically by the front door like a sentry asleep on duty and that is where he woke up the following morning. "The last bit of that story is true," admits Redvers. "I did wake up standing by the door. I'm just a notoriously heavy sleeper." DECEMBER 18, 2007

EVE JOHNSON HOUGHTON, the third generation of her family to train at Woodway, Blewbury, is enjoying a cracking first season. On Sunday she sent out her 14th winner, just one short of her target of 15 in year one.

However, she achieved a long-held ambition recently not by reaching any targets on the racecourse but by hosting a fancy-dress party. It was, depending on how you look at it, either a dark exercise in the child psychology of some of our up-and-coming trainers or it was an indication of what clothes, in adulthood, they keep handy in their wardrobes as the dress code was: 'When I grow up I want to be.'

So, for the benefit of anyone not there, we'll run through some of the runners. John Francome's ironic sense of humour was at work because he went as a policeman. Andrew Balding looked like he had stepped straight out of Siegfried Sassoon's Memoirs of An Infantry Officer as an army captain while his trusty assistant, Chris Bonner, turned a few female heads in an immaculate white American naval officer's uniform.

Anna-Lisa Balding was one of a number of naughty nurses likely to raise rather than lower the temperature of any male patients while Alice Plunkett went as a slightly clumsy fairy. Her wings kept knocking people off the dance floor. The hostess went as a circus ringmaster – obviously there's precious little difference between what she's doing in adulthood and what she wanted to be when she grew up. Francome suggested she went like that because she has a big top.

Ralph Beckett went as John Noakes of Blue Peter fame but it looked awfully like he'd stuck a wig on, asked someone who he resembled and gone as that man. Harriet Smyly went as a particularly authentic punk with bolts strategically pierced about her body. Her husband, the former trainer Mark, went as an Aston Villa footballer but was badly let down by the sparrow-like thickness of his legs.

Gordon Johnson Houghton, another former trainer, was the spit of Sid Vicious while Martin Bosley went as another pop star of that sort of era, Adam Ant, although I had him down as General Custer after a dust-up with a chicken due to the feathers attached to his American cavalryman's jacket. I haven't seen him since but I hope the DIY face paint – Tippex – has not left too much of a scar across his nose.

Charlie Hills and his wife Pip went as Barry and Penny Hills but the best-dressed couple were undoubtedly Jonny and Sophie Portman, who went as an airline pilot and trolley-dolly (respectively – thought I'd just clear that up for anyone who knows Portman). However, with his Mr

Bean looks and a masterful moustache I wouldn't have wanted to fly a kite with him let alone a plane. AUGUST 21, 2007

THERE is a God and he proved it in the most unlikely of locations on Saturday night – at a racing charity auction in a Cotswold village hall attended by Michael 'Corky' Caulfield, racing's resident sports psychologist.

For those of you who don't know him bachelor Corky has, by his own admission, short arms and long pockets and his living expenses for the week (any week including the one before Christmas) rarely amount to more than £20. His round in the pub is likely to be the first – before everyone's arrived.

It is in his good gregarious nature, however, at charity auctions to get the bidding going by putting his mitt up for the first bid safe in the certain knowledge that the item is either vastly undervalued or that his bid will be superseded.

Throughout the auction a pattern, therefore, began to emerge. "What am I bid for a fortnight in an alpine chalet? Who'll start me off at £2,000?" Silence. So the auctioneer drops his asking price to £500, Corky puts his hand up and the auction is suddenly up and running. Holiday house in Florida? Morning on the gallops with Mick Channon? A well-bred greyhound pup? You name it, the first bid's with you, Mr Caulfield.

So after the serious stuff like holidays and dogs came the less serious which are not practical and whose value, if any, is purely sentimental. "Who'll give me £2,000 for an England rugby shirt signed by Ben Cohen, his uncle George (aunt Mavis etc)?" Again silence. "Who'll give me a grand, then?"

It was here that Corky made a fatal error of judgement in his belief that everyone would want an England rugby shirt collectively soiled by the extended Cohen family. He stuck his paw up at a grand. Whether everyone thought (unlikely) that he'd been 'trying' so hard all night they should let him have it or (more likely) thought 'rugby shirt, worth maximum £100' it is not clear but when the auctioneer scanned the room for another bid he sought but could not find. "Going," he said. "For the third time. Gone. Mr Caulfield. Thankyou very much." It's bread and water for his foreseeable future. SEPTEMBER 21, 2004

THE stop smoking campaign, you may have noticed, has finally hit race sponsorship. Racegoers at Newmarket last Saturday, Doncaster this coming Saturday and at Aintree on Becher Chase day at the end of November will be given 'advice and support' on how to quit smoking. Pneumonia from taking an outside fag break in the cold is not, it seems, proving a persuasive argument.

The company putting up the money for the sponsorship is pharmaceutical giant Pfizer, which has teamed up with the charity Quit so, one imagines, part of the advice is one of its products that replicates the kick or the taste of nicotine.

However, the name they have adopted for the campaign is Seriousquitters and, you wouldn't have to be even one percent dyslexic – you could just be in a hurry – to think that the Seriousquitters.co.uk Rockfel Stakes on Saturday was sponsored by either a reformed group of ex-lax chocolate abusers or a British holiday-makers in India helpline. OCTOBER 22, 2007

THEY may not be fully paid-up members of the Racehorse Owners' Association but two of the four lunatics who recently crossed 1,100 miles of ice and snow to reach the Pole of Inaccessibility – the furthest point inland on Antarctica – are just that, racehorse owners.

You may have read a paragraph here and there about their trip recently because, having left home in November, Rupert Longsdon, Rory Sweet, Henry Cookson and their lead-horse/hand-holder, Paul Landry, finally made it to their destination over the weekend.

They were yesterday picked up by a plane – having used a shovel to iron out the creases in the ice for a runway – to begin the long journey back to South Africa, which will include several plane hops and a ten-day journey across the Southern Ocean in a boat – easily the worst bit of the trip in my book.

Longsdon is brother of successful rookie trainer Charlie and owner of recent 33-1 Ludlow winner Royal Katidoki. He also, in his guise as landlord of the Tunnel House, a pub near Cirencester, promoted the 'Pummel in the Tunnel' otherwise known as Andrew Balding's charity boxing thrashing of Windsor clerk of the course David Mackinnon last summer. Six weeks before he left Longsdon married Davina Brennan, daughter of stipendiary steward Terence Brennan and a wife of extreme understanding to let him go on a three-month honeymoon with his mates and without her.

Sweet owned Frenchman's Creek (winner of the National Hunt Handicap Chase) and Marble Arch (runner-up in the Champion Hurdle) and is step-son of Hughie Morrison. For all I know Henry Cookson, the third member of the team, doesn't know what a horse looks like. They had form, however, having won the Scott Dunn Polar Challenge in 2005.

Unlike Richard Dunwoody, who has undertaken similar ventures, these lads had the good sense not to man-handle their 18stone 'pulks' all the way; instead they were pulled along by kites (the size of a small parachute on a 50ft line) for most of the journey and reached speeds of ten mph. On their last day, when it was -58C in the wind chill, they covered 150 miles in 18 hours.

Sweet was so tired he began hallucinating and believed there was a fifth man on the trip. Shackleton, they say, had the same experience when he was on his knees. Great but fuddled minds, it seems, think alike.

Only one group has ever been to Inaccessibility before, a Soviet expedition using large tracked vehicles in 1958. When they got there they built a hut and stuck a bust of Lenin on a tall pole. When this lot got there Lenin, of all people, was waiting for them but the hut, in which there is a visitors' book, was ten feet under snow – however, they managed to excavate a hole to the front door. "They must be mad," is Morrison's succinct diagnosis of the team's principal ailment. January 23, 2007

FOR a long time the National Trainers' Federation would have struggled to put together the semblance of a basketball team. A lot of trainers, at some stage, rode and by virtue of the weight-for-height scale it goes without saying that the sport is not populated by huge numbers of six-footers.

At the moment I'd say, guessing, the tallest is probably Ed Dunlop at about 18.3hh. If he had any hair to speak of John Gosden would probably give him a run for his money while James Fanshawe's height is purely an optical illusion. He looks taller than he is because he's so narrow in much the same way The Chair looks so much bigger than the third fence in the National when, in reality, there's only an inch between them.

However, in the space of a few weeks, like the old London bus scenario, we now have two giant additions to the training ranks and, just to confuse the issue, they even look similar. Within days of David Pipe assuming the mastership of Nicholashayne, we now have 6ft 5in Charlie Longsdon, one of the few people capable of seeing eye-to-eye with David, applying for a licence.

"David came up to me recently," says Charlie, "and said how pissed off he was because someone had just mistaken him for me. I'm glad it happened to him. It happens to me every day. People call me 'Dave' at the races all the time."

After five years of assisting Nicky Henderson, during which time the yard sent out seven Festival winners, Charlie, like a condemned man, had one last breakfast (a Tessa Henderson-cooked fry-up) on Friday before leaving the comfort zone of Seven Barrows. Now, with just a HRA interview to pass, he will start training from the Cotswold Stud near Broadway in the autumn.

Relations are normally the first port of call for an aspiring trainer. His parents, great racing fans but hitherto never owners, look like being presented with something purchased from Doncaster sales this week and, crucially, the bill while his brother, Rupert, a rather successful publican, will also be tapped up along with his customers.

Longsdon has the relevant experience. Henderson apart he spent a 'gap' year with Nigel Twiston-Davies, three years with Kim Bailey and won the Alex Scott Memorial Fund Scholarship, which took him to Todd Pletcher's in America.

His irrelevant experience includes a degree in history of art and anthropology from Oxford Brookes and a spell in the Lewa rhino reserve in Kenya. At the 60,000-acre park, the rhino were fenced in and the poachers, theoretically, fenced out. Failing that, Charlie was licensed to kill should he come face to face with a poacher, an event luckily for all concerned that never happened. It is always handy when training certain jumpers, though, to have some experience of looking after big, ungainly, thick-skinned beasts. JUNE 23, 2006

RICHARD JOHNSON is from the school of thought that reckons training racehorses is not rocket science. Like most top jump jockeys from Scudamore to McCoy if they don't win, they think you gallop them faster, further or steeper – until they do.

Consequently, he is frequently left baffled by the number of 'experts' employed by Adlestrop trainer Richard Phillips. And in a small way he may have a point as the only 'expert' Phillips hasn't had round there lately is someone specialising in feng shui.

Currently, the trainer retains Corky, Woody and Yogi. That's sports psychologist Michael Caulfield to make the staff feel good about themselves. That's Richard Dunwoody to make the pretty girls in the yard feel good about him and Yogi Breisner to make the horses feel good about their jumping.

Second jockey Warren Marston, who is also sceptical about this retinue of retainers, was watching racing on television recently when he noticed Yarmi, the well-known Newmarket horse whisperer, load a difficult horse into the stalls. He thought to himself: "That's the sort of person Phillips would employ," and saw an opportunity for a practical joke on 'Dickie' Johnson, so he rang him.

"That's it," said Warren. "That's the final straw, Dickie. I'm not going to ride out for Phillips again. He's only gone and got Yarmi to look at all the horses."

"Who the hell is Yarmi?" replied a flabbergasted Dickie.

"He can tell if a horse is nervous," explained Warren. "He's only been round, touched every horse and picked out the nervous ones."

Though peeved at the thought of it Dickie gave it little more consideration until his next visit to Adlestrop last Monday. Having been primed by Warren, the assistant trainer tied some baler-twine into the forelock of a strong chasing type as the jockey was saddling it up.

"What the **** is that all about?" asked Dickie. The assistant explained that it was a result of Yarmi's visit and it was to 'soothe' his nervous mount. Dickie just raised his eyebrows heavenwards.

Circling outside the yard Warren nodded towards Dickie's mount's head decorated with baler-twine and winked. "Don't even go there," said Dickie. "That freak who came round the horses on Saturday told them to put it in. I'm not even going to mention it."

However, at the top of the gallop after the first canter Warren asked Dickie how the horse had gone with the baler-twine. "Well between you and me," confided Dickie, "it didn't pull as hard as it usually does. But I'm not going to tell anyone else. You know how this sort of thing winds me up."

Shortly afterwards one of the girls riding out asked him what was with the baler-twine. "Either," said Dickie, returning to his pet subject of criticising the 'experts', "it got its head stuck in its hay-net last night or Phillips has paid another freak £500 a month to speak rubbish and he believes them."

However, he was so convinced by the soothing powers of the dangling baler-twine he tied some in himself for second lot – without being asked. As yet, although the rest of the weighing room is in on it, Dickie is still none the wiser. "As he writes for *The Times* and doesn't read the *Telegraph*," says Warren, "he probably won't be any wiser when you write it either." OCTOBER 25, 2005

DINNER with Kingston Lisle trainer Charlie Morlock was cancelled last week when the principal ingredient of the meal, a pheasant, went missing in unusual circumstances.

Morlock, enjoying a good season with several winners, is one of those people who could live off the land or, indeed, the road. He had acquired the bird not, as you might expect, as a souvenir brace at the end of a day's shooting but because it, flying west to east, had met a vehicle travelling south to north, same time, same grid reference. Partial to roadkill myself, I've always maintained it disproves the theory that there's no such thing as a free meal.

Anyway, he stuck the fatally damaged bird in his car and, as you do, forgot about it when he got home and the creature was unintentionally left to 'hang' (as it were) under the passenger seat.

During the night, however, his car/game larder, a black Passat, was stolen. Two things were striking at this stage. One was that the thieves left the 'hot hatch', a high-performance Subaru WRX, parked next to it and, secondly, that there was enough diesel in the Passat plodder to get it to where it was discovered by police the following morning just along the Ridgeway.

Apart from the bumper Morlock had to explain (which took some doing) to incredulous detectives that only two other things of value were missing from the car: a bag of coppers (two-penny pieces as opposed to policemen) and one dead pheasant.

In return the thieves left a ski jacket and, while you can be pretty sure they won't have dined on pheasant hotpot, you can rest assured Morlock will wear that jacket until it's worn out. NOVEMBER 28, 2006

IT IS, in several respects, a long way from the Slad Valley to St Tropez as trainer Tom George has found out somewhat to his embarrassment.

The Stroud-based trainer was on a day trip 'en famille' (since we're in France) to the pricey Riviera resort and had just had an exceptionally good but not overly cheap lunch in a snug little back-street restaurant.

He was returning to his conveyance for the day – not unnaturally in that part of the world, a boat – when he and his two sons, aged two and four, were caught short.

They noticed in the marina sea-wall, to which were moored some of the world's most expensive gin palaces, a steel door above which was the sign 'toilette 1 euro'. Tom, his wife Sophie and boys turned their pockets out and could only come up with a solitary one-euro coin between them.

The loo, looking not unlike an elevator internally, was all-singing, all-dancing. It was cavernous, made entirely of stainless steel and by some primitive Mediterranean standards (a couple of footplates and a hole in the ground) positively 22nd century sci-fi. Despite the fact that it would fit a family of 14 let alone four, Tom stubbornly decided he'd let the wife pee the children first and he'd go in next while she dutifully put a foot in the door to prevent it closing.

Well, all was going to plan until the George children took off in the direction of the sea and Sophie had little choice but to withdraw her foot and make sure none of her offspring, as little boys are prone to do, jumped into the marina. As she did the door clunked shut.

Inside Stroud's most famous trainer was just unzipping when the lights went out and the contraption began to whirr and vibrate so much that, in the belief that he was on an Alton Towers horror ride, he clung to the walls – even Sir Edmund Hillary couldn't cling on to stainless steel walls – lest the floor gave way to open sewers. Then it began to spray jets of disinfected water from the ceiling, the walls and the floor like the world's most advanced shower/bidet.

Inside, after what seemed an eternity, the washing cycle came to a halt. Outside, of course, film stars, world famous celebrities and the mega-rich, all potential racehorse owners, were promenading back to their yachts from their restaurants for their post-prandial kips when they were startled, from a hole in the wall, by the appearance of a green thing – stinking of disinfectant. "Incroyable," they whispered and hurried on.

The green thing started running past them towards the marina and, when he came to the edge, just kept going and dived in. "We have a rule in our family now," says the trainer with the moral of the story, "that when abroad everyone keeps a one-euro coin on them at all times." AUGUST 30, 2005

YOU didn't honestly think David Loder would never train another horse when he handed in his licence for the last time, did you?

One way or another he has caused a bit of a stir since he left Newmarket – or was it Evry or Dubai, no I'm sure it was Newmarket – and returned to his Cotswold roots.

Anyway, the background to the following tale is that when he and his cousin Roddy Fleming formed a private pack of hounds to 'hunt' parts of the Heythrop country in Gloucestershire, it caused a certain frisson with the local branch of the pony club. You may even have read about it in the papers.

That's all happily shaking itself out now but Roddy thought it might be rather nice, for old times' sake, to win the members' race at the Heythrop point-to-point a week ago on Sunday.

To add a bit of all-too-seldom-seen style and class to the occasion he would then take the winner's trophy, the doubled-handed silver Brassey Cup, fly to London from Chipping Norton in a helicopter and celebrate by drinking champagne from it in a private box at the Emirates Stadium while watching Arsenal later on in the same afternoon.

To pull off the long-hatched plan he roped in cousin David on the advisory side – a bit, we think, like Simon Crisford at Godolphin – to help with the training of the useful ex-Paul Nicholls-trained Lord Anner, although the placing of the horse was, so to speak, already a done deal.

The jockey was the experienced point-to-point pilot and safe pair of hands Jon Trice-Rolph, who has ridden more winners than most of us have had hot dinners. He is also whipper-in to Mr Fleming's Hounds so, in effect, was doubly qualified to take the mount.

But the best-laid-plans of mice and men ... went astray at the open ditch. The race went to 25-1 outsider Sandmartin, a first winner from virtually a first ride for apprentice blacksmith Charlie Sands.

But it doesn't end there. This bit may be apocryphal but in the confusion of catching up loose horses, battered jockeys and bits of tack scattered around the point-to-point course, as well as the tight timings of reaching the Emirates Stadium in time for kick-off, Roddy 'forgot' his bloodstock adviser/cousin on the helicopter flight. In order to make it David had to, cupless as he was, belt down the M40 to London in his motor – somewhat less stylishly than anticipated. JULY 31, 2007

THERE has been mole trouble at The Pheasant Inn, the popular watering hole for racing folk just outside Lambourn run by expert fly-caster Johnny the Fish.

Inside, under the steely gaze of great trainers past like Fred Winter, a mole has been caught passing on information about various people to tabloid gossip columnists.

Careless talk costs lives and in this case it's highly likely to be the mole's life which is costed if he continues to pass on news of little local indiscretions.

Ways of getting rid of him are currently under review. The introduction of Chatham House Rules to normal pub rules is one suggestion, although it is too late for another prominent option, to entomb him in the foundations of the Pheasant's new hotel annex. The concrete's long down and the wing is already open for business.

While that has been ongoing, an outside mole problem has arisen. Little eruptions of soil started appearing on the lawn where the marquee for Johnny's daughter's wedding is due to go up in the summer.

So he sought the expertise of the only man to call in these situations, the figure feared the length and breadth of the Lambourn Valley by the little black velvety digger – big Pete Walwyn, the former champion trainer who caught 400 moles on the gallops in his first season at Seven Barrows.

"Yes," recalls Big Pete taking up the story, "Johnny rang saying he'd got a spot of trouble and I said I'd have a look. It's a knack really, practice and knowing what to do. I put on a pair of rubber gloves and prod around until I find a tunnel. The mole is a very shy animal. You need to trap them because then you know you've caught the buggers. Do you know the Queen decorated her molecatcher?"

So, armed with marigolds and traps the master molester arrived, prodded and set his traps. Moles may have eyesight only marginally better than Andrew Thornton but they are canny creatures with a keen sense of smell and for a long time this particular fellow appeared wise to the whereabouts of the Walwyn trap's steel jaws. Time after time Big Pete returned empty handed from his inspections.

Recently, however, he finally got a result and, not shy about his proficiency in the mole-catching department, he sought a suitable platform to proclaim the fact. As you know Big Pete's stance, even since his knee/hip operations, is a bit like John Wayne's after a long hot day in the saddle and, to the astonishment of lunchtime diners in the restaurant tucking into the soup, he stood before them thus, swinging the little limp monster around his head. "Got one, got one," he bellowed to the startled customers and a dismayed chef. JANUARY 27, 2009

JOHN 'MAD' MANNERS, the man from Highworth, has never been in complete love with authority. Once after returning from a lengthy ban he named a horse Spambruco after the three stewards (Sam Vestey, Bruce Hobbs and Robert Waley-Cohen) who had imposed the suspension.

Now, though, he won't have a bad word said against the BHA. You're probably thinking the old boy's a couple of years the wrong side of his 80th birthday and showing signs of mellowing but not a bit of it. In these difficult times for farmers he's just been done a huge turn by the BHA.

Recently when Robin Gow, the former trainer-turned-BHA yard inspector, called in on a routine inspection Manners, himself, was not in. He was down the fields on his horse with a Charolais cow who had been struggling to calve for hours. It did not look good from anyone's perspective; the farmer's, his accountant's, the cow's and, most immediately, the calf's, which looked odds-against seeing the light of day.

Its two feet were protruding from the cow's back-end, its head was 'back' – a term that equates to 'stuck' – and, compounding the issue, all the vets in the area were busy elsewhere.

Audrey Manners conveyed the news of her husband's whereabouts to the inspector, saying that if he wanted John he had two options: wait or help. To her astonishment he took the second option, stripped off to his waist and put on his BHA-issue waterproof trousers.

"He's got quite a nice body," says Audrey in an aside to the story. "A bit skinny possibly but quite nice – I don't get to see that many these days."

But like James Herriott in his pomp, Robin shoved his arms up to his elbows in a place I dare say not many others on the BHA payroll have been and, by pushing and pulling, slowly but surely straightened the calf out and, just like Shane Warne's first ball in a English Test match, it was the perfect delivery.

"There's no question he saved its life," says Audrey. "The BHA has gone up in John's estimation no end. He thinks they've got a proper man working for them now. Normally when they come if there's a cowpat they step round it – but not Robin." JULY 15, 2008

WINNING a race could soon carry a government health warning. The last time we encountered Giles Bravery and his long-suffering wife Fiona the pair were on a fitness drive in the gym. On that occasion the Newmarket trainer, who had warmed up nicely on the treadmill, tried to take off his jumper as he continued to run.

He lost his balance and the conveyor belt spat him out backwards into a wall while he was still wrestling his way out of his jumper. Naturally the other users of the gym assumed that the tangled, twitching mass was a man in the final stages of cardiac arrrest. As everyone else went to his rescue, his embarrassed wife kept her head down on the bicycle machine at the other end of the room.

This time he was in a Cambridge garden listening on his mobile to his horse Bustan win a race at Beverley. As the gelding crossed the line, a length to the good, Bravery leaped for joy.

It's not clear whether it was on take-off or landing when the damage, a snapped right Achilles tendon, was done but yet again his antics – this time rolling around in the border of a rather smart garden in agony – embarrassed his poor wife. Hearing his cries of 'hospital, hospital' only as 'wolf, wolf', a cry she had heard often before, she whisked him off home with a rollocking.

"She did take me 48 hours later," complains Bravery, who has yet to master the basic concept of crutches, "but only because she had to go shopping and could throw me out at A&E on the way. They can only operate on an Achilles within 12 hours so that particular medical option was no longer open. Now it's got to be in plaster for three months."

Mrs Bravery's version is, naturally, slightly different. "The doctor said he couldn't operate because of the three Fs: fat, fags and unfit," she says. JULY 15, 2008

RICHARD PHILLIPS, the trainer, has never learned to swim and on five occasions, much to the amusement of his close friends, he has nearly drowned.

There is, a psychiatrist would probably tell you, a deeper reason for his inability to swim other than the patently obvious: laziness. His father, a merchant seaman, couldn't swim either. When his boat was torpedoed in World War II he assumed he would not make it so he handed his life-jacket to a sailor with a family – which earned him a mention in despatches – and clung to a piece of wood. While he was later rescued those who swam for it never made it.

"It didn't do him any harm so I've never worried too much about it," says Phillips. "I've nearly drowned several times much to the hilarity of many people. John Francome once tried to teach me to swim by going through his legs, which put me off more than the water. Anyway he's hardly Mark Spitz himself."

The latest incident came when Phillips fell in a lake at Welcombe Golf Course near Stratford at an owner's golf day last week. Playing with his swimming coach, his assistant Gordon Clarkson and an owner, Rick Allen, he teed off at the eighth.

Initially his shot looked good before it faded left towards the deep water hazard. "I didn't see a ripple," said the visually challenged Clarkson, helpfully. "With your eyesight I'm surprised you can see the lake," suggested Francome.

There, however, 100 yards from the hole but six inches from the water's edge Phillips' ball had come to rest in an empty swan's nest. While any normal human being would have taken a penalty shot and moved the ball a club's length, there was money riding on this so he opted for a precarious wedge shot.

As soon as Francome congratulated him on a cracking shot, the un-reinforced banks began to crumble under his not insignificant weight and, plop, he was gone.

Before effecting a rescue, Francome unselfishly rang the two other members of the fourball to tell them to come and watch because he didn't want to be the only one to enjoy the sight of the trainer drowning. In his wet shorts Phillips spent the rest of the day looking like a sweaty Don Estelle in It Ain't Half Hot Mum. MAY 5, 2009

BOOKMAKERS don't always get a great press but Sportingbet deserve a pat on the back for putting a five-figure sum into Heros, the Homing Ex-Racehorses Organisation Scheme, which is based at North Farm Stud near Great Shefford and run with enthusiastic drive by Grace Muir.

Heros now finds homes for more ex-racehorses than the other three rehoming charities put together and has been so busy that the old stud office was no longer big enough to cope.

A very good-looking, hunky electrician, much fancied by all the female members of staff, was putting the finishing touches to a light fitting in the new office the other day. Our Gracie, who has moments of formidableness, was on the phone to an owner discussing an imminent operation to geld his colt but she was oblivious to the electrician's presence.

"His testicles are big enough now and ripe for the picking," she said in her own down-to-earth way. "I think we should do it tomorrow."

On overhearing his end of the conversation the panic-stricken electrician fled to the hills and hasn't been seen since. MAY 27, 2009

Chapter Four
MY FAMILY AND OTHER ANIMALS

NORMAL village life was suspended in Wildhern, Andover, recently when William Johnson went missing. William is the working (a fact disputed by her husband) cocker spaniel belonging to Marty Johnson, the long-suffering wife of *Daily Express* racing correspondent Rolf.

Like a lot of racing households, the basis for the pecking order is number of legs, four being infinitely preferable to two. To put her love of William into context, having nursed Rolf through serious illness, Marty recently went away on a short break leaving the dog, suffering from a small tumour, and her husband, undergoing radiotherapy, at home.

Among other instructions, recalls Rolf, was the order that when she returned she had no desire to find William in an urn. "What about me?" he asked. "Oh," she replied, "I'm not bothered about you."

When William disappeared Marty formidably threw herself and the village into finding the dog. A number of emergency services, like the police and the council's dog warden, were alerted. Emma Lavelle's stable lads were requisitioned to form a search party, telecom engineers who had been halfway up a telegraph pole had no chance – they came under orders to get down and get looking – while light aircraft with thermal imaging were prepared to scramble at Thruxton.

Rolf, meanwhile, was unaware of the state of emergency that had been declared in North Hampshire. He spent the morning at Ascot sales purchasing a store horse – he's nothing if not positive about his illness – before an afternoon visit to his oncologist for an update on his progress.

Meanwhile Mrs Johnson was about leave the house when she stuck her head into the larder where, patiently but sheepishly, sat William, who had followed her in on a previous visit earlier in the day.

"You'd have thought," shrugged her husband, "he'd have had the sense to bark." November 11, 2008

EXTREMELY good news about Little Knickers who, after finding herself drawn next to Primed And Poised on her racecourse debut at Lingfield, was withdrawn after coming down in the stalls. She's completely recovered and due to run in the 6.10 at Kempton tomorrow. JUNE 5, 2007

OTHER PARTS of this newspaper have been taken lately by entertaining epitaphs. As a former jump jockey mine would probably be something along the lines of 'Fell at the last – not for the first time.'

But what about the other, less morbid, end of our short stay on this earth? If you are on the ball you will have noticed last Friday in the births section of the 'hatch, match and dispatch' announcements that Angus Loughran, the *Telegraph*'s punting expert, has just sired a colt, Benedict Henry James.

As a postscript to the announcement the golf-mad pundit added: 'A future Open champion.' Two above him in the same column under the name Heaton-Armstrong the father (maybe it was the wife) announced a fourth child but with the more dire prediction 'snip, snip!' I see a trend developing.

Ben's mum, Blanche, gave birth to him in a hospital just round the corner from Ibrox, home of Rangers, the Protestant team in Glasgow. "We don't get too many Benedicts in this part of town," confided the midwife.

Having also bumped into the prime minister Gordon Brown just before the birth, Angus, leaving nothing to chance, persuaded him to sign two cards, one for a boy and the other for a girl. He gave the discard to his racing producer at the BBC, Carl Hicks, who had a little girl the same day.

On the subject of offspring I ran my own son in a two-year-old maiden at his nursery last week. He was well schooled for the stalls (having had it drummed into him to start running on 'steady') but I knew he'd be a bit green if left out in front on his own for too long. A proverbial fence clear he threw himself on the ground four strides from the finish – he'd been watching too much jump racing on television. My admiration for trainers who get juvenile horses to win first time out has just gone up. JULY 31, 2007

THERE goes my summer holiday. Anyone watching the BBC's latest Sunday night Jane Austen costume drama *Sense and Sensibility* – described in one critique as a 'breeches ripper' – cannot have failed to have been charmed by the wonderful location of Mrs Dashwood's cottage on the North Devon coast.

In real life – as revealed last week in the *Daily Telegraph*, which even offered readers the chance to win a week at the place – it is a holiday cottage called Blackpool Mill at the end of a long track belonging to Sir Hugh and Lady Angie Stucley of nearby Hartland Abbey.

Without casting aspersions (in the style of Mrs Dashwood's unsubtle innuendo-riddled cousin Sir John Middleton) on their daughters, the two Miss Stucleys, I'd hazard a guess that a few breeches had been ripped there long before the BBC arrived – both are married to jockeys.

Boo, the eldest, is better known as Mrs Tom Scudamore, currently expecting their second child, while Louby, an artist who used to ride out for Nigel Twiston-Davies, was recently married to titan of the tartan turf, point-to-point jockey Ranald Morgan, a winner at Larkhill on Saturday.

Plenty of their racing friends, like Tony Dobbin, Rose Davidson, Joe Tizzard and Twiston-Davies, have spent holidays there and I even took it for a glorious week a couple of summers ago. I have a feeling it'll be out of my price range now especially as it has both electricity and heating, two luxuries it didn't have then.

In the Austen drama one of the Dashwood daughters, Elinor, is 'sense' while the other, Marianne, is 'sensibility'. Which did Ran think he'd married? "Definitely sense," he said diplomatically before adding, "with a fringe of sensibility! The best of both worlds."

Louby, who specialises in horse and dog portraits, has had to take time out from painting because of a badly broken collarbone after a nasty fall while riding – riding on the shoulders of a tall friend at a dance.

But despite unprecedented demand for the cottage since it appeared on television, Mr and Mrs Morgan are hoping to take Blackpool Mill for a week in the summer. "Louby's entered the *Telegraph* quiz," revealed her ever hopeful husband. JANUARY 8, 2007

RIDING FOR A FALL

THE HILLS twins, Michael and Richard, learned to cope with it out of necessity but for point-to-point brothers Ranald and Luke Morgan, sibling rivalry proved highly expensive at the Haydon point-to-point last weekend.

For the first time in their ten years of riding together the brothers, from Dumfriesshire, landed upsides over the last fence together – in the men's open at Hexham. "I have to say sibling rivalry got the better of us and the whip rules," admits Ran, 28, who finished runner-up on Hoh Tel to Luke, 26, on Starbuck.

"We had it planned beforehand to dominate proceedings and all went to plan except that the little bastard won," says Ran. "I was fined £100. It's bad enough being beaten by your little bro but when they only fined the little sh*t £50 – that was just rubbing salt to the wound."

I don't think our hearts should bleed too much for them. Despite being born in Scotland they both operate as property spivs in the south now. Round two in the hunter chase at Cartmel yesterday looked incident-free. JUNE 10, 2006

Siblings

JOHNNO SPENCE, public relations consultant to many in the racing industry, has just pulled off a huge PR coup even by his own standards. One of his 'employees' or rather Johnno's angels, Anna-Lisa Balding, wife of trainer Andrew Balding, has just called her first born Jonno James or 'JJ' for short. Only the 'h' is missing.

JJ, who was due to come under starters' orders in mid-December, was clearly quite comfortable where he was and delayed his entry into this world by nearly a fortnight.

In some respects his timing was perfect, on his father's birthday last Friday, but in others it was not so good. His sports-mad father had to miss a lads' night out – in fact with the other Johnno, his own assistant Chris Bonner and Charlie Vigors – to the quarter-finals of the Ladbrokes PDC World Darts Championships at the Circus Tavern in Purfleet. (Just as an interesting aside – the PDC is the only sporting venue that I know of which hosts one round of a world championship one night and lap-dancing the next – it would be like Cheltenham closing for a day during the Festival for a gentleman's smoking evening.)

Anyway, the action in the maternity ward of Basingstoke General did not prevent the new father getting home in time to watch the 'arrers' on Sky. Just as Phil 'The Power' Taylor got to the stage to tumultuous applause the camera, much to Balding's delight, caught three blokes holding up a banner that read 'Push Anna-Lisa'.

While on the subject of Balding medical notes we can also report that grandpa Ian, who broke his neck and back in a fall out riding a week before Christmas, is now back home but confined to barracks. Martin Dwyer, former stable apprentice, brought round some DVDs that he described as 'raunchy' in parts to aid Ian's recovery, so the retired trainer is currently busy fast-forwarding through these films.

"We've told him he can teach JJ cricket, rugger and tennis," says Andrew. "But he's not to take him riding." JANUARY 2, 2007

AS I seem to spend most of this column plugging things for other people I might as well plug something of my own before I stick them on eBay. From a litter of five I have two male black and tan terrier pups, aged six weeks, for sale. They are impeccably bred, by Sir Michael Stoute's Rocky, out of my own top-class rabbiter Turpentine – and were conceived in a car boot at David Nicholson's memorial service. Good homes only need apply. JANUARY 2, 2007

I APOLOGISE for bringing my family into this column for the second week running but after one of the wettest winters on record and with a genuine prospect of heavy ground at a Festival for the first time since Desert Orchid's Gold Cup in 1989 – the last time it was heavy for a Champion Hurdle on the first day was when For Auction won in 1982 – scholarship material Arthur Armytage, 2.5, awoke to a new concept in his little world last Friday. He saw a visible sunrise and asked the following pertinent question: "Daddy," he said, "where's raining?" MARCH 6, 2007

SIR PERCY is a huge advertisement for Angela Sykes who, in her first season as a fully fledged bloodstock agent, selected him for trainer Marcus Tregoning for 16,000gns.

So we appear to have two options here. Either it's incredible beginners' luck or it is the start of a spectacular career. But with Strategic Prince due to represent her judgement in the Coventry Stakes, it looks like the latter and, as if to confirm that yesterday, she was really getting into the mode of serious bloodstock agent – fishing on the Spey. Tomorrow it'll be large cigars.

I have always admired those who can spot potential in full-size horses let alone a half-grown one, although this admiration is not universally shared in the press room. I'll let you in on a little secret here but, in the pecking order of pond life, if there is one profession that racing journalists consider ourselves superior to in the food chain of respectability, it is the poor old bloodstock agent. (There could be an ancient jealousy at work here as, essentially, it's always slightly galling to see someone getting paid for spending someone else's money.)

They also seem to lead two distinct lives in that they are omnipresent in the winner's enclosure after a purchase triumphs, unashamedly nudging up to the winning owner, but they melt away into the undergrowth if the same purchase has to unsaddle with the also-rans.

It has been a long apprenticeship for young Angie, whose mother, Pamela, used to train jumpers near Ludlow. Angie used to train pointers herself and in the summer, armed with her vet's and blacksmith's bills, would take off for Scotland with her Magimix and lurcher Smudge in the back of the car and cooked until she had paid them off.

Far from being a girl's best friend, Smudge proved a constant let-down. Once after chasing a stag over a moor he jumped in the famous Arndilly beat of the Spey to cool off which, as you can imagine, went down with the local fly-fishermen about as well as lobbing in a hand-grenade. On another occasion when she cooked for a man fastidious about his garden, to the point where the gardener was made to blow the leaves off the lawn, the dog dug for Australia the evening before she was due to leave.

She spent two years at Ballydoyle and a year with Tom George. She still has not given up on training one day but took the logical view that there's little point in training unless you have the right stock in your yard. In order to learn what a good horse looks like she joined James Delahooke, the man who bought Dancing Brave and Quest For Fame, as his assistant for five years.

In the early days this involved some fairly menial tasks, like holding a coat on a hot day or the umbrella when it was raining, but it was his methodical approach that ensured she did not miss Sir Percy, who is by the unfashionable Mark Of Esteem. JULY 6, 2005

WHEN Christophe Soumillon, the French jockey, won the King George VI and Queen Elizabeth Diamond Stakes on Hurricane Run at Ascot a year and a half ago, instead of Churchill's V-for-victory sign or something equally dignified, he made a hand gesture to his backside.

I don't want to get into the precise meaning of this signal – you wouldn't need to be a hearing dog for the deaf to work it out – but I believe it had something to do with what he thought of the British jockeys behind him, in that nine times out of ten, they bury him in a race if they can. Obviously, on that occasion, they couldn't get close enough to Hurricane Run.

On Saturday, after winning the Victor Chandler on Tamarinbleu, you may have noticed Tom Scudamore repeating something he first did when Lough Derg won the Long Walk Hurdle at Ascot just before Christmas. He transferred his whip from his left hand to his right after crossing the line and with his free arm stretched out towards the crowd made a snapping movement with his hand and repeated it several times.

What's it all mean, this novel celebratory salute? "It's a message to Margot, my young daughter," says modern father Tom Scu, not a bit embarrassed. "When you ask her what a lion does, she roars. When you ask her what a dog does, she barks. But when you ask her what a crocodile does, she makes this snapping movement with her hand. So that's it really – it's a crocodile snapping. I was sort of dared to do it by my wife, Charlotte, but only when I win a race big enough."

I think we've just about heard it all now. JANUARY 22, 2008

STORKS have been busy in the Lambourn area this past week and the local registrar is going to be asking 'and how would you be spelling that?' when it comes to issuing birth certificates.

One has to hope Jim Culloty's timing on Best Mate in the Gold Cup is better than it was last Wednesday. After a night in the delivery suite he was told that wife Suzie would, one way or another, give birth at about midday – just long enough for him to pop home, freshen up and return. He returned in plenty of time or so he thought but it turned out to be ten minutes after his son had been delivered.

A couple of weeks after newspapers carried stories about the largest baby born in the country for eight years Art Culloty, as he shall be called, weighed in not far behind at a thumping great 9lb 6½oz. In the likelihood that he is a sportsman his options look limited to rowing, rugby or Gaelic football.

"Art is an Irish name," explains Jim before giving a slightly American explanation. "As in Art Garfunkel. It's not short for Arthur. He arrived on Suzie's birthday so he saved me having to buy her a present." When questioned as to what proportion of his 9lb 6½oz might be attributable to his father's greatest attribute, his nose, Jim was reticent. "Let's just say the parentage was confirmed," he says.

Meanwhile Lambourn trainer Ralph Beckett's wife, Izzie, has given birth to a little girl on Saturday. In what appears to be an effort to give the Beckhams a run for their money she is to be called Katinka – a cross between Katherine and Tinkerbell – which is a new one on me. "And on me, too," says the happy father. MARCH 8, 2005

NOWADAYS winning the Derby doesn't exonerate you from life's normal chores like the occasional school run or, most recently for Michael Bell, helping his mother move house. And just like he did with Motivator he threw himself into the job with a certain amount of efficiency and confidence.

Mike's mum's biggest worry about moving was her tortoiseshell cat, Polly. Cats don't move quite as well as dogs and to remind Polly that she was now living elsewhere, Mrs Bell decided to do what all good cat owners would do and keep Polly shut in the house for the first week. You really have to drum it into cats don't you?

Anyway Mike was in the garden when he noticed the cat slip across the road. "Hell," he thought having read somewhere that moving house was the next most stressful thing after divorce, "there could be no greater drama at this stage of proceedings than Polly going AWOL." And off he set in subtle pursuit.

Cut to Mr Motivator, lying in the middle of the street, hand held out and calling: "Here pussy! Here pussy." Curtains in the close-knit village of Stourton, as you can imagine, twitched and the neighbourhood watch scheme was activated. The cat, meanwhile, responded much like Motivator to his animal magnetism and came to him, whereupon he scooped her up.

Meanwhile Mrs Bell's new neighbour had just seen her own tortoiseshell 'catnapped' from under her nose by a stranger. Mike returned to his mum and proudly presented her with the neighbour's cat at exactly the same time that the neighbour arrived to claim it back while, oblivious to the commotion, Polly slept soundly in the sitting room. It is one way, I suppose, of breaking the ice with the neighbours. NOVEMBER 8, 2005

LAWNEY and Alan Hill have been well known in the point-to-point world for years, for both riding them and, latterly, training them. The start to Lawney's professional training career could not have begun any better, although there was a give-away clue that she came from pointing – she made Robert 'Choc' Thornton wear woollen colours on the hottest day of the year.

Her first runner, Bell Rock, won not only the race at Uttoxeter but, led up in the parade ring by their daughter, Gaby, won £50 for the best turned out. That was, by my calculations, two winners from one runner so it can only be downhill all the way now.

But not everything went as smoothly as it looked. As it was her first runner as a grand professional trainer she was not expecting to have to break up a squabble between Gaby, 12, and her nine-year-old brother, Joe, over the £50. As Gaby is too young to go into the racecourse stables she thought £50 for ostensibly leading a horse round the paddock four times was money for old rope. Joe reckoned he deserved at least a 50 per cent cut of the unearned income. Lawney's solution was simple – to take the money for herself. AUGUST 9, 2005

I HAVE romantic news from the most unlikely of sources. The form book has been completely shredded on this one because Anthony Stroud, former racing manager to Sheikh Mohammed and successful bloodstock agent, has become engaged. Until now he has, for years, been second top-rated confirmed bachelor in racing after Sir Mark Prescott. However neither he nor onlookers – in this case a herd of gazelle – were totally sure he'd got the nod from his girlfriend, Camilla Courage, when he popped the question.

On the last day of a riding safari in Kenya he and Camilla had dropped off the main string when he pointed out that her horse looked lame. Gallantly – and despite the horse being sound as a bell – he said he would see if it had a stone in its foot. While looking for the non-existent stone he got down on bended knee and took off his hat – he burns easily I seem to remember – and proposed.

With that Camilla uttered an "Oh my God" and galloped off leaving him on his knee in a cloud of dust. Surrounded by giraffe, zebra and who knows what else lurking in the bush, he was unsure quite whether that exclamation and manoeuvre was a 'yes' or 'no'. His uncertainty was prolonged because his own mount wouldn't, having been left on its own, stand still long enough for him to remount. When he finally caught up he was given the thumbs-up.

That was last Thursday, but back on duty at the sales in Kentucky yesterday Anthony was receiving calls of congratulations from around the world. "But I'm expecting a wreath from Sir Mark," he added. JANUARY 11, 2005

IT COMES to something when a trainer, with recourse to all-weather gallops, horse walkers, work-companions, the best crushed Scottish oats – you could go on forever – struggles to get his son's pony fit but that had been perplexing Lambourn's Dominic ffrench Davis until very recently.

He had bought a 13hh jumping pony for his son, Ben, five months ago and, having reached the jump-off at Lambourn show recently, the trainer had been somewhat disappointed that the pony, when the chips were down, was not as fast as he had been led to believe and, though it jumped an exemplary round, was well down on the clock.

"I did think she was a bit dip-backed and carried her weight a bit low down," says the master of Windy Hollow in his defence. For on Friday he received an early morning call from his head girl on her feeding round to say that beside Ben's pony was a nice chestnut colt foal asleep in the straw.

"The thing is," says Dominic, "I bought her off a vet, lo and behold, and when I rang to tell him the happy news he seemed to have gone ex-directory. She was flying up the gallops only last week."

The little chap has already been christened by the ffrench Davis family. "He's called Bog Off," he says. "Buy one, get one free." SEPTEMBER 11, 2007

RETIREMENT is clearly not a word in the vocabulary of Chives, the former chaser. You may recall owner Trevor Hemmings found a nice hunting home for him with Aintree managing director, Charles Barnett, and that he first made the Diary for rolling in a ploughed field with his new jockey on board.

Having been under two stern headmistresses, Henrietta Knight and Sue Smith, during his racing career he's clearly finding his new home a soft touch because he continues to play tricks.

A week later, while the Barnetts were out for Sunday lunch, Chives took his new stable companion, another former racehorse, Aghawadda Gold, on a little adventure.

Next door to the Aintree supremo resides Bangor racecourse's robust chairman, Sir Charles Lowther. Sir Charles's pride and joy at Erbistock Hall are his two-tier gardens famed for their topiary and lovingly maintained since the year dot.

Chives, in complete denial that his racecourse career is over, decided to take Aghawadda Gold on a little tour down the hall's drive, over the cattle grid and into the gardens to see if the chairman's 'Bangor' turf was up to scratch. In the process they took in a couple of hedges.

"When they left home they had a lot of options but took the drive to

Erbistock Hall," says Barnett. "We had to do quite a bit of repair work."

Indeed. Aintree's treader-inners were diverted on their journey home to Wolverhampton via Bangor-on-Dee for a bit of filling-in, although Sir Charles's lawn still isn't quite as level as it was before this escapade.
NOVEMBER 14, 2006

IT IS a scene straight out of a modern Black Beauty – except for a few minor details. For 'Beauty' substitute Blowing Wind, placed third in the Grand National twice, and for the little girl looking after Beauty stick in Amanda Sweeting, who has been given the horse to hunt in his retirement.

Amanda was hacking Blowing Wind out last week, getting his back down for the following day's hunting, which he has taken to like a duck to water. After a while she passed a car in which sat a plain-clothes policeman from what would appear, in light of subsequent events, to be the Not-Very-Special Branch. This, though, is how immigration is dealt with at the sharp end.

Our man had been following a lorry in which he and his colleagues reckoned were what he termed 'illegals' – vernacular, it transpires, in those circles for illegal immigrants, although when he first mentioned it Amanda thought she was being asked to deal with a consignment of ill eagles.

To put you in the picture, illegals are no longer kicked out of their transport at the first lay-by out of Dover. It's a bit more subtle than that. Membury, above Lambourn, is a popular spot and many an illegal's first port of call is Marcus Tregoning's. But Bicester seems to be equally popular. "Scuse me, madam," said the opportunistic copper getting out of his car. "I have reason to believe there are illegals being unloaded from that lorry over there." The trouble was that he had done such a covert job he'd parked the wrong side of a hedge and a field away from the lorry. Even if he'd had binoculars – which he didn't – his view would have been obscured by blackthorn.

"A horse," he continued, "is just what the doctor ordered. Could you ride up the field and tell me what you see being unloaded from that lorry?"

So Blowing Wind and Amanda swept into action, at the canter, to investigate. There, sure enough, were dark, hunched figures jumping out of the lorry and legging it into local woodland. Blowing Wind, who can now add police horse to his CV, reported back. Other covert coppers sprung out of the woodwork and another batch of illegals and a lorry driver were apprehended – all thanks to a racehorse. FEBRUARY 15, 2005

LEICESTER staged a couple of pony races, under the auspices of the Jockey Club, on Sunday. The 13.2hh heat was won by Jack Sherwood – son of Simon so no surprises there – and the 14.2hh by Jake Greenall, son of Lord Daresbury so no surprises there either.

Most of the Jockey Club officials volunteered to stay on but the starter was unable to. In the event Capt Nick Lees, the racecourse chairman, stepped in and did his career prospects of becoming a starter no good by getting Tom Wallace, son of the Jockey Club's director of regulation Malcolm Wallace, left five lengths.

His problems are nothing compared to Cathy Twiston-Davies. Her sons, Willie and Sam, have both qualified for the final, at Aintree in October – on the same pony. "I've got World War III on my hands," she says. AUGUST 15, 2006

JUST as most of us are getting warmed up for this year's Cheltenham Festival, the champion jockey has already been approached to ride in next year's Totesport Gold Cup.

In National Velvet meets Jim'll Fix It, one of his younger fans, Miss Ellie Eastwood, 11, from Reading, has written to AP McCoy inquiring as to his availability to ride Chester, her 11-year-old 13.2hh pony, in 2008.

AP, however, is not stupid. He replied that he'd like to see a photo of Chester before committing himself. However, Ellie might have blown it in the letter she sent back with the photos – not just of Chester but also her old horse from a fancy dress competition to which he went as the National Lottery Rollover Unicorn (with apologies for the horn which had fallen off). In it she asked whether AP could give her any advice on getting Chester over ditches, an obstacle he will face four times in the Gold Cup. Speaking on Sunday night, Britain's youngest trainer was in a bullish mood. "He just doesn't like ditches and refuses," she says. "But I think AP would get him over them. I'm pretty confident he'll win." JANUARY 16, 2007

PATRICK MULLINS, 17, recorded his first win against professionals when Adamant Approach got up on the line to win the Pertemps Hurdle qualifier from a field of 27 runners at Leopardstown on Sunday. Trailing in his wake were Ruby Walsh, AP McCoy and most of the Carberry family.

Having his first ride against the leading professionals, young Patrick likened it to a boy playing football with David Beckham at Old Trafford but, while he left his dad in the bar celebrating, he was back at boarding school, Clongowes Wood College, by 6pm.

"I'm not sure whether he had permission or not," says his father, "but I think after winning, the game's up."

The production line of the next generation of Mullins is now in full spate. His cousin Emmet, 16, son of George Mullins, won his first point-to-point in west Cork the same day. As long as it's not during term time it can't be too long before they're riding at Cheltenham. JANUARY 16, 2007 – PATRICK WON THE FESTIVAL BUMPER THERE ON COUSIN VINNY IN 2008

JENNY PITMAN is going to the dogs, increasingly. It's a brave man, I hear you whispering in admiration, to write those words about the former trainer who won a brace of Grand Nationals and Gold Cups and now writes novels entitled 'Vendetta'.

However, Jenny has indeed turned her attentions from horses to greyhounds. In Moonstone Magic, trained by Terry Dartnall, she has a potential champion. Not that she, after a quarter of a century training horses, is one to count her chickens. The dog, one of six she has in training, has run in eight races at Reading and won five, the last two of which have been in open races despite technically still being a 'puppy'. The experts tell me puppies aren't usually good enough to win opens.

"When you train horses you become addicted to an adrenalin rush," she says, "and when I stopped training I missed that. I also missed the social side of talking to animal people. As far as Moonstone Magic is concerned I am taking it one race at a time. I know jolly well the folly of building hopes up. It's like a young horse, the world's his oyster but we'll have to keep our fingers crossed."

Her involvement does not stop at turning up to Reading dogs. "We have the pups at home," she says, "and as my brother is a butcher you can imagine they get fed nothing but the best."

As for Moonstone Magic, he can expect immortality of a sort no matter how good he turns out. The horses in Jenny's thrillers are all named after her greyhounds. JANUARY 17, 2006

THERE HAVE been a couple of high-profile pocket-denting (relatively) National Hunt racing weddings in Ireland lately. Arthur Moore saw his daughter Anna, a bloodstock agent, married off the weekend before last while, as reported by Charlie Brooks yesterday, JP McManus invited his 1,500 closest friends to his daughter Sue Ann's nuptials last weekend.

However, it is an upcoming wedding at the end of August that is causing some consternation at Michael Bell's Fitzroy Stables in Newmarket. We don't often delve too far into pedigrees in the Diary but – concentrate – Michael is married to Georgina (nee Lillingston) and many of the yard's top horses have been bought by Georgina's brother, Luke, who, along with his American business partner Lincoln Collins, is part of the Kern Lillingston bloodstock agency responsible for the purchase of current stable stars Red Evie and Hoh Mike.

In August Georgina's brother Andrew, ergo also Luke's brother, marries Serena Beckett, younger sister of Whitsbury trainer Ralph, and the feeling now is that once the knot is tied, Kern Lillingston's best purchases will have to be split evenly between Fitzroy and Whitsbury. "Hopefully," says the brother of the bride, "although they all seem to be going to Mark Johnston at the moment, so it may be an irrelevance."

By strange coincidence Bell and Beckett are already vaguely related as Bell's grandmother was a Beckett. "It's not that rare," confirms Bell, "most of racing's inter-bred. However some even say Ralph and I look alike."

There are two men, apparently, who confuse the pair: the gateman at Kempton who always wishes Beckett "good luck, Mr Bell" and JP McManus. The latter was once chatting to Beckett in the foyer of the Carlton Tower Hotel before the Derby dinner. He talked for five minutes about how well Beckett's career as a trainer was going but as he left he said: "Good to see you, Mike, give my love to Georgina."

As for the wedding Beckett comments as only a brother can: "Andrew," he says, "is two stone in front of any other boyfriend Serena's ever had." JULY 17, 2007

A RETIRED Classic-winning trainer was updating a friend on what the rest of his family were up to these days and said that his eldest daughter had just split from her second husband. "I'm sorry to hear that," said the friend. "I'm not," said the retired trainer. "I used to call him Thrombosis ... he was a slow-moving clot." JULY 18, 2006

THE PRECOCIOUS three-year-old niece of an up-and-coming trainer, who takes more than a passing interest in her uncle's profession, was recently dictating her mum a letter to Father Christmas, to post up the chimney, with her wish-list of presents for 2005.

Halfway through she came to an abrupt halt. She walked over to the coffee table and picked up a Tattersalls catalogue. "What are you doing?" asked her mum. "I'm going to pick a horse for Father Christmas to give me," she replied, "which I'm then going to send to Uncle Paul." DECEMBER 21, 2005

MUCH HAS been made of David Elsworth's successful move to Newmarket but less has been said about the man who replaced him at Whitsbury, Ralph Beckett.

The trainer has recently hit a rich vein of form. He sent out three winners last week and his 16 winners for the season put him on course for, at least, equalling last year, his best season to date.

If his standing with punters is currently good then it is positively stratospheric with his in-laws, the Adams family. Last Thursday he saddled an almost unique across-the-card double with Lipocco, part-owned by his mother-in-law Kaye Adams, winning a nursery at Leicester and Carloman, part-owned by his father-in-law Arthur, winning the last at Epsom.

"I think I'll be welcome Chez Adams for Christmas this year," points out Ralph. "Lipocco is beginning to look like a smart two-year-old and Carloman has been hard to win with."

Arthur is a proper man. I once met him in Dubai when he and a friend had, during the course of a long evening, polished off nine-tenths of a bottle of Scotch. "Hell," he exclaimed eyeing up what was left in the bottle, "we must have got through a lot of water this evening."

However, Ralph denied rumours that picking out the maiden handicap at Epsom had more to do with the fact that Arthur's favourite band, UB40, were playing shortly after the race than careful race planning on the trainer's part. "UB40 was a nice bonus for him," says Ralph. JULY 25, 2006

THE FOLLOWING story would not be believable if one of the syndicate that leases a certain two-year-old filly in Newmarket was not the highly respected vet Richard Greenwood, who has subsequently penned an as yet unpublished letter to the Veterinary Record under the title: 'Differential diagnosis of head-shaking.'

Head-shakers as the name suggests are horses who constantly shake their heads as if there's something in their ears, although vets have discovered it is more commonly the side-effect of an allergy. Not much notice is paid to it in racing but, obviously, if you have a dressage horse who is a head-shaker then you're in big trouble.

Anyway, one morning recently the unraced filly was uncomfortable about having her bridle fitted but, as her lad couldn't see anything outwardly wrong, she completed a normal exercise that included a trot up to one of Newmarket's all-weather gallops and a canter. On her return she was head-shaking with rather more vehemence so the head lad was called and what appeared to be a worm was found to be dangling from her nostril.

He pulled and found, attached to the end of the 'worm', a rather dazed young mouse who had mistaken the nostril for its hole. It had then heroically resisted all attempts to shake or blow (it must have been like residing in a wind tunnel at the top of the gallop) it out.

The head man didn't have the heart to stamp on the mouse and, having been revived, it was released in a neighbouring stable and the filly was miraculously cured of her affliction. "Maybe," says the eminently rational vet, "it is for the same reason that elephants don't like mice." SEPTEMBER 26, 2006

AN IRISHMAN, who used to ride against my sister Gee, was inquiring after her health recently. "Oh," I said, "she's not long since had a baby, Thomas, and he's doing well but he's quite low down in the pecking order. When it comes to getting attention Thomas comes after her dogs and her boss, AP McCoy."

"Ah, to be sure," he said in full approval. "'Tis a grand t'ing to finish in the first three." FEBRUARY 27, 2007

MY four-year-old son Arthur came to Sandown on Saturday and his resemblance to his father is very much in the 'mini-me' category. "Ah," said an Irish acquaintance on eyeing Arthur up, "the mare didn't jump into the wrong paddock on that occasion!" APRIL 28, 2009

MUCH HINGES on one man and his dog regarding racing at Newbury on Saturday. Stephen Higgins, Newbury's newish major-domo, ordered the fleeces to go down last Friday and, yesterday, it was raceable – under the covers and several tonnes of snow.

Having just arrived back from a skiing holiday in the Alps, Higgins found conditions more suitable for the Game Spirit Langlaufing Championships than the Game Spirit Chase but he remains optimistic.

Current conditions are not ideal for his thin-skinned travelling companion, Fernie the whippet, who is finding the cold snap something of a two-coater.

Fernie's toilet habits have been keeping the staff at Newbury amused ever since he arrived in the office and promptly cocked his leg on a neatly stacked pile of members' renewal applications.

Unfortunately for Fernie, while the rest of us have been doing our utmost to keep our long johns on, he has suddenly found the sap rising and has been going through that most awkward of stages, the whippet's teenage years.

Not content with sexually molesting a 15-year-old dog in the office, he has now taken an unhealthy interest in roger-ing his basket. "It's been a major distraction for all concerned," admits Higgins. Today's the day, alas, and Fernie is off to the vet for an operation. Animal, vegetable or mineral, it should put an end to further amorous advances. FEBRUARY 3, 2009

LOOK AROUND you. Not, obviously, at your own household but in the wider world, at work, on the way there. It is fact that considerably more thought goes into the breeding of thoroughbred horses these days than it does into the breeding of many humans.

It is not an exact science though and, for all that, you still get horses bred to be six-furlong sprinters winning the Grand National just as two non-musical parents might produce someone with the voice of angel.

This is not to cast aspersions on the sporting prowess of Dale Gibson outside of the saddle and I am sure had he not been a jockey he might well have played football to a very high (well, 5ft 6in anyway and width-wise he could always have made a good goal-post) standard but his son, George, 9, just happens to be one of the most precocious young sportsmen in Yorkshire.

George had two trials with Leeds United but turned down a third because it clashed with his under-11 county cricket, quite apart from his position in the county development squad for tennis.

So riding at Wolverhampton on a freezing night is not so much a chore for Gibson snr – it's a relief from the taxi service he provides young George to winter nets.

As northern safety officer he also is a spokesman on any issue that might be construed as dangerous but it is, apparently, not a job he takes home with him because, these long winter nights, George has set up some stumps on the landing and Dale has to bowl at him. "We've lost a couple of lightbulbs so far," he says. "We just have to grin and bear it."
JANUARY 12, 2009

IT IS a well-known fact that when you have a child it starts costing you from the moment it's born until the moment you leave this mortal coil behind. So when Jonny Portman's wife, Sophie, gave birth to twins (Jack and Eliza) last week it did not take the Compton trainer long to work out that, in his case, everything would cost double.

Even he, however, was surprised on leaving the maternity ward of the John Radcliffe Hospital in Oxford, after a three-hour visit, to find that on feeding his parking ticket into a machine it tried to bill him for £1,844.00.

"I'm all prepared to do my bit for the NHS," he says, "but not to that extent."

The trainer, who has a striking similarity to Mr Bean, has already been tangled up trying to put the baby seats in the car for the baby Beans' homecoming on Sunday night. "I think I'm reasonably intelligent and able-bodied," he says, "but can I install a couple of baby seats? I've told Sophie the twins won't be travelling much during the early part of their lives." JANUARY 12, 2009

HENRY PONSONBY, the successful owner and syndicate manager, has some form regarding dogs who steal.

In the 1970s Ponsonby, also known as 'the SAS major' on account of the fact that his most significant job in the army was as a 'live target' for Britain's Elite forces on Otterburn Range (they missed), went to the pub for lunch with his then girlfriend leaving his Labrador in his London flat.

When they returned it had nabbed £100 worth (£500 at today's values) of fillet steak, which the girlfriend had bought to cook at an important directors' lunch later that day. The dog had the good grace, at least, to leave the wrapping paper.

His present black Lab, Rupert, is similarly prone to theft when egged on by his nose and stomach. His speciality is Camembert cheese left anywhere within a six-foot range of the ground.

On one occasion he chomped his way through not only a whole wheel of cheese but the wooden box that it had comfortably filled since it had left the Normandy farm of its origin. Evidence that it was Rupert? The three staples that held the box together were in his basket.

Now, if you follow racing at all closely you'll know the most common jockey's name these days is de Sousa. There's Nelson, Jose and Silvestre, plus a million more waiting in the wings in Brazil until Ponsonby's good mate Paul Cole, who employs most of them, gets his next vacancy.

And where Ponsonby comes into his own with respect to keeping them happy is that he employs the various Mrs de Sousas to clean his house and if he's not there when they've finished scrubbing and hoovering, he leaves their wage on the table. Recently when Ellie de Sousa, wife of Nelson, had finished her morning's work she went to pick up the money only to find it wasn't there.

Later in the day her husband knocked on the door, drew himself up to his full height of 4ft 11in and asked the SAS major if he could have his wife's money. Ponsonby argued that it had been put out as usual but the jockey insisted that his wife had left the house empty handed.

The mystery, however, was solved the following day when Ponsonby was on his pooper-scooping round of the garden and discovered on the end of his shovel a half-digested Adam Smith, who normally decorates the back of the £20 note, looking more poppy-eyed than normal. JULY 12, 2008

WHEN Curtain Call, part-owned by Jimmy George and winner of the Group 3 Mooresbridge Stakes at the Curragh yesterday, disappointed in last year's Derby, finishing tenth after all the pre-race hype, there was a certain amount of deflation in the camp.

"Tell me," said George's boss at Tattersalls, Edmond Mahony, to George's young daughter Charlotte at the rather flat post-race picnic, "what do you make of it all?"

"Well," she replied, "I'm just glad daddy bought my pony before the race rather than after it." MARCH 5, 2009

THE TATTERSALLS golf day at Woburn is an event seldom short of incident. Last year there were many schemes afoot to prevent Jonno Mills winning the competition for the umpteenth time. They reckoned without Mills himself, however, who brained himself on the 13th when a rebounding ball, which he'd whacked into a nearby tree, hit him in the temple.

The event – it's taken him considerably longer to win it than the Derby – was won by William Haggas and his owner Bob Scott. But it was another Derby-winning trainer, Michael Bell, who caused a stir.

Bell was given a lift to Woburn by Nick Wright, a director of Newmarket, in his BMW and when Wright scrunched to a halt on the gravel in front of Fitzroy House, the trainer flung his clubs in the boot without a second thought.

Fast forward an hour and when Bell arrived at what his well-trained secretary described as "a very important meeting – you won't be able to contact him today", he opened the boot to discover Harvey, his son's terrier pup who had hopped in and stowed away. If there's a 'no dogs' policy at Woburn, the car-proud Wright was also adamant that he wasn't having Harvey chew his way through his Beamer for as long as it takes to play 18 holes.

But here Bell's draw saved the day because he had been selected to play with the Duke of Bedford whose back garden, for want of a better description, Woburn is. Thus Harvey spent the rest of the day attached to Bell's golf bag. "He proved a very adept ball cleaner," said Bell without being any more specific. MAY 13, 2008

THE Jockey Club change of address card has just arrived and, one is bold enough to presume, the invitation to the house-warming party at 75, High Holborn has merely been held up in the post.

Once the Jockey Club seemed immovable from Portman Square, although some older readers may even remember the days when a summons to Cavendish Square often foretold bad news for a trainer or jockey.

After a quarter of a century at Portman Square, Shaftesbury Avenue lasted just five years – just long enough to get settled in. Now they have moved from 'luvvie-land' to one of the legal centres of London, where the BHA will join them in the autumn to form a racing one-stop-shop along with the Racehorse Owners' Association and the Racecourse Association. Ben, otherwise known as Racing Enterprises Limited (REL), will also be saving the world from his office there.

So why the hasty move from Shaftesbury Avenue? Well, reports suggest that apart from being all-singing all-dancing, 151 Shaftesbury Avenue is also an all-squeaking Mickey Mouse operation and, no matter that the local pest control officer makes more visits to the place than Jamie Spencer, it is plagued by wee timorous beasties. The Jockey Club, it seems, were sped on their way by mice.

Barely a day goes by at this prestigious address without staff receiving a courtesy visit from their four-legged friends and many a meeting has been disturbed by a yelp from down the passage as one of the various PAs or secretaries about the place has come face to face with a mouse.

One Jockey Club official's afternoon nap was even disturbed by a scrabbling noise near his desk. It was a brazen mouse climbing into his dustbin checking out the leftover sandwich situation. It was Rabbie Burns who wrote Ode To A Mouse after he disturbed a nest of mice while ploughing but there was nothing 'cowrin' or 'tim'rous' about this individual.

Having been confirmed on floors one and seven it is fair to assume they also colonise two to six. MAY 19, 2009

GUY WILLOUGHBY, chief executive of the mine-clearing charity Halo Trust and Corinthian amateur jockey, has retired – true to his word – on a winner. When he made the idle threat to go out in a blaze of glory, luckily he didn't specify that it had to be his own winner for otherwise he might have hung around the weighing rooms of Scotland considerably longer.

As you'd expect of the chief executive of such an organisation

Willoughby, 47, who has just returned from a fortnight in Afghanistan, is less hands on at clearing mines these days and the most potent lethal weapon he's handled lately is Oliverjohn (it said in the form book before he bought him he was apt to 'blunder'), with whom or from whom he hit the deck three times this winter.

His wife Fiona was planning to sponsor the aptly named Guy Willoughby UR Retiring Handicap Chase at Carlisle, in which all the other jockeys would be briefed to let him win, but it was the astounding success of his son Jamie, 9, in a different sphere that has precipitated his retirement.

Jamie joined the local Dumfriesshire bike club where he was spotted by the local big biking cheese, who suggested he should have a run out in the local round of the Scottish Cross-Country Mountain Biking Championships.

This is so Willoughby it's not true: while all young Jamie's rivals turned up in lycra, special biking shoes and on state-of-the-art machines that only just resembled bicycles as we know them, Jamie pitched up in cords, plimsolls and a woolly jumper riding a bike bought from eBay for £40 and proceeded to win by a distance. This Sunday he won another round, this time in a forest somewhere north of Inverness, by a similar distance and two more wins will secure him the Scottish title.

After a round trip of nine hours in the Land Rover, however, Jamie's sisters are of the opinion that going to Carlisle to watch Daddy fall off wasn't so bad after all. MAY 27, 2008

CHRIS MAUDE'S daughter Nell proved something of a show-stopper at school recently. After retiring from the saddle, the former jump jockey bought out John Buckingham's jockeys' valet service. It is largely thanks to him and his team that many a modern jump and Flat jockey looks the part when he goes out to ride in a race with sparkling boots, clean breeches, silks that don't flap in the wind, caps that don't come undone and tack that doesn't break.

The question (nothing changes) was put to Nell's class at school recently: "What does your father do for a living?" One child spoke about his father being in the army, another said his dad was a solicitor, and one even innocently admitted his father was an estate agent.

Then it came to Nell's turn. "Oh," she said, "my dad washes dwarves' underpants for a living." And with that there was a stunned silence. MAY 27, 2008

Chapter Five

THE
DISTINGUISHED
ORDER OF MERIT

IT'S rumoured that Keira Knightley, star of recent film *The Duchess* (of Devonshire), may follow in the footsteps of Dame Helen Mirren by being invited to Royal Ascot next summer to present a trophy. It is through the connection with the present Duke of Devonshire, who lives at Chatsworth where the movie was filmed on location and is also Her Majesty's Representative at Ascot.

Ascot has a brief history of these little reciprocal arrangements. Fiona Bruce, the glamorous newsreader, presented the prize for this year's Albany Stakes at the royal meeting. She came into contact with Ascot when filming an episode of Antiques Roadshow there earlier in the year and agreed to come back and present a prize. I'm sure the duke regarded this arrangement very much as a case of tit for tat. SEPTEMBER 16, 2008

THE best advice is to book early for restaurants in Cheltenham to avoid disappointment this week. A well-known northern punter, working on short notice, was unable to get into his favourite Chinese restaurant in town. "No table flee, sir," he was told when ringing.

With little going the punters way this week he turned to all he had left, his wits. A couple of minutes later he rang back. "I'd like to order a table in the name of Souness," he demanded. "That's Graeme Souness."

"No problem, sir," came the reply. "What time you like? How you are? I amazed. You knock us out of FA Cup, lose your job, then come back to Cheltenham?" MARCH 16, 2006

WHILE there was a delay to the start of the last, Barry Dennis, the well-known bookie, was barred by a security guard from leaving the betting ring to enter the Club enclosure. As he sparred verbally with the guard a large section of the crowd, by this time bored of waiting for the bumper, started cheering him before chanting: "Who are you?" and "6-4 you don't get in." MARCH 15, 2006

IT WILL go down as one of the great social put-downs. Becky, Marchioness of Blandford, has a wide-ranging role at this Ascot as assistant-trainer-cum-waitress to trainer and car park picnic king Jamie Osborne. At after-racing drinks on Wednesday evening she was introduced to the friend of a well-known east end millionaire who professed to have met her husband Jamie (from whom she is now divorced) before. "Where was that?" she asked, "in jail?" JUNE 19, 2008

NICK SMITH, Ascot's head of public relations, has faced some tough questioning from the world's media since it was announced York would host this year's royal meeting. However, it took a nine-year-old called Leah on a 'press packers' assignment for the BBC's Newsround to stump him. "What type of weaponry will you be employing to protect the Queen at York?" she asked innocently.

"I've given about 15 interviews a day for about 15 months of build-up," said Nick, "but never a question like that. We immediately took her to see Clare Balding in the BBC's outside broadcast unit." JUNE 14, 2005

THE London Festival of Racing, two Wednesday evenings at Kempton on July 4 and 11 and, sandwiched in the middle, the two-day Eclipse meeting at Sandown on July 6 and 7, is about to be launched.

Kempton starts with an American-themed 'Independence night' to coincide with some holiday they have in the States and ends with a 'Best of British night'.

Last week John McCririck was roped in to pose for London Festival of Racing publicity shots dressed up as a Beefeater standing outside (should be banged up inside) the Tower of London. At the time a party of schoolgirls was passing. "Oh look," said one to another, "someone dressed up as Henry VIII." JUNE 5, 2007

THESE are confusing times for Robert 'Chocolate' Thornton, the 27-year-old jump jockey attached to Alan King's yard. At Andrew

Thornton's (no relation) recent wedding he was refused a drink because he was considered too young by the barman. For a fellow that is not necessarily a compliment but, apparently, it saved him a few quid.

Contrast that with an incident at Market Rasen recently. I thought this sort of thing only happened to David Beckham, possibly in light of recent events Freddie Flintoff. Choc was meandering out to the paddock quietly minding his own business signing his autograph on racecards for two young kids when he heard, behind him, a polite female asking: "Can you sign this, please."

As he turned round, she offered him a felt pen, lifted her T-shirt and asked him to sign her partially naked breasts. The felt pen – it was, he insists, the only thing he felt – was in his hand before he could either leg it or decline and, thus ambushed, he was obliged to sign while turning scarlet with embarrassment. "I had to shut my eyes," he says.

There has since been speculation in the weighing room that had either Carl Llewellyn or Mick Fitzgerald been approached to do the same they would have made up some longish middle names and included their telephone numbers. JUNE 5, 2007

CHESTER has just been voted Travelling The Turf's 'racecourse of the year' and much of that must be down to its immaculate formal garden look. It employs two full-time gardeners just to tend the paddock. Rightly proud of the job they do, it will be eyes down for this week's meeting because chief executive Richard Thomas defies anyone to find a weed.

Last year a new centrepiece to the paddock was installed, a life-size wire climbing frame in the shape of a racehorse, up which ivy grows. This year they have commissioned a chicken-wire sculpture of a jockey, also by artist Rupert Till, to enhance the place. It's based on measurements of Jamie Spencer and Tom Queally. "It was embarrassing all round," says Till. "They thought I was fitting them up for a coffin."

According to Thomas the sculpture is doing what even bad jockeys do well – posing outside the weighing room. MAY 3, 2005

Sign this please

FRANKIE DETTORI, as you probably already know, is to be a father for the fifth time. On hearing the news Liverpudlian Martin Dwyer, his weighing-room colleague, was stunned and probably thinking if you had that many kids in Liverpool there would be a shortage of cars to nick: "Blimey, Frankie, how many you going to have?" he asked.

"Seven," replied Frankie, "And I'm gonna call the last one Ascot!"
AUGUST 24, 2004

THE QUEEN will miss the Derby for only the second time in 50 years when she attends the 60th anniversary of D-Day in Normandy this weekend. The last time she missed it was for the 40th anniversary. Without D-Day, of course, there would be no Derby.

So what about the Derby 60 years ago? Very little, it turns out, is written about war-time racing. During World War II the Derby was moved to Newmarket and racing continued on a small scale because of a determination by the public not to be disrupted.

Most racecourses, including Newmarket's Rowley Mile, were requisitioned by the military authorities – Epsom's Princess stand became an officers' mess – so the race was run as 'the New Derby Stakes' on the July course.

In 1942 the King, George VI, had the favourite Big Game. The wartime restriction on travel made it difficult for the King and Queen to make a special journey to Newmarket but their absence could not be contemplated so an agricultural tour of Cambridge was planned for the period, enabling the King to take in both the Oaks and Derby, although Big Game finished a dismal sixth.

In 1944 the New Derby was run on Saturday, June 17, just 11 days after the D-Day landings. The result would not have been lost on those fighting their way across Normandy after their bumpy trip across the Channel. Ocean Swell won with Happy Landing a long neck away in third. The King's horse, Fair Glint, was unplaced.

One famous Derby-winning jockey once said after the war that such was his dislike of the Derby's infamous gradients and turns, that if he'd been in touch with the Germans he would have asked them to flatten the course, and in fact his wishes were partially met. The stand opposite the number board was badly damaged by a bomb and Tattersalls was littered with craters. JUNE 1, 2004

AP McCOY couldn't make an engagement to open a new function room at the Irish Oak, a pub in Cheltenham's Lower High Street, last Friday so sent along three jockeys in the fervent hope that their aggregate fame would equal his.

The jury, however, is out on whether the combined talents of Mick Fitzgerald, Carl Llewellyn and Mark Bradburne (an Irishman, a Welshman and a Scotsman – which sounds like the formula for a bad joke) have the same appeal as one McCoy. So well known is Mark, despite two Festival winners, among Cheltenham's Irish that he spent most of the evening being addressed as Mark Bradbury. SEPTEMBER 7, 2004

CHESTER racecourse – motto: racing on the city's doorstep – has produced, along with its jumping sister Bangor-on-Dee, a calendar for 2005. It is glossy, colourful and highlights the racedays at both tracks. Below the racing pictures are a photo of the main movers and shakers at each course, Jeannie Chantler, manager at Bangor, Richard Thomas, chief executive at both tracks, Ed Gretton, clerk of the course, Melanie Simms, sponsorship manager, and Melissa Hatton, communications manager. It's a management identity awareness thing I imagine. My complaint that I could put up with a picture of Richard Thomas for one month a year but not 12 has been echoed somewhat closer to home. Mrs Thomas has also complained to the management. "Do I need to see a picture of you every day of every month?" she asked. JANUARY 11, 2005

IT HAS not been a great week for Graham Cowdrey, head of public relations at Cantor whose 'Spreadfair' is the world's first sports spread-betting exchange. Firstly he fitted up the three jockeys (AP McCoy, Mick Fitzgerald and Carl Llewellyn) which Cantor Fitzgerald sponsor with Cantor Spreadfair kit.

Bookmakers cannot sponsor jockeys – though a financial spread-betting firm can – a policy that, after a tip-off, the Jockey Club has reiterated to all parties. So good old Graham, who is somewhat more spread than any jockey, found himself with a car-load of logo-ed up polo-neck shirts into which he can't fit.

If that isn't bad enough he thought he'd pulled off a right stunt at the Masters snooker tournament at Wembley when he was tipped off by the player's agent that Paul Hunter – also sponsored by Cantor and a course and distance winner at Wembley so a good thing to beat Steve Davis on Sunday – was going to break new ground in the world of pot black fashion by wearing a bandana.

Although Hunter wouldn't be able to wear Cantor's Spreadfair logo Graham, who had been assured he'd be wearing a gold bandana, hit on the great idea that yesterday at Wembley they'd hand out 5,000 free gold bandanas to spectators emblazoned with the Spreadfair logo.

Two points to make about this: Hunter rocked up with a black bandana and, worse still, lost 6-5 to Davis so that on top of polo-necks that don't fit Graham also has 5,000 gold bandanas to wear. "We'd give 'em away, ten for the price of one," says Graham – if he could. FEBRUARY 15, 2005

WHAT other sport brings people together like racing? At yesterday's Anglo-Irish Jump Racing Awards 2006 (at which Brave Inca was named Horse of the Year), the BHB's chairman, Martin Broughton, whose proper job is chairman of British Airways, gave the prize for champion three-mile chaser to War Of Attrition's owner, Michael O'Leary, chief executive of Ryanair. "Normally," quipped O'Leary, "he wouldn't give me anything other than abuse." MAY 16, 2006

ONE of the more interesting scenes at the Gare du Nord in Paris on Sunday was a be-whiskered gentleman berating the world's most efficient travel agent, Ian Fry of Horse Racing Abroad, about the declining standards of first-class travel on Eurostar. Needless to say it was John McCririck who was wrong – again.

At Waterloo he had noticed his ticket said Seat 28 Club 4 so he hopped on the train, turned left, which on an aircraft pretty much guarantees you'll end up in Club class if not the cockpit, found seat 28 and settled in for a trip during which he expected a French maid with a low-cut top and high-cut bottom to deliver hot croissants, some filtered coffee and a complimentary brandy to his table. None of the above happened – what's more yobs lounged on the floor and children screamed.

One look at his ticket proved to the world's most efficient travel agent what he'd suspected. Big Mac sat in the right seat but wrong coach.

"It was an utter, incomprehensible disaster," explained Big Mac yesterday. "Am I stupid, am I thick, do I have no brain? It says Club 4 – that's got to be Club class hasn't it? Of course I never saw the bit on the left of the ticket that said Coach 10. They should have had a guard on the door saying: 'Why, non monsieur, you are too important for this carriage' instead of shuffling me on to cattle class!" OCTOBER 18, 2004

THE HONG KONG JOCKEY CLUB'S hospitality knows no bounds. But however much money you can throw at something it is still the small things that count.

A dinner party was organised last Friday on the eve of the financially upgraded Champions Mile to entertain connections of runners on a 150ft yacht cruising Hong Kong harbour.

For a long time, however, it looked like Attraction's owners, the Duke and Duchess of Roxburghe, would be non-runners on account of the duchess's predisposition to seasickness combined with the harbour's inclination to choppiness.

Forget what happened to Attraction the next day, the prospect of the duchess lobbing one over the side midway through dinner was considerably worse. Even that, though, in the opinion of the HKJC was preferable to their Graces' non-attendance. What finally persuaded the duchess to go was the delivery, mid-afternoon, to her hotel room of a small package. With heroic thoughtfulness Joanna Arculli, wife of the Jockey Club chairman Ronnie, had sent seasickness pills. MAY 18, 2005

THE Cheltenham Gold Cup is not the only thing Henrietta Knight does in threes. Every three years she has to have a tack sale because she is a compulsive buyer of the stuff and, tomorrow week, the local racing fraternity will descend on West Lockinge to buy her nearly new, worn-once rather than worn-out, rugs, bridles, boots, bits and bobs as well as a big selection of schooling fences and hurdles.

Just in case you think she has had a change of policy and is either moving to the Flat or going to send her jumpers to the races without having schooled them, she is moving over to plastic schooling obstacles because they are easier and lighter to move about to fresh ground.

While the tack was being lotted up by Pilgrim Bond, the auctioneers, recently Hen took a cold call on her mobile phone from a firm trying to sell not pensions, pvc windows or overdrafts but hospitality chalets at, of all places, the Cheltenham Festival.

Cold calling must be one of the most demoralising jobs in the world. Reading from a crib sheet, the caller explained to the trainer of Best Mate that the 'Cheltenham National Hunt Festival takes place in March and lasts four days' and the highlight of it 'is a race called the Tote Cheltenham Gold Cup on Friday, one of the most important, eagerly awaited races in the jumping calendar'.

"You're talking to the wrong person," said Hen politely. "I'm usually too busy on Gold Cup day [saddling horses] to be interested in hospitality." But the experienced cold-caller only knows one language, the clunk of the phone going down. Leave the door half-open and you're inviting trouble. As she hadn't, your man obviously registered her polite 'no' as what Aidan O'Brien calls a 'definitely possible'. A week later a girl from the same firm called, reading from the same crib sheet. "I think you should know," said the ever-polite trainer when the importance of the Gold Cup had been explained to her for a second time by someone clueless about the sport "that we won the Gold Cup – three times. I know all about it, thank you."

"Oh," replied the girl – and for the first time in history a cold caller put the phone down on a recipient of their unwanted attention. SEPTEMBER 18, 2007

HAVE you ever wondered where the hundreds of horses bought by Sheikh Mohammed's bloodstock adviser John Ferguson, bred by Darley or subsumed into Godolphin – 77 individual runners so far this season – go to?

We thought we were on to one possible outlet for them the other day when up-and-coming trainer Ed Vaughan's Minnis Bay rocked up into the paddock at Goodwood owned by John Ferguson Spares Ltd. However, subsequent investigation revealed we were barking up the wrong dead-end. These aren't spare horses at all, they're spare parts for amusement arcades but it was a nice try. SEPTEMBER 18, 2007

THE CONTINUING stand-off between John Magnier and Sheikh Mohammed is still overshadowing the bloodstock world and making life difficult for the smaller breeder. Does he use Coolmore, or Darley or, to save the bother, neither?

Last week an Irish breeder, who has seldom, if ever, sent his mares across the Irish Sea to be covered in England was weighing up these issues. While in Newmarket for the sales he decided to have a look at Cheveley Park's stallions. "I'm off," he told a bloodstock agent before going, "to have a look at some Protestant stallions. It's a bit complicated using the Catholic and Muslim ones at the moment." OCTOBER 18, 2005

132 Turn Me On Guv

HAYDOCK, where Lester Piggott rode his first winner, The Chase, as a 12-year-old boy in 1948 and his last, Palacegate Jack, in 1994 as a grandfather, is to unveil a 1/3 life-size bronze of both winners on Saturday. Lester will be doing the honours himself and presenting a maquette of the sculpture to the winning owner of the Lester Piggott Start-to-Finish Handicap Stakes, a race to commemorate the two landmarks.

The artist is Willie Newton, best known for sculpting the Derby winner's bronze each year. Originally he was commissioned by Susan Piggott to do The Chase and Palacegate Jack with the hugely differing styles of the young and old Lester on respectively for the great man's 70th birthday.

At the ensuing party Peter O'Sullevan was so impressed with the work he suggested to Bill Whittle, chairman of Haydock, that he commission a larger version for the racecourse.

When told that the race to go with it would be perpetual, Willie asked Bill for how long it was really intended it would be run. "A hundred years," said Bill.

"In 100 years people won't know who Lester Piggott was," said Newton before adding without thinking: "I mean you already have the Tommy Whittle Chase and who was Tommy Whittle?"

"My father," replied Bill.

Thinking he might have been offensive, the polite sculptor rang back to apologise and said he'd meant to say the Tommy Wallis Hurdle at Wincanton. "Oh," said Bill, "You mean my godfather." So there we have it, a sculptor good at digging holes too. SEPTEMBER 19, 2006

WHILE on the subject of bloodstock agents – the manic sales season has already begun – David Redvers did not have the greatest of weekends. On Saturday morning he was 'field mastering' – in charge of the rampaging hordes on horseback – for his local 'trail' hunt for the first time and keen to make the right impression. However, he was unceremoniously dumped in front of his 'field' by the horse he was riding when it spooked at a bale of hay. Having got rid of him it bolted over the horizon. In the afternoon at Newbury Flashy Wings, the speedy filly he bred, was beaten for the first time.

He trumped this in August, however, when he was on his way to Deauville via Portsmouth. At the ferry terminal he realised he had not got his passport. Keen not to miss the boat and no doubt aware that half the people arriving in Britain these days don't actually have passports, he found getting out harder.

Though it's nice to know you're wanted, he tried everything from pleading to finally resorting, as no bloodstock agent can resist, to self-importance. "I'm a well-known bloodstock agent," he said. The immigration officer was clearly impressed. "Tell me," she said before turning him back, "what is a bloodstock agent?" SEPTEMBER 20, 2005

LOIS DUFFEY, the owner of Grand National winner Mr Frisk, died recently aged 95. Mentally sharp to the very end, when she was being moved from her Maryland home to the American equivalent of an old peoples' home, she turned to those taking her. "At last," she said, "I get to go to finishing school." NOVEMBER 20, 2007

WHAT'S in a name? Stan James are, if you didn't know, the bookmakers who sponsor this year's King George VI Chase, highlight of the Stan James Christmas Festival run this year at Sandown on Boxing Day, and have signed up for a long-term (five years) commitment – that's long-term by recent standards – to the 1,000 and 2,000 Guineas at Newmarket.

When Stan James opened his first ever betting shop, in Compton, Berkshire, in 1973 the surrounding villages of East and West Ilsley boasted numerous trainers like Ken Cundell, Dick Hern, Fulke Johnson Houghton, Gavin Hunter, my father Roddy and Charlie Dingwall and, more particularly, enough stable lads to ensure healthy profits from the outset. In reality, of course, the lads became middlemen between trainer and bookmaker by donating their wages to Stan's cause.

His next wise move was to open a betting shop in Marlborough where he could cut out both middlemen, trainers and lads, by receiving his profits directly from the sons of rich owners who were in attendance at the well-known public school of that town.

Stan James now have only 19 shops, which means they have hardly spiralled out of control. But – and it is quite a major but – they turn over £10m a week on internet and telephone betting and in a recent Sunday Times 'rich list' were number 40 in the fastest growing businesses in Britain and number 112 in the top 250 companies.

So Stan James? He could only have been a wizened old bookmaker with a name like that couldn't he? Stan, himself is, in fact, fictional and the name came about much like the 1981 Grand National winner Aldaniti's did. His name was an amalgam of the breeder's children's names – ALastair, DAvid, NIcola and TImothy.

Originally the bookie's shop was going to be called Steve James after its founding partners, Steve Fisher, who is still in charge, and the late James Holder. However, women's lib was a prominent movement at the time even though, then as now, bookmaking is a male-oriented business. Thus Steve's wife, Anne, also a partner, was having none of it. She put in a claim for Anne to be used in the title, hence Steve and Anne equals Stan.

This year, apart from giving the lad or lass of the best turned out runner in each race a cash prize, good old Stan will also give them a free £100 bet on their horse. DECEMBER 21, 2005

IT ALWAYS pays for a trainer to send out a few winners for his yard sponsor. It helps keep them sweet. At Newbury on Friday Jonny Portman excelled in this department when Russian Rosie, in which his sponsor Jeremy Brownlee has a share, was the particularly impressive winner of the two-year-old maiden fillies' race. She has a bright future. Jonny has also won for him this season with Odessa Star and Inflagranti.

Of course, part of the sponsorship package at Hamilton Stables is to have the horsebox decked out in the logo and livery of the sponsor, in this case Jeremy's company Pump Technology Ltd. But therein lies a minor problem. Pump Technology Ltd is a company that makes pumps for the sewage and waste water industry and its logo, which Jeremy would like to have plastered all over the lorry, is 'pumping poo with panache'.

"I've told him it's not quite the image I'm trying to foster," insists Jonny dryly. "I've said he can only do it if Odessa Star, which he bought out of a claimer, wins a Listed race. I think I'm safe." AUGUST 22, 2006

PETER DEAL is one of racing's most prominent owners under both codes. His current string includes jumpers Mamlook and Jaunty Flight and the fastest thing over five furlongs, Amour Propre.

The other day Peter shot into the yard of his local timber merchant, H.J.Webb & Son. He was on his way from his home near Swindon to Faringdon, and had forgotten his wallet. To save him having to return ten miles home, he asked the 'And Son' in the partnership (Jez Webb, a keen racing man) if he could borrow £20.

They then had a brief chat and one of the timber merchant's employees (a racing enthusiast who knew who Peter was) came into the office at the back end of the conversation.

After a few moments Peter said: "Must be off, thanks for lending me the 20 quid." As the door shut the employee turned to his boss. "Christ," he said, "this credit crunch really is biting deep, isn't it?" NOVEMBER 11, 2008

THERE'S a strong likelihood that your sitting room will be invaded this Christmas by Sarah Aspinall. There are, you'll be pleased to know, considerably worse people with whom to spend Christmas.

Sarah is the next hot thing when it comes to painting racehorses and her 'Three Winter Kings', a study of Kicking King, Moscow Flyer and Hardy Eustace, was commissioned by Sir Peter O'Sullevan for his 2005 charity Christmas cards.

The original will be auctioned at his big charity lunch tomorrow and some of her work is on show at the Osborne Studio Gallery in Motcomb Street until later this week.

As 70,000 cards have been produced one is sure to plop through your letterbox in the next five weeks and it will bring Sarah, 41, from relative obscurity to a mass audience.

Having spent ten years in Rome, until 2000, working on the restoration of old masters, it is only now that she is becoming better known here than she was there, where she was the Italian Jockey Club's official artist and exhibited at the Capannelle, Rome's racecourse.

It was while manning her stand at the Capannelle that she got her lucky break. The Duke of Richmond, something of an old master himself though in no need of restoration, bought a drawing she had done of Goodwood. He asked her to bring it up to the house when she was next over and told her she should charge more, a policy he has successfully applied to his own racecourse. When she did bring it he suggested she have a stand at Goodwood and, thus, her foot was firmly planted in racing's door.

Far be it for me to comment but the noted art critic Robin Gray says: "My personal opinion is that Sarah Aspinall has only Susan Crawford as a rival among contemporary equine painters." Well, Susan Crawford was asked but was too busy to do Sir Peter's card this year so has she, inadvertently, let Sarah Aspinall slip up the inside rail?

The commissions are now flowing and next year it's likely that Sarah will also be too busy to be doing Christmas cards. One of her previous jobs was to paint Grand Lodge at Coolmore. After the stallion had been pulled out, walked up and down and made to stand impeccably for her, she was so impressed she tipped the lad a tenner for his trouble.

A while later she was in McCarthy's Bar when she was horrified to be introduced to the 'lad' whom she had just tipped – Tom Magnier, the owner's son. NOVEMBER 22, 2005

AFTER being given the *Daily Telegraph* Award of Merit for services to racing at the Cartier Awards last week Henry Cecil described it as a surprise, especially as it had come at the end of his worst ever season.

With typical modesty he recalled going to Leicester races on a weekday back in July. He didn't recognise anyone, the filly he expected to win finished third, it began to rain, he wasn't enjoying himself and was heading for his car when he was approached by an elderly man who asked him for his autograph. He was chuffed to be asked and said of course he would. After he had scribbled his name on the racecard the old man said: "Thankyou – Sir Michael."

"I think," said Cecil, "that was probably the highlight of my year."
NOVEMBER 22, 2005

IT WAS, it has universally been agreed, a poor start to the afternoon for Martin Belsham, chief executive of the leading interactive bookmakers, Blue Square.

On Saturday Blue Square were sponsors of both the racing and the 'beautiful festival' at Chester where racegoers were treated to demonstrations of such interesting things as personal tanning kits and Frankie Dettori's men's toiletry range.

However, not even the prospect of a bikini-clad Miss UK 2004, Amy Guy, 'enjoying herself' – as the racecard rather ambiguously put it – in a hot tub or a reviving whiff of 'Dettori' could improve Belsham's day after the way it started.

He woke up to find that Blue Square were pinpointed as the bookmaker to be mugged by the *Racing Post*'s Pricewise column in regard to the great tipster's nap of the day, Ashkal Way. Having offered it at a tad over-generous 13-2 in the morning, Belsham received the call that he didn't want to hear at just after 3.15. The beast had won by six wickets at Beverley having been backed down to 2-1 at a six-figure cost to his firm. Thus battered he retired to the main sponsor's box at Chester where the caterers promptly offered a revitalising fruit elixir – produced by, of all the appropriate people, the Looza Juice Co. AUGUST 23, 2005

SIX MONTHS of competition among small- to medium-sized Irish enterprises comes to its climax at Cheltenham on Saturday when Lily O'Brien, purveyor of smart but affordable chocolates, wins the prize to 'sponsor' the £30,000 two-and-a-half-mile novice hurdle.

There are, of course, certain dangers in running such a competition. Last year it was won by a breadcrumb business and came dangerously close to being called the Mr Crumb 'Get Stuffed' Novices' Hurdle but the only danger when Lily Wonka and the Chocolate Factory come to town is to one's bathroom scales.

The business, named after her daughter, is run by Mary Ann O'Brien, wife of Jonathan Irwin; daughter of legendary horseman Phonsie O'Brien; niece of legendary trainer Vincent O'Brien; and sister-in-law of Noel Meade. She is one of only two O'Briens – the other is David who went into vineyards and is now a successful wine-maker – to ever escape horses.

She started making chocolates while she was commercial manager at Phoenix Park in 1992, rented the kitchens at the Dublin racecourse, set up a packing facility in the hospitality boxes, and for two years Lily O'Brien's only employee was also the lady who used to clean her office. One minute she was persuading Cartier to sponsor Europe's first £1m race, the next she was up to her elbows in hot cocoa.

It now turns over £15m, employs 100 people, can make 30 tonnes of chocolate a week and, supermarkets apart, supplies chocolates to ten million passengers on a dozen different airlines. Chocolates being chocolate, that is the next best thing, let's face it, to supplying in-flight sex.

Unfortunately this weekend Mary Ann has to attend what most females I know would consider an alternative vision of heaven on earth, a chocolate trade fair in Cologne so large that it would take three days to walk it. "You never want to see another chocolate again afterwards," says a weary Mary Ann.

Instead she will be represented at Cheltenham by her husband, Lily herself, and David Wright, Noel Meade's nephew and the company's sales executive. Meade is under very strict instructions to win the race.

"It's not exactly making screws for washing machines," says Mary Ann. "It gives people so much pleasure. I might as well be running a brothel. It's only food but it's the food of the gods. When people ask what I do and I tell them I own a chocolate factory they go mad." OCTOBER 24, 2006

ED POWNALL, who recently left Blue Square to be appointed head of PR and sponsorship at *The Sportsman*, the new sports betting paper due to hit the newsagent's shelves some time this spring, has not only taken on a new job but a wife.

Ed has become engaged to Charlotte Jones, a former employee of the BHB and daughter of former Lambourn trainer Merrita Jones. Charlotte is now an estate agent.

Ever aware of image, Ed concludes: "It's a good thing one of us gave up our jobs. A bookmaker marrying an estate agent is not conducive to a good press." JANUARY 24, 2006

THE recruitment of former detectives and Sherlock Holmes types is clearly having the desired effect on racecourse security. John Maxse, the Jockey Club's 'director of special projects' and crack Corinthian amateur rider, had ridden in a hunter chase recently and when he came to get dressed afterwards he found he had mislaid one of his shoes.

One of the weighing-room security officers was called in and the following was overheard: "Well John," he said, "did you have the shoe with you when you arrived at the course?" APRIL 24, 2007

I AM not sure how Cheltenham will get on with its veterinary inspection of certain horses at the Festival in March. One Irish trainer, very successful there in the past, is of the view that there are two things in this life you should never feel: a man's wife or his horse's legs. OCTOBER 24, 2006

EVIDENCE has come to light that medium wave is not reaching some of the more rural parts of Lincolnshire. On Saturday Cornelius Lysaght, Radio 5 Live's racing presenter, did a favour for a couple of friends who wanted to go to Market Rasen by arranging to have two tickets left on the gate for them.

When the couple arrived they went to the owners' and trainers' entrance in search of their complimentary badges. "We've come to pick up two tickets in the name of Cornelius Lysaght, please," they asked politely.

"And what race does that horse run in?" replied the lady dispensing badges. SEPTEMBER 27, 2005

WHEN Nigel Payne left Aintree after a long and glorious career as spokesman and PR fixer – he'll be in action organising Sir Peter O'Sullevan's lunch at the Dorchester today – we wondered who would replace him and whether it would be someone with the same slightly dishevelled look.

Alas, they have failed on all counts and another, that the best results required the colourful language of an effin' British Army trooper. For starters, 'he' is a smartly turned out, youthful, she. Emma Owen, an internal promotion after six years at Aintree, had her first public outing in Nigel's role on Sunday and took it all in her stride.

Her background is in racing but the wrong type of racing. Her father and uncle, Tom and Joe, were household names in Newcastle during the seventies and, lest you jump to the conclusion that their names are still reverentially whispered in pigeon lofts the length and breadth of the Tyne, it was speedway at which they excelled.

She was brought up on the road between speedway meetings and, just as it is most jockeys' fervent wish that their daughters don't marry jockeys, so it was Tom's that Emma did not get involved with a speedway rider. After a nine-and-a-half-year courtship his wish finally didn't come true earlier this month when she tied the knot with Australian speedway star Mark Lemon.

I say 'star' but I can think of plenty of other words for someone who rides a bike at 70mph with no brakes round a 300-metre oval track made of cinder and shale for 30 weeks of the year. His injury profile is remarkably similar to a jump jockey's – with extra knee ligament damage thrown in for good measure. For example, he could give Ruby Walsh good advice on shoulder reconstruction.

But it was while he was riding for Poole and she was on work experience with a speedway magazine in Oxford that their paths first crossed. "That was the end of it or, rather, the start of it," says Mark, who is remarkably understated for an Australian professional sportsman. NOVEMBER 27, 2007

SINCE taking out a trainers' licence last summer Lawney Hill has frequently been compared to Henrietta Knight. This is, I believe, not because she's trained a triple Gold Cup winner but for the simple reason that they are both female and came into racing through the point-to-point field in which they both enjoyed success.

To be brutally honest, however, such comparison is beginning to grind with Lawney who regards it as no longer original.

Having to deal with her books means her accountant, formerly a non-racing man, is at last getting to grips with the ins and outs of this complicated sport. For example he knows now that she is no longer 'point-to-point' but 'under rules' and in a short space of time his grasp of racing has become almost as good as his encyclopaedic knowledge of British cinema.

When he arrived at the Hills' yard near Kingston Blount recently his opening line was: "I'm really getting into racing now and [to prove it] I gather you are frequently compared to ... "

"Oh, no," thought Lawney, "not that old chestnut, frequently compared to Henrietta Knight?"

"I gather," he said, "you are frequently compared to Keira Knightley."

Close but no cigar. "It's made me appreciate being compared to Hen again," says Lawney.

Her accountant's confusion is not dissimilar to the old *Sporting Life* ad-man whose grasp of advertising was clearly better than his grasp of racing. He once famously rang the world's greatest trainer, Vincent O'Brien. When the great man answered the ad-man asked if he was speaking to Vincent Price. O'Brien put the phone down on him.

Of course his confusion may have been caused by the fact that Ryan Price was also a well-known trainer at the time, but by marrying the two together he too came up with an actor. FEBRUARY 28, 2006

WILLIE MACAULEY, manager of Burton Agnes Stud, was having his hair cut (a process that doesn't take long these days) by his barber in Taylors of Jermyn Street recently. In the chair next to him was a man he thought he recognised as an acquaintance from Scotland whose wife is called April. "How's April?" inquired Willie politely.

Slightly taken aback the man replied that she was fine and shortly after got up to go, whereupon Willie saw that it was a case of mistaken identity and it wasn't his acquaintance after all but someone completely different. Meanwhile, the well-known master and huntsman of the North Cotswold Hunt, Nigel Peel, having tipped his barber also posed him the following question as he departed: "Tell me," he said. "How the hell does he know I've got a hound called April?" JUNE 30, 2006

ANNUALLY, a leading, financially astute trainer puts together a syndicate to buy a few expensive yearlings who he will train. He scours the world's various rich lists to pull in a few likely punters but usually it is the same old loyal owner who has to stump up the lion's share of the costs if the other millionaires fail to show.

This autumn the trainer thought the purchase of the yearlings should be celebrated with dinner after the sales in an expensive Dublin restaurant. At the end of the meal the bill was, as usual, placed in front of the loyal owner who, fed up with annually bailing out the syndicate, thought it only fair that he should pass it to the trainer.

On being handed the bill, the trainer carefully and slowly scrutinised the figures before handing it back to the owner. "Here you are," said the trainer, "I can assure you it's fine." NOVEMBER 31, 2006

SPARE a thought for Newbury racecourse, which has just increased the value of next month's Juddmonte Lockinge to £250,000.

As you know these are hard times and, after years of resisting it on the off-chance of a royal visit, officials finally took the plunge and let the royal box out commercially for the first time on Saturday.

So it must have been greeted with a mixture of delight and horror when the Queen, spending a long weekend at Highclere, announced she would be attending racing on both Friday and Saturday. She was, apparently, amused and pleased to try out the Champions' Suite instead. APRIL 21, 2009

IF YOU are the head of communication and international racing at Ascot, as Nick Smith is, then it is important you are seen at the world's great meetings be they at home or abroad.

The father-to-be recently attended, with his wife Kate, the 20-week scan of their first child due in late March. It was the wife's show and he was there merely to hold her hand.

Following the scan the gynaecologist said: "I've good news, Mrs Smith, we can bring the birth date forward a few days – it's due on March 13."

Well, as you can imagine Mrs Smith was delighted with the news but it set alarm bells ringing in her husband's head. That, he rightly remembered, is Cheltenham Gold Cup day. "Any questions?" asked the gynaecologist. "Yes," said Nick, "can you tell me whether that'll be morning or afternoon?" DECEMBER 9, 2008

WHEN Edward Gillespie, managing director of Cheltenham racecourse, took the Gloucestershire Gypsies to St Moritz last winter for the annual cricket-on-ice tournament, the authorities there made it clear that the name 'gypsies' was not quite in keeping with the town's status as the world's most expensive ski resort.

It is, after all, a place which describes its climate not as 'bloody cold' – which it invariably is – but as 'champagne' and, to avoid any resident getting the wrong end of the stick about the arrival of gypsies, the side's name was changed, in transit, to the Cheltenham Cavaliers. FEBRUARY 3, 2009

AN OWNER, who had recently developed an aneurysm, was about to undergo surgery to have a stent inserted into the offending artery. He was warned by the specialist that, at his age and with some 'previous' in the heart department, there was a one-in-ten chance that he wouldn't come through the operation.

Being a betting man, he worked out that meeting his Maker was only a 10-1 shot and the odds were heavily stacked in favour of a full recovery. That consoled him greatly until a friend unhelpfully pointed out that the horse, which the owner currently has in training, recently came in, well backed, at 25-1. FEBRUARY 3, 2009

MIKE BELL, the royal trainer no less, also trains a horse for Chelsea footballer Ashley Cole. Harty Boy, an unraced three-year-old, is due to make his long-awaited debut in the next few days.

Trainer and owner have struck up a good rapport and each time Bell has supplied the international left-back with a winning tip Cole, in return, has supplied his trainer not with tickets to the next game but, much more tantalisingly, another digit in the mobile telephone number of his attractive wife, Cheryl.

"The winners were coming thick and fast," explains Bell, "but I feel I've been slightly led up the garden path. The first two numbers he gave me were 0 and 7, which I could have guessed, and when I got to the moment critique she changed her number." JANUARY 27, 2009

THROUGHOUT racing's history, meetings have been abandoned or postponed for a wide variety of reasons ranging from wind and fire to pestilence and even a shortage of horse food (Moscow in the 1980s). War has also put paid to racing and, of course, there is always the human cock-up element to fall back on or a simple phone call like the one that delayed the 1997 National.

But usually we get by. In the early 1960s racing was merely held up a short while at Flemington in Melbourne when notorious whip protester Wally Hoysted – a man 40 years ahead of his time – arrived at the start with a shotgun threatening to shoot the starter unless the jockeys laid down their sticks. Nowadays, of course, they'd call that an attempt at police-assisted suicide.

But, forget war, give peace a chance and it has brought racing to a grinding halt in Randwick, Sydney, much to the un-amusement of its resident trainers. For the first time, to the best of my knowledge, it is a case of Pope stops play.

The racecourse, one of the largest open spaces in the capital – the neighbouring SCG is, of course, a sacred shrine to Australia's principal religion – has been requisitioned for the visit later this month of Pope Benedict XVI.

With half a million pilgrims expected to attend, the 16 trainers and 1,000 horses have had to evacuate to temporary accommodation at Warwick Farm for ten weeks and some 15 Randwick fixtures have been spread around Queensland. Because of the damage expected, trainers are not allowed back until August 24.

You might think, after racing in the state was ravaged by equine influenza, a visit from His Holiness to sprinkle a little holy water around the place was well timed but no – couldn't be worse apparently.

One of the trainers affected is Kevin Moses who, as a jockey, was popular in Ireland. With a name like that, quite apart from a personal audience, you'd have thought the bare minimum he'd be in line for was a front-row ticket.

"Listen, mate," said Moses who now has to struggle through rush-hour traffic to get to his horses, "the only religion I practise is karma – being nice to people. All I know is the Popemobile arrives today so the big fella can't be too far behind it." JULY 10, 2008

CLARE TWEMLOW – that's the correct spelling, you haven't just developed an inability to pronounce your 'r's – who won this year's John Smith's People's Race at Aintree is to take out a category A amateur riders' licence to ride over jumps.

The category A – no relation to prisoners of the same grouping although both are regarded as highly dangerous unless confined – means, initially, she will be restricted to riding against other amateurs.

At Aintree she showed admirable coolness for a debutante to come with a beautifully timed run on Barney Curley's Zabeel Palace not only to land £50,000 to the charity of her choice – Curley's Direct Aid for Africa (DAFA) – but a whacking good gamble.

Newmarket-based Clare, 30, is a chief financial officer for a pharmaceutical company but would like one day to return to a similar job in racing. There she could possibly follow in the footsteps of the accountant who, on his first day working for Sheikh Mohammed, had to write a cheque to Keeneland Sales for $56 million. JULY 28, 2008

THE Kildare Street and University Club, Dublin's nearest equivalent to the Turf Club, is celebrating its 225th anniversary. I rather liked the story about one of the old waiters, no longer with us, who minded the room service to the upper floors for years. An ancient man, keen on his racing, behind his back he was known as 'Scrotum' to the members on account of the fact that he was a wrinkled retainer. MARCH 8, 2004

CONVERSATION overheard at a recent charity dinner for the Watermill Theatre, Newbury, just as the auction was getting under way. Lady with a mild warning to her sports-minded husband as both were perusing

through the 14 lots, which included holidays, boxes at the races and
sporting memorabilia: "You once bought me Ian Botham's sweater,
worse still it was unwashed – I don't need Frankie Dettori's breeches
thankyou very much." MARCH 8, 2004

Chapter Six
GOOD SKILLS

THE last race at Sandown on Saturday was a Flat versus jump jockeys' challenge over a mile. It just so happened that three of the six jump jockeys' mounts – quite apart from their riders – needed blindfolds on to get them into the stalls. "What do I do with this?" asked jump jockey Chocolate Thornton, being unfamiliar with the process whereby Flat jockeys usually hoick them off just as the stalls open. "Don't worry about that," replied one of his Flat colleagues, "just so long as you take it off before you get to the bend." APRIL 26, 2005

THE SPIRIT of free enterprise is alive and well in Yorkshire. A racegoer in a smart car blagged his way into one of the car parks closer to the action by dropping the gateman a crisp £50 note. "Find this man a good spot," yelled the gateman to his colleague across the car park. "He's given me £20 and we'll split it between us." JUNE 16, 2005

THE TITLE most accident-prone trainer used to belong, unequivocally, to Peter Walwyn. But Big Pete's almost forgotten the way to Oxford's John Radcliffe it's been – and let's cross our fingers here – so long since his last encounter with Paris (plaster of).

The title now goes north to a man who, for the last week, has been trussed up in a straitjacket, not unlike an over-ready chicken, to keep his shattered upper humerus steady. The man with a wing down is Mark Johnston.

He was nearing the end of a family skiing trip to St Moritz with Markus Graff, the owner of his Goodwood Cup winner Darasim, when he took a purler. In fact it was so near the end of the holiday that his next move, had it been possible, would have been to return his skis to the hire shop. Looking on the bright side though, better the last day than the first.

The Middleham trainer was trying to lay up with his children when, travelling at great speed, he was presented with options: a piste to the left or a piste to the right. A momentary delay in the decision-making process meant, effectively, his right ski went for the left slope and his left ski for the right slope and he ploughed, somewhat recklessly, straight on. Even among the clatter of skis, poles and ice wife Deirdre heard the crack as the top of his arm divided into what she describes as "orange segments". Ouch.

But then – I suppose being a Flat trainer he can be excused this – he completely disregarded the old steeplechasing maxim: 'There are fools, damn fools and those who remount.' Looking 'terrible' as well he might, he remounted and skied to the nearest restaurant, presumably for a stiff one, and from there he was transported to hospital by snow-mobile.

Of course, this is not entirely bad news for the trainer who can be expected to tip the pilot handsomely if he avoids any turbulence on his way to Dubai today. When he was kicked and broke his wrist Mister Baileys won the 2,000 Guineas. Last year when he fell off his mountain bike crossing a cattle grid resulting in another broken wrist he won the 1,000 Guineas with Attraction. Given the seriousness of this accident one suspects the 2005 Derby winner must be lurking somewhere around Kingsley House.

Big Pete was magnanimous at the loss of his title. "To be honest," he said, "I never got beyond the nursery slopes skiing and I kept having altercations with Germans or, at least, people who I thought were Germans." MARCH 1, 2005

IS IT a bird? Is it an avalanche? No it's just the BHB's marketing director making his way down the mountain. It is mildly ironic that a group of Flat jockeys, including Steve Drowne and Alan Daly, should go skiing and, somewhat surprisingly, survive in stark contrast to Chris John – the equivalent of a skiing blackbelt and an athletic sort who was probably captain of all the school first XIs. He made his way to the bottom of the first mountain of his winter sojourn courtesy of the bloodwagon.

Though the Flat jockeys possess a gift of balance their inexperience on the slopes combined with an almost suicidal daring and pencil-thin legs which, in Daly's case, tend to snap when the wind gusts at more than 40 mph means that any skiing holiday where there is no recourse to their travel insurance is something of a miracle.

Hosting last week's BHB Flat Racing Awards at the Café Royal on crutches, Chris has done what all trainers dread in their horses – severed a tendon. On the first day of a family holiday to Courcheval he turned on a rock, touched the void as it were, and ended up dazed in a pile of scree. A deep cut to his knee required a small operation and stitching.

The lack of snow meant the doctor's surgery was busier than a casualty clearing station on the Somme. "It's a busy day but a good day," said the docteur.

"And what, then, is a bad day?" inquired our marketing director.

"Oh just death and paralysis," said the docteur matter-of-factly, putting a cut knee and six weeks on crutches into perspective.

So while the rest of his family skied Chris moped around Courcheval and undertook the first stage in a Jockey Club apprenticeship – long lunches on a daily basis. The timing of this injury has not been good. Restricted to following the hunt – it is now into its final month – in the car rather than on a horse, he was at a meet of the Minehead Harriers recently. It took him so long to get in and out of the car that when he finally thought he had caught up with them he discovered it was another hunt altogether, the Devon And Somerset Staghounds. JANUARY 25, 2005

FOR much of his adult life former jump jockey Andy Orkney has been trying to prove that knights of the pigskin are not just a one-trick pony, men so concussed that outside of getting a horse from A to B their only achievement is a single-figure golf handicap.

When he was riding he combined that profession with running an optician's shop in Leyburn – he celebrates 25 years as an optometrist this year – and it still amazes me that the good burghers of that town entrust their vision to someone who had such trouble seeing a stride.

Possibly his greatest feat of horsemanship was in the 1985 Aintree Fox Hunters. Riding Golden Ty, his stirrup-iron broke on the approach to Becher's Brook. Seldom in the history of catastrophic equipment failures has there been worse timing. Heroically he completed the course in third, his voice rising an octave at every obstacle, and afterwards he squeaked the stewards into believing that Johnny Greenall had committed some heinous breach of the rules up the run-in and was promoted to second.

Off the course he was a member of the three-man 'jockeys' team' that famously triumphed against hairdressers and AA patrolmen on a round of the 1980s low-budget game show Busman's Holiday.

Last winter he became part-time amateur huntsman of the West of Yore Hunt and on one occasion the joker laying the trail took his hounds into the middle of a full-on moto-cross rally. As 300 bikers skidded around a muddy hillside Orkney stood gallantly in the middle of them blowing his trumpet to retrieve his hounds.

And, of course, the highlight of any huntsman's summer is his puppy show, which in Orkney's case took place in waist-deep mud on Sunday. The judging was over and, as tradition dictates, one of the visiting judges, a huntsman from a local pack, was just getting to the punchline of a very borderline joke that was even making male guests blush, when the West of Yore's champion doghound and champion bitch decided to get it on in the showring.

But that is all an aside to the crux of this article. About a dozen years ago Orkney and his wife Barbara joined the Wensleydale Bridge Club – average age then 85 and they are all still playing. However, a couple of weeks ago the couple were presented with a pair of claret jugs after becoming national bridge champions following victory in the Marie Curie Cancer Care National Bridge Tournament in which there were 1,800 runners.

It is quite a result for jockeys this because bridge, as anyone who has ever played it will know, is a bookmakers' game. "We thought there was more chance of us getting the national wooden spoon," says a modest Orkney. "We were lucky the cards fell as they did."

The achievement did not go unnoticed locally and the Darlington and Stockton Times carried a nice picture of Mrs Orkney and her jugs. JULY 3, 2007

GOING out to Paris on Sunday morning Richard Hannon jnr fell foul of the new regulations preventing passengers from flying with toiletries in their hand luggage. His whole washbag was confiscated with the exception of his toothbrush, which was handed back to him. However, not to be completely outdone, he showered himself with a good part of a bottle of his designer after-shave. "At least," he reflected with some satisfaction, "I was the best smelling man on the plane." OCTOBER 3, 2006

best smelling man on plane

AS YOU know our top jockeys are some of the fittest athletes but one of their time-honoured, pre-race warm-up exercises went west on Sunday when smoking was outlawed in weighing rooms across England. The job had already been long gone in Ireland and Scotland.

Just because he's lost a bit of habitat, however, the wheezing, coughing jock who you just want to pat on the back as he returns from a hard ride is not about to be endangered. The nicotine stick is an appetite suppressant and nearly every jockey-smoker who has tried to give up the weed has found himself, in common with the rest of the population, putting on weight.

One colleague described Simon Whitworth as not so much a smoker but an "eater of cigarettes". It'll hardly help his climb back up the ladder after a brief sabbatical. "When I gave up before I put on 6lb overnight," he recalls. "But it's the law, end of story."

Being a regular at Hamilton and Musselburgh, Jimmy Quinn said he was already well practised at loitering by the nation's weighing-room backdoors. "There are," he says, putting it into context, "considerably worse rules in racing than not being able to smoke in the changing room." JULY 3, 2007

YOU have to hand it to Sandown's sales supremo, Ben Gibson. He probably didn't realise the difference a digit made either.

Last week, before everything at Wembley was put on hold until 2007, he issued what in the PR world is known as a 'joint mail out' with the new stadium to promote Sandown's Betfred meeting.

The idea is that the two sporting locations share their database on the basis that those interested in sport at Wembley wouldn't be averse to a bit of horseracing and vice versa. Simple enough?

However, on Sandown's mail out, to a mere 10,000, although the main part of Wembley's box office number was right, it was prefixed with an 0207 central London area code instead of 0208 outer ring as it should be.

Somewhat harrowingly for those who responded to Wembley, the 0207 prefix is for a hardcore porn line. To save you the call because, I'm told, such lines are charged at a premium rate, I've checked it out (twice) and the only thing 'Kitty' says that is remotely printable is her opening line: "Are you dirty?" It's rapidly downhill from thereon in until she sobers you up with news of how she intends to invoice you for the call.

"Quite a few grannies rang Sandown and said they thought there was something wrong with the phone line," said a spokesperson. Things just aren't going Wembley's way at the moment. APRIL 3, 2006

THIS is a classic of the genre and fairly typical of racecourse catering which, for the big occasion, ships in a lot of part-time or student staff to swell the number of full-time employees. Last week at Goodwood Peter Deal, part-owner of Derby winner Motivator and outright owner of Champion Hurdle winner Make A Stand, was overcome one afternoon by the need for a pink gin.

Pink gin, for those who don't know, may sound like a cocktail served at gay bars but it is in fact more of a man's drink. It's a couple of measures of Plymouth Gin with a dash of Angostura bitters which give it the distinctive colour and was made popular by Royal Navy officers in the mid-19th century. Even until pretty recently it was the drink of choice on a ship as soon as the sun was above the yard-arm for everyone from old admirals down to petty officers

Confronted by a barman who'd yet to start shaving, Peter realised that asking for a pink gin might be asking too much and that it might be met by a blank stare. So he thought he would dumb it down (I think that is the right expression) a bit and give the barman half a chance by asking if he had any of the vital ingredient, Angostura bitters.

"I'm terribly sorry, sir," replied the barman. "We only sell Worthington's here." AUGUST 2, 2005

CHARLES CHURCH, one of our foremost equestrian artists and a man brave enough once to spend a year under the same roof as Eddie Hales (now training in Ireland) in Lambourn, is holding an exhibition entitled 'Great British', a celebration of our rural heritage at the Arndean Gallery in Cork St, London W1, all this week.

The exhibition has the full backing of the Prince of Wales who is patron of the Rare Breeds Survival Trust and the organisation will receive a donation for every painting specifically of a rare breed sold at the exhibition. In his introduction Prince Charles describes Church as a "very remarkable young artist" before going on to talk about vegetables.

The exhibition also includes the Prince's 'Shetland Cow'. On a trip to Highgrove to sketch the creature Charles the artist accepted an invitation to tour the gardens a month later. While on the guided tour he saw the Shetland cow again but this time in a different paddock grazing underneath the Prince of Wales's bedroom.

Keen to get another look at it before he completed the painting in his studio he vaulted, sketchbook in hand, the gate out of the garden. His feet had barely landed before nine policemen clad from top to toe in body armour emerged from the undergrowth to arrest him.

In among the Portland Ram, Suffolk Punch, Gloucester Old Spot and selection of foxhounds, however, are a few thoroughbred horses including two paintings of Best Mate, a novice chaser and a paddock scene from the Cotley point-to-point in Devon. He is not sure whether to take a call from Henrietta Knight's office recently inquiring about two paintings as a compliment or not. She was after the 'Trio of Buff Orpingtons' and the 'Farmyard Goose' from his poultry section, not her famous horse. "She's the type of trainer who wouldn't hang a painting of a horse while he was still racing," says Charles reassuring himself. NOVEMBER 1, 2005

BY ANYONE'S standards the 2007 season has gone pretty well for young apprentice William Buick with 51 winners. Taking an avuncular interest in his progress has been Ian Balding, father of Buick's employer,

Andrew. Whether this is because the former trainer hasn't been able to do much else since he broke his neck or because he has backed him at 500-1 to be champion jockey within the next ten years, it is not clear.

Ride Buick may be able to do with style, but drive? Not yet. A fortnight ago he failed his driving test in Basingstoke for cocking up his reversal round a bend. "I was driving quite well," he says. "I thought they'd let me get away with it."

He is now scheduled to retake the driving part of his test in December, when he might be in either Dubai with trainer Doug Watson, or back in Florida with Todd Pletcher where he spent last winter.

And while every day of suspension this summer has been spent crammed with driving lessons, the end result may have had something to do with his final tutorial, given to him by Ian Balding, on the A303 on the way to Salisbury recently, the day before his test.

At the wheel Balding was going through a number of practical items that are not generally discussed in regular driving lessons up the cul de sacs of Newbury. "A lot of racing people drive fast," he explained, trapping past a white van parked up in a lay-by, "and there's nothing wrong with that. But the trick is to always be on the alert and look out for the police and hidden speed cameras."

It was a good case of 'do as I say, not do as I do'. The white van was the police. A week later a speeding fine plopped through the Baldings' letterbox – for doing 80mph down the A303. NOVEMBER 6, 2007

IT IS approaching Christmas so that can only mean one thing – online bookmakers Blue Square and their public relations chief Ed Pownall incurring the wrath of some major organisation defending helpless minorities. When he organised a turkey race and announced that the winner would be spared the Christmas table, World Poultry Concern leapt down his throat in defence of the also-rans.

When it was alligators it upset the Born Free Foundation and the RSPCA took a dim view of his hamster dragster and, last year, the Little

Peoples Athletic Association were up in arms – make that halfway up, in arms – about a race for elves. This Monday, having found enough little athletes not affiliated to the LPAA, Santa's elves will get their race – a 150-yard obstacle course – at Copthall Stadium in Barnet live online this Monday. "I've done animal rights to death," says a weary Ed, "so now I've moved on to human rights." The winner's cup is 38 inches high, about the same height as the smallest elf, so there must be some doubt as to whether the victor will be able to lift it aloft. DECEMBER 6, 2005

THERE is not much of this earth, let's face it, which is left uncharted. Most places on land have been visited by man – and if not Richard Dunwoody's on his way there right now – and only the floors of the great oceans remain harder to reach than neighbouring planets.

It was, therefore, in this spirit of exploration that Richard Hunnisett set off on Motcomb Jam in the 'confined' race at the Burton point-to-point held at Market Rasen the weekend before last.

At the first Richard, a 40-something pawnbroker whose green colours sport the pawnbroker's shop sign, three gold balls, lost his irons. He'd got one back at the second but as he reached down ostensibly to put foot in stirrup his shifting weight caused his saddle to slip. At the same time with his arms (ergo: brakes) otherwise engaged, Motcomb Jam reached a speed commonly known as 'lickety split'.

Knowing a lost cause when he saw one – they must walk into his shops on a daily basis – he opted out of the race and (how Market Rasen's greenkeeper must love horses) on to the golf course where he had nine fairways not to mention the odd green to gallop up and down until he came to a halt.

Unbeknown to that man or that beast there is a ditch up the middle of Market Rasen, the depth of which is more commonly associated with plate tectonics than drainage channels. Horse and rider spotted this obvious obstacle to their progress at roughly the same time and those following the situation through binoculars from the stand say they both wore the same facial expression. "Oh, shit" would not be nearly strong enough.

At that stage they disappeared out of sight. Motcomb Jam had tried dropping anchor with the result that he slid into the ditch's murky depths while Richard executed a perfect shallow dive. Both were completely immersed to the extent that the jockey's boots were full of water, while his underpants were wet through and contained weed. Even the hair under his helmet wasn't dry – and he was riding in the next race. When they emerged on the far back side, completely green including the golden balls which were indistinguishable from any other part of him, the crowd was overcome with laughing and cheering.

Having borrowed kit for the next race Richard finished third which, as trainer Caroline Bailey pointed out, was somewhat better. "Well," replied her intrepid owner-rider Richard and master of understatement, "it's something just to finish dry."

On Friday Mallards, Richard's pawnbroker, is the main sponsor at Leicester and next week, you'd imagine, must be a busy one for his trade. "Not noticeably so," says Richard who once took a saddle as a pawn. "But, unquestionably, our best shops are the ones situated next to bookmakers. There we get customers in and out twice in an afternoon." MARCH 7, 2006

IT IS disappointing that great racehorses cannot now be buried, as they have traditionally been, because of a directive from Europe and the steadfast insistence of government agencies here, in Best Mate's case the Trading Standards Office, to adhere to such regulations. We all know perfectly well the first people to ignore these rules, bend them or, now, set fire to them, would be those who made them, the French.

In Australia if you want to dig a hole and stick a horse in it, that's fine by everyone. And there is the recent example of the aptly named Mummify.

As winner of the Caulfield Cup in 2003 – no matter that it's a Flat handicap – Mummify was, by Australian standards, a great horse and accorded the same respect down under as a Grand National winner here.

This year, aged six, Mummify hit form again winning the Singapore International. Having heroically made every yard of the running under top weight in this year's Caulfield Cup he was collared in the last strides to go down by the uniquely Australian margin of two short necks.

However, 20 yards past the post, having given his all, he went lame with a fractured leg. The kindest solution for the old warrior was to have him put down.

Lee Freedman, his trainer, took the dead horse home and buried him in the old Red Indian tradition – standing up and facing east. As superstitious as she is, this bit might interest Henrietta Knight; the theory is that the spirit of the horse lives on with his connections. So in Freedman's case, and I dare say Big Chief Sitting Bull's before him, they end up getting another, Timeform 130-rated, great horse.

You're probably sitting there thinking 'pinch of salt' time. Now, as it happens, not all went entirely to plan in Mummify's case. Either the compass wasn't working or they didn't have one but there was a minor cock-up of sorts. Mummify doesn't face due east.

However, maybe it's the thought rather than the deed that kicks off the superstition in a positive fashion. Freedman cleaned up at the Spring Carnival. He won the Cox Plate, the Victoria Derby, the Oaks and the Melbourne Cup for a third time with Makybe Diva. It is the first time for 70 years that a trainer has won the Derby, Oaks and Cup in the same year.
NOVEMBER 8, 2005

WHILE Tom Scudamore popped up with his most valuable winner to date – Desert Air in Saturday's Ladbroke Hurdle at Sandown – it will come as good news to (well, I'm not entirely sure who in actual fact) genealogists perhaps that the really talented Scudamore sibling is about to hit the saddle.

Hitherto Tom's younger but bigger brother Michael, 21, has expended his energy on the rugby pitch, firstly for Gloucester and, until last season, for Ebbw Vale. Unless you're Gavin Henson when it is a matter of suntans or hairstyles, rugby is, as you know, life or death stuff in the Valleys. So it was no mean feat playing open side flanker for a Welsh Premiership side and under-19s for the national side.

At Cheltenham College he was playing for the school against Clifton College while his mum, Marilyn, watched from the touchline next to two coaches. "That's Peter Scudamore's son," said one without realising who she was. "He's not too bad," replied the other, "but playing rugby? You'd have to question the parentage."

Well, the paternal genes are coming to the fore at last and Michael, who has dispensed with the hymns and arias, has joined the family business and is assisting his grandfather Michael with a view to taking over the licence one day. He has slimmed down from a chunky 14st to 11st 5lb and, before the fortnight's out, will have made his debut in a point-to-point.

"He was always more talented but less interested than me," says Tom, though he dismissed Michael's not inconsiderable achievement of shedding two and a half stone as the result of having a proper job for the first time in his life. Michael, for his part, says it was easier shedding it than it was putting it on.

"At Pony Club," recalls Tom, "I was always focused on winning, getting the angles right in the jump off and he'd rock up, chase the girls, show no interest – then beat me. When we rode out for Nigel Twiston-Davies he was always the one that looked like Cash Asmussen."

Michael's debut is likely to be in a deep, dark corner of Herefordshire on one of his mother's ten pointers. Depending on how things go he could be seen under rules before the season's out in a hunter chase. But don't you just love older brothers. "I think," said Tom, "after schooling a few he's got half an eye on Cheltenham and a ride in a National."
JANUARY 10, 2006

FULL marks to Cheltenham for opening its doors to a very successful full day of pony racing organised by the Cotswold Vale Hunt a week ago. The first race, it seems, was for the coolest 'pegs' in the changing room – AP McCoy's, Ruby Walsh's and Choc Thornton's.

However the lad I'm tipping for the top is George Saunders, 13, grandson of Grand National-winning amateur, Dick. He was had in by the stewards – for swearing at the starter. His mum, Tik, denied it was anything to do with her. "He didn't learn it off me," she insists. APRIL 10, 2007

THERE are certain career moves that look like financial suicide. Top of that list is, unquestionably, training racehorses.

So when Ollie Stevens, the Winchester-educated second head lad to James Fanshawe, decided he wasn't going to take that route after all, his accountant and, no doubt, family breathed a huge sigh of relief. That was the good news but his accountant must have felt like a man who has just been missed by a train but steps back into the path of a car when Ollie gave him the bad news. He wished to convert an old fishing tackle shop on All Saints Road, Newmarket – from the slime to the ridiculous – into a delicatessen.

Though slightly off the beaten track the fact that the shop had survived selling rods and bait for as long as anyone can remember when there isn't anything more substantial water-wise within 20 miles of the town than a cattle trough can only be good news. It's shopping's equivalent of a lucky yard.

The English Kitchen opened a few weeks ago and is now doing good trade during the sales. Of course in the deli world when you're selling a few slices of this and a few slices of that the biggest problem, and therefore cost, is not what is sold but what is wasted. To combat this and reduce prices he's installed a kitchen to knock out pies with leftovers at the end of the day.

"Racing was my work and food a big interest," he says. "Now it's the other way round." Shopkeeping is in his blood, though. His granny,

Bunty Richardson, ran a shop at the top of Newmarket's High Street and his sister, Rosie, runs a deli in Brixton that was recently voted the best delicatessen in London by the *Observer*.

However old habits, it seems, die hard in Newmarket. At his launch a fortnight ago someone walked in and ordered a pint of fresh maggots. He was pleased not to oblige them. OCTOBER 11, 2005

IT'S been a trying few days for the BHA, let's face it. Last week before the Fallon trial exploded in its face, Lawney Hill, the Aston Rowant trainer, dutifully rang in, as she is required to do by the rules of racing, to report a broken blood vessel at Folkestone the previous day. Having briefly digested the information the really smart girl on the end of the line then asked the trainer whether it was the horse or the jockey who had suffered this unfortunate occurrence. At that point the trainer burst a blood vessel. DECEMBER 11, 2007

NIGEL and Carolyn Elwes shouldn't need too much of an introduction, especially in breeding circles. They breed Flat horses although, as is sometimes the case, one of the best, and certainly the most fun, horses they have bred is David Pipe's Puntal. He's the Whitbread winner, a standing dish in the National and ran a phenomenal race in the cross-country at Cheltenham in November when a close third after going about a furlong in the wrong direction.

Nigel is a former chairman of the Thoroughbred Breeders' Association, remains chairman of Racing Welfare and the British Racing School, on the board at Kempton and on the committee at Sandown.

Carolyn is an experienced steward and still sits on the panel at Kempton, Sandown, Newbury and Salisbury. But when they moved to within six miles of Wincanton a few years ago she reckoned, after a suitable amount of time, that she should offer her services as a local steward and consequently put in a call to the management offering just that.

She was slightly taken aback to be asked to apply in writing with a CV attached. Hastily she and Nigel knocked out the required information and posted it. Pretty sharpish she received a call from Rebecca Morgan, Wincanton's clerk of the course. "I'm terribly sorry," she said, "we thought you were applying to be a steward in the car park." December 11, 2007

BEING talented at one thing isn't enough for some people, which is grossly unfair when you consider how many people aren't talented at anything. But there's a slight twist to the case of Tolly, a man so well known in Newmarket that, a bit like Pele, he's known by just the single name.

The twist is this: he combines the macho with the artistic in much the same way an SAS sergeant major who has a part-time job hairdressing might. By day Tolly is a stallion man at Dalham Hall Stud; by night he's arranging flowers. His equine charges have included Dubai Millennium and, now, Best Of The Bests. But Limerick-born Tolly, 38, also owns a thriving flower shop in Newmarket called Tolly's Flowers.

What is more annoying about his talent for arranging is that he is untaught, a natural who, unlike most of us who fall into a rose bed and come up cut to ribbons and smelling of muck, took his chance when it came. At one of Sheikh Mohammed's first stallion parades ten years ago a load of flowers were dumped in the office. The then secretary sighed and said: "What are we going to do with them, Tolly?"

The rest is hippeastri gloribunda. The business has grown like, well, giant hogweed. So one minute he's leading Best Of The Bests to the covering shed for passion, the next he's firing off a bouquet of flowers to a girl from a Flat jockey who hopes that it will also lead to the same conclusion.

Last week Sheikh Mohammed paraded his 22 stallions at Dalham as well as entertaining everyone to a lobster brunch and chocolate fountain. The first things to hit you were not lobsters stacked ten high but the delphiniums (2,400 of them) in all hues of blue arranged up the marquee poles by Tolly. For him it was a doubly proud moment, Best Of The Bests parading in front of his delph's. July 13, 2004

SLAVERY is making a bit of a comeback in the north. The West of Yore Hunt, whose territory includes Middleham, held an auction of slaves to raise funds and putting themselves up for sale from racing were Charlie Stebbing, the clerk of the scales, station announcer Andy Orkney and trainer James Bethell.

As a man who spends most of his working life watching other people's weight it is slightly incongruous that Charlie was offering himself as a chef. However, such is his reputation in Yorkshire that the biggest certainty was that he'd be top lot and knock an eye test with Orkney and a morning yawning on the gallops with Bethell into a cocked hat.

His 'dinner for eight' was knocked down to Mark Johnston for £280. If the trainer has any sense he and Deirdre will go back four times. They can expect a starter of smoked salmon terrine, followed by grouse, homegrown vegetables and, perhaps, a Seville roulade. The wine will be changed between courses and, as he drove to France just to get the cheese for his own 50th birthday dinner, you can imagine it won't just be a lump of Wensleydale Blue to finish with.

After that, according to Orkney, who regularly samples Stebbing hospitality, the dogs get to lick the plates, which, I believe, Gordon Ramsey might have something to say about.

So Johnston has a bargain. Not that his waistline suggests he's undernourished but could it be that Deirdre isn't so handy with a saucepan? At the auction Mark bought every slave offering to prepare food. JULY 13, 2004

SINCE it was born of the Jockey Club one always assumes the BHB to have inherited a few of its traits, among them a certain amount of crustiness. However, with more departments than Harrods and plenty of jobs for young go-getters in designer specs, it couldn't be further from the truth.

Take, for example, bloodstock marketing executive Caley Wilson, 30. The first time the 6ft-plus former rugby player from New Zealand was interviewed by the BHB he failed to get the job – because the interviewee before him was an attractive, busty brunette. However, his degree in marketing earned him a second chance and, before he knew it, we had a Kiwi promoting British thoroughbreds.

Last week, though, he took an evening off from Doncaster Sales to return to London and perform with his band 'Flow' at the Half Moon in Putney, a venue where U2, the Rolling Stones and the Who cut their plectrums in the early years. Bopping away in the audience listening to the acoustic rock was the BHB's impossibly trendy head of marketing, Chris John. The Jockey Club's PR man Paul Struthers had dusted off his winkle pickers and tight jeans for the occasion too, along with half a dozen other colleagues.

Wilson first came here in a sulk because he'd smashed his shoulder playing rugby at home and denying a New Zealander the right to play rugby is like denying a fish water. He sought consolation in his guitar but his music is far from melancholic and after listening to Flow you don't, like you might with some singer-songwriters, want to commit suicide.

Flow have also cut a CD which includes songs like Summertime, Swimming In Your Sea and Freedom, familiar song titles but different songs. It's a bit like Caliban, the horse who famously beat Park Top in the 1970 Coronation Cup, and Caliban, the modern-day plodder trained by Ian Williams – they're a different kettle of fish.

"There's nothing very George Michael about our Freedom," says Wilson. 'Swimming In Your Sea' is not about a New Zealander trying to surf on six-inch waves off Devon. Written by Wilson, it's about a girl he fell for on a pre-BHB visit to Japan that came to nothing. In actual fact it did come to something. As a result he backed, with complete disregard to form, Made In Japan at the 2004 Cheltenham Festival, the 20-1 winner of the Triumph Hurdle. SEPTEMBER 13, 2005

THERE was an interesting two-year-old maiden at Lingfield on Friday, or would have been, when Little Knickers was due to race against

Primed And Poised. Little Knickers was withdrawn after nearly coming down in the stalls. JUNE 15, 2007

TOBY BALDING, the recently-but-hardly retired trainer, is many things. After handing over Kimpton Down to his son-in-law, Jonathan Geake, one suspects he still pays more than a passing interest in the way the horses are trained. Like the Queen he is never too far from a Corgi and on top of all this he's on every committee God invented.

It is unlikely, however, even he contemplated the latest addition to his CV: father of a celebrated pornographer. Yes, at an age (45) when you'd think most children were beyond embarrassing their fathers, his son Gerald, once an elephant trainer in America and now taking time out as ringmaster at Gifford's Circus, has produced the quadruple X-rated film *The Avlon Lady*.

It was filmed, and more off-puttingly the sound effects recorded, in a room in Toby's house using puppets Gerald and his partner in crime, Luca Garcia, a resting clown, made themselves. Imagine the Wooden Tops on Viagra and you have it.

The Avlon Lady is part of Gerald's touring (it tours stag nights) Delicia Show which is (using puppets) like the Trisha Show meets Punch and Judy. In it one of the puppets is a guest on Delicia's daytime show to discuss her making of the film and it cleverly alternates between film and live action. It was runner-up recently in the Erotic Awards (performance category) – that would be quite something to boast to your girlfriend – and, probably a truer reflection of its class, it went down a storm when premiered at the Geake stable lads' Christmas party. It was particularly a hit with the blacksmith, apparently.

So the smartest yard in the south now has a sideline in porn? "No," says Gerald, "it's more a sideline in puppets with a bit of porn involved. We also do children's shows but we strive to keep the puppets separate. The Delicia Show is meant to be funny though some do find it sexy. There's no accounting for taste. I don't find it sexy but then I've spent far too long handling their private parts."

While one of Toby's daughters, Serena, is the wholly innocent Mrs Geake, another, Camilla, was roped in to do part of the voiceover for the bonking puppets. So far Toby has only been called on for the use of his spare bedroom. "As adult entertainment goes," says the supportive ex-trainer, "it's a must." May 16, 2006

IT IS early days – and by that I mean we're still in Plymouth Sound on a round-the-world yacht race – but setting a strong early pace in the point-to-point riders' championship is Nicky Henderson's assistant trainer, Jamie Snowden, 26. For a man named after a large mountain he has remarkably few weight problems.

The most remarkable thing about Jamie's burgeoning career is that he was not put off when, as a ten-year-old at Pony Club camp, Joe Tizzard broke his nose by mistake in a sack-race or, as a 12-year-old, when he lost his four front teeth in a fall over a hedge from his pony. Without his plate in, apart from it detracting from his looks, he's not much good for anything other than sucking a boiled sweet.

After a year at Sandhurst he was commissioned into the King's Royal Hussars, a cavalry regiment with a rich history in horses. However it had, by his time, swapped its traditional mode of transport for Challenger II tanks, vehicles programmed to take on obstacles with much the same mental approach as Iris's Gift.

Despite the fact that his mere smiling without his teeth in would have had six battalions of Iraqi soldiers in swift retreat, the nearest he got to the Middle East conflict was Tidworth. He did, however, represent England in the Elephant Polo World Championships in Thailand, a sport taken so seriously that one of the opposing teams was made up of ladyboys. Don't get too many of them at Larkhill.

When he was based in Harrogate on a job teaching recruits, his sergeant only knew of his whereabouts if he bought the Racing Post. And in Northern Ireland, where soldiers were forbidden to leave their barracks in South Armagh without weapons, he and Alex Michael, a fellow captain, used to be smuggled over the border to ride out for an Eire-based trainer desperately short of staff.

His commanding officer, with the aim of winning the Grand Military Gold Cup, sent him on secondment to Paul Nicholls for five months and the end result was a whole load of silverware for the officers' mess. Teaming up with the quirky Whitenzo for the trainer, he won the Grand Military and Royal Artillery Gold Cups plus another race at Exeter before the pair finished fourth in the Betfred Gold Cup. JANUARY 17, 2006

AT AN age, 42, when some of his old City banking colleagues are considering retirement, George Baker has decided to jump off the financial equivalent of the Clifton Suspension Bridge and take up the noble art of racehorse training.

He passed the licensing department's 'chat without coffee' last week and our newest dual-purpose trainer will shortly launch from Moreton Morrell in Warwickshire with 20 horses.

That's as much as you need to know about the future; it's the past we're interested in for this is the Hughie Morrison approach to training – get experience in another business first. Morrison, of course, ran a lighting business in Manchester during the last recession.

Baker's first venture into the big wide world was at Edinburgh University where he studied the Sporting Life for a year. I'm sure degrees in Scotland normally take four years, but, whatever. He then hit the Square Mile in no uncertain terms. It was during his time with Barings that the old family banking firm was pretty much wiped out by Nick Leeson but it was at BZW that he excelled.

At a Monday morning meeting on the trading floor, BZW's oil analyst stood up and confidently announced that the oil price was about to rise sharply and that everyone should invest accordingly. Baker duly returned to his office and went in long – as they say in the City – in a Danish oil company.

Sure enough a few days later there was high-fiving and war-whooping in offices across the firm as the price of oil began to go through the roof and, accordingly, the share value of oil companies. There was high-fiving everywhere, that is, except for Baker's office where the share price of his Danish oil company remained resolutely static. "Don't worry," he reassured colleagues, "it'll come. Obviously there's a time lag between here and Denmark."

A couple of days on and the price still hadn't budged one way or the other and a colleague insisted they conduct some deeper research into the state of Denmark's oil where, it appeared, something was indeed rotten.

Of course when they skimmed the surface it transpired that the business Baker had gone long on was indeed in the hands of Danes – unusually as it turned out – because its proud claim to fame was that it owned three olive oil refineries in Tuscany and was, therefore, singularly unaffected by the price of crude.

It was a tipping point for Baker. He then spent three years in Vietnam and time as assistant to Paul Webber. But if the name sounds vaguely familiar it is because he was Lambourn correspondent and feature writer for the duration of the ill-fated *Sportsman* and although the economics of the paper – 150 employees in a swanky office, five readers – didn't quite pan out as budgeted, Baker proved himself to be one of the stars of the show. Now, we hope, he'll be making his own headlines.

November 20, 2007

PIP KIRKBY, managing director at Market Rasen for the past eight years and Nottingham since last July, is set to go far in racecourse management. Jockey Club Racecourses, for whom she works, will almost certainly already know about her ability to think on her feet.

The weekend before last she was seconded to Aintree where, for seven years now, she has been one of a number of other racecourse executives who are roped in to help out at the Grand National as a 'sector manager'.

This year that involved being clerk of the course Andrew Tulloch's sidekick.

Normally before a Market Rasen fixture (there was one the day after the National) Pip, short for Claire (no explanation), does an interview with BBC Radio Lincolnshire's breakfast show. They rang Pip on Thursday and arranged to speak to her at 8.20 on Friday, primarily about Market Rasen's Sunday meeting but, given her location, they requested that she be standing by one of Aintree's famous landmarks for the interview to give the breakfast show some added excitement.

With plenty going on Pip completely forgot about the interview and on Friday morning, at the appointed hour, the phone went. However, she was not standing beside Becher's Brook, Foinavon's fence or the Canal Turn, she was instead queuing up for a full English with a number of other Jockey Club employees in a canteen in the car park.

The first question put to her was: "Pip, where are you standing?"

"I'm standing beside the chair," she replied, accurately, although the 3ft high, 1ft wide plastic seat on wobbly legs beside her was not quite as formidable as 6ft wide, 5ft high The Chair, which, later that day, was to ensnare five runners in the Topham Trophy. She went on to describe the fence, from memory, in considerable detail.

The interview continued to go well with the National and Market Rasen's upcoming meeting getting plenty of air-time – albeit in Lincolnshire – until the final question was delivered. "Well, Pip, so that our listeners can get a real sense of the fence," concluded her interviewer, "can you rub the spruce so we can hear it?"

"Hang on a moment," she said, exiting the canteen and heading for a nearby privet hedge into which she plunged her mobile phone and ruffled the branches. And to this day rural Lincolnshire remains blissfully none the wiser. APRIL 24, 2007

LUKE HARVEY, erstwhile morning racing bulletin man for BBC 5 Live and an ATR presenter, can be thankful for friends in high places. The first indication he had of the gathering severity of Friday's floods came while eating a sandwich (they're free) in the press room at Newbury after racing had been called off.

A security man came in to the press room, asking the few in there to leave. "Why?" they asked, not wanting to hurry their lunch. "Because," he replied, "the water in the press car park is up to the doors on your cars."

When he returned home to his newly built cottage in Fawler near Wantage he found the kitchen, two steps down from the rest of the house, filling up like a scene from Titanic. The quick-thinking former jockey removed all the white goods, unscrewed the doors from the cupboards and legged it to neighbouring trainer Charlie Morlock, up the hill in Kingston Lisle, to borrow two buckets with which to start bailing. "It was like peeing against the wind," he said. "The road was a river one side of the house and the stream was a river on the other."

But after the tidal wave came the brainwave. He rang former trainer and farmer Chris Nash, who arrived with his industrial-sized chemical sprayer and, unlike the rest of us who fought with little girl-sized pond pumps if we were lucky, the manful machine was able to pump out 10,000 gallons (not a particularly large amount of water unless it's in your kitchen) in a matter of minutes.

"I managed to save some beer too," said the former publican Harvey, "and we stood there with a can watching with incredulity as it sucked it in one end and pumped it out on to the road at the other." It has dried out already. July 24, 2007

A CHARITY called Heros, the Homing Ex-Racehorses Organisation Scheme, was launched at Newbury on Saturday. It is the fourth such charity and joins the three other rehoming centres, Moorcroft, Greatwood and the Thoroughbred Rehabilitation Centre in Lancashire. All four are supported by racing's own dedicated organisation, the Retraining of Racehorses.

With the 'O' and 'S' of Heros sounding a little bit contrived one of the guests at the launch suggested that Grace Muir, the founder and chief executive who has already rehomed some 300 racehorses from North Farm Stud, near Wantage, could easily have come up with the acronym Heros from the equally apt 'Helping Ex-Racehorses Out of the Shit'. October 24, 2006

BEN ORDE-POWLETT, hitherto best known to this column for being the only conditional jockey in the country who could bike home to a castle for lunch after third lot, has retired from riding at the age of 25.

Having, like his father Harry (now Lord Bolton) piloted horses with some success – particularly those who appeared to be named after French aristocracy like Enzo De Baune and Idalgo De Guye – he is now in the process of learning to pilot something that hopefully goes slightly further than the width of an open ditch between take-off and landing: an aeroplane. It is, I believe, just a coincidence that the jockey's employment training scheme goes by the acronym Jets.

Ahead of him are numerous visits to Teesside Airport and at least 700 hours of flying – the equivalent of 14 trips to Australia and back – before he can even be considered for a commercial flying licence and probably even longer before near-neighbour Mark Johnston gives him the leg-up in his Piper.

Ben has the pedigree. His uncle, Michael, gave up farming, aged 35, to become a pilot and now flies for British Airways and, while I don't suppose he'll put this in his CV come the day, his dad once landed a Tiger Moth in some electric fencing and, on another occasion, landed a light plane upside down.

"I did bend one once," confirms Harry whose private pilot's licence has since elapsed but retains a keen knowledge of the skies. "Flying an aeroplane is a bit like driving a car with a couple of flat tyres, you need a feel for it. Flying is something that lends itself quite well to people changing direction later in life. Unlike me, it is something you really want to do beyond, rather than during, your hooligan days but in Ben's case he seems to have kept most of his cars upright, which is a start."

Of course, in the intervening 700 hours he might also have to neutralise the English/Irish racing patois he has picked up working in the Middleham yards of Ferdy Murphy and George Moore before he's allowed to say: "This is your Captain speaking" for BA.

It's all change with the Bolton boys. Ben's older brother Tom, who you may recall getting mentioned in these dispatches for the MC he won in Iraq, is to leave the army and is to enter the renewable energy business, which is probably where we should all be going. It is a great surprise, though, that he wasn't sent to Afghanistan to put the wind up the Taliban first. January 9, 2007

NEVER let it be said that British racing lacks variety. The BHA has just issued an opera-singing cowgirl from Alabama with her training licence and she hopes to have her first runner within the fortnight.

Heather Main, wife of Newbury vet James Main, is about to embark on her training career with a mix of two-year-olds and jumpers at their farm in Kingston Lisle, Oxfordshire.

As a teenager she was crowned 'Rodeo Queen of Alabama' for her barrel-racing victories. But she transferred from her studies at Atlanta University to complete her degree in Southampton and never went home again.

She spent the next ten years studying singing, much of it at Trinity College of Music in London, and after he heard her singing to the horses in the barn one of her former stable lads turned up the next day with an entry form for Britain's Got Talent – the only stumbling block being her nationality.

She should know a thing or two about speed. Barrel racing involves galloping round three barrels laid out in a clover-leaf pattern. You come into the arena at full tilt and if you are going right-handed round a barrel your right foot should be skimming the ground, such is the ability of the quarterhorse to turn on a 'dime'.

Naturally she met her husband through horses. She was pre-training a racehorse called Cool Temper for Paul Cole who was lame and after the trainer had seen it trot up he said: "I think you need James."

"He turned up and I nearly burst into tears when he said the horse may never run again and I was determined to prove him wrong," she recalls. "I followed his instructions to the letter though and the horse won its first race back for Paul and two weeks later I won an amateur race at Newmarket on him. Our relationship was purely professional at that stage although I did think it was rather sweet that my equine vet was called Mr Mane!"

The singing is now restricted to the occasional recital, weddings and she is not averse to belting one out at a dinner party. Whether she does an Oliver Brady, the Irish trainer renowned for breaking into song in the winner's enclosure, remains to be seen. "I was wondering if anyone had ever done that," she says – so she has clearly given it some thought. APRIL 21, 2009

PAUL WEBBER has been training winners like they have been going out of fashion lately and one of them, Edgbriar, who won the CSP Novices' Handicap Hurdle at Newbury the week before last, is clearly something of a character.

A few days before he was due to run, Edgbriar got loose on the gallops and as loose horses do 99 times out of 100, he headed for home, rapidly. (Richard Hannon once had a loose horse who did not go home and was lost on Salisbury Plain for three days.)

Webber, in his Jeep, picked up the horse's jockey and drove back to the yard expecting to find Edgbriar already back in his box munching hay. However, the box was empty and no-one back at the yard had seen Edgbriar return, so they were detailed to go and look for the six-year-old.

He was eventually found standing outside Webber's equine pool, his rugs and tack all in place if a little wet, looking very pleased with himself.

He was waiting to be scraped down having just taken himself for what he obviously considered a well-earned dip.

"They don't need me," says Webber, "they know what the routine is round here." DECEMBER 9, 2008

WHAT do Richard Hannon and Dr Jeremy Naylor have in common, apart from training on Salisbury Plain? Both were drummers in a band though it has to be said so far that Hannon, who was briefly drumming for the Troggs in the swinging sixties, has been more successful on both counts.

In his youth Naylor was the Mr Sticks to the very un-PC named band 'Old People Are Mad'. Their non-hit single 'Trust' and 'Violent and Unknown' – in reality a double B-side – was played on Capital Radio a couple of times in the early 80s.

In a bout of optimism Wrinkley Records produced more of these 45 rpm vinyl records than they sold and Naylor still hands them out to anyone who expresses an interest, even though you'd need to go to a museum with a gramophone to listen to it now. "It'll make a good ashtray if nothing else," he said, handing over the priceless piece of pop memorabilia.

The rest of the band were mainly City boys and the nearest they came to rebellion was when, unknown to security, they had a late-night rehearsal in some City offices which resulted in them having to scarper before being arrested by the City of London Police, probably on charges of corruption.

Naylor still makes music though. His wife, Enid, also a practising vet, made the mistake of giving him a guitar three years ago. "Now he's got three," she says. "We're hoping to make Jeremy a soundproof office to practise in above my small animal veterinary surgery." God help recuperating hamsters. JANUARY 12, 2009

Chapter Seven
THE PASTIMES OF THIS NOBLE BREED

IT HAS been in Eddie Ahern's mind for some time to convert some of his Flat colleagues to the joys of hunting and, to this end, he took Tom Queally and hunting 'virgins' Adam Kirby and Hayley Turner out with the Grafton last week.

While Miss Turner looked straight out of the Pony Club, it is still unclear from whence the day's hero Adam Kirby took his sartorial inspiration – Elton John? Boyzone? He certainly had his own take on hunting pink.

For the top half he wore a pink shirt with the top button undone, and a pink tie with an unbuttoned, borrowed black jacket. One of the weighing room's size zeros, there was enough slack for several more colleagues in breeches borrowed from his valet Dave Mustoe, who has a 34-inch waste. Underpinning the whole ensemble were his American Kroops riding-out boots complete with Cuban heels and pointy toe.

As he led his horse, an ex-hurdler of unknown repute, down the horsebox ramp its eyes were popping out of its head. "I don't expect it's seen a pack of hounds before," commented someone knowingly. "I don't think it can have seen a ****ing dog before," replied the nothing if not game Kirby. The way it took to hunting, however, it turns out it must have been Kirby's tie that was causing it such distress.

The first to go a purler was Queally, who had the misfortune to come down on gravel and is still, a week later, picking grit from his hands. "You know some horses go long and some go short," says Henry Cecil's jockey. "Well, this did neither."

Next down was our leading lady jockey. Her confidence up after pinging gates, she went for the high part of a post and rail. When, later, asked by her boss Mike Bell, why she hadn't helped it defy gravity by sitting back and picking its head up off the floor, she pointed out: "Because it was doing a somersault at the time, guv'nor."

Third down was Ahern. He claims to have been brought down. Up to a point it seems he was right; he was brought down by some sheep-netting about a yard out beyond a hedge.

"When I came round the corner and saw horse and jockey skidding across the turf I just somehow naturally assumed it was Adam," says Mustoe. "But he was the only one not to fall – his horse is legendary."

Since then both Turner and, regrettably, Kirby – because hunting's somewhat stuffy image could do with a few more people turning up like they'd taken a wrong turning on the way to a gay wedding – have been on shopping sprees to get all the kit. It's unlikely the Grafton have seen the last of them. NOVEMBER 18, 2008

DINING ROOMS are apparently going out of fashion in Britain but not so in Ireland. A former Irish trainer, who is giving his house a major renovation largely to his own design, was recounting how pleased he had been with the way the dining room – the piece de resistance of his extension – was coming on and how much he was looking forward to some entertaining dinner parties in there in the future.

As Paddy the plasterer (no relation to Forpadydeplasterer, fourth in yesterday's Ballymore Properties Novices' Hurdle) was artfully applying the finishing touches he turned to the trainer. "Boss," he said, "this'll be the finest room in the house – I bet you cannot wait to be getting the plasma screen up." MARCH 14, 2008

THERE are several specialist racing books out this Christmas including *The Jockey Club Rooms* – an upmarket inventory and potted history of the Jockey Club's art and artefacts – and the purple-bound *The Derby Stakes – the Complete History 1780-2006* by Michael Church.

No other sport has been recorded on canvas quite like racing during the last 250 years and the Jockey Club houses its finest collection. Although a picture is supposed to paint a thousand words, where they don't David Oldrey fills us in.

Writing about the painting of Crucifix, the 1840 Oaks winner owned by one of the Jockey Club's great administrators, Lord George Bentinck and trained by John Day snr, he alludes to Day's sharp practice and how the owner and the ironically nicknamed 'Honest John' eventually fell out over the trainer's 'devious' handling of Crucifix's breakdown.

However, Oldrey does not recall quite the full story due to doubts about its authenticity – something that has never discouraged this column. At the time, though, Lord George, almost as big a figure in the annals of Jockey Club history as Admiral Rous, was on a mission to clamp down on the well-known shenanigans within racing. At the same time he was a pretty serious punter, which didn't quite tally with his crusade but, hey, that's the Jockey Club for you.

Anyway, in plotting another of his shenanigans, Day wrote two letters. One was to Lord George telling him to have what he liked on one of his horses who was shortly due to run because it would win. The other letter was to Lord George's bookmaker telling him to lay Lord George what he liked on the same horse because it wasn't off and wouldn't win. The idea was that the horse wouldn't win and he would draw from the bookmaker.

The moment when, I think it's fair to say, Honest John Day went wrong was when he made the schoolboy error of putting the letters in the wrong envelopes so that when Lord George opened his at breakfast it read, Dear bookmaker. And vice versa. It is believed that this led to the terminal breakdown in relationship between owner and trainer.
DECEMBER 5, 2006

ONE of the great sporting moments – that is how it is being described in Newmarket. "Made losing bearable," was the comment of one slightly disloyal team member. Julian Wilson, the former face of BBC racing, one of Newmarket's greatest spinners – by his own admission – and a man who takes his bowling average more seriously than life itself, joined a select band of bowlers on Sunday.

Unfortunately for 'Wiz', that select band includes the hapless Malcolm Nash, another left-armer, who was famously hit for six sixes in an over by Garry Sobers. Playing for Newmarket in a team that included Mike Bell, Ed Dunlop and William Haggas, on his home pitch of Burrough Green,

Newmarket were cruising with three overs to go. A couple of mere boys hardly out of shorts were at the crease and Newmarket had 35 runs in hand over a visiting XI when Wiz brought himself on in the hope of a cheap wicket to bolster that average. Instead he was smote to all parts of the village as he went for six sixes.

Instead of glory, he snatched defeat from the jaws of victory to complete a bad day for himself. Earlier one of his own team had landed a six on the bonnet of his wife's car. It is one way into cricket's history books but not the way he would have wished.

He's not taken it well. Muttering about having coached the boy who destroyed his bowling figures "since he was 12", he refused to join the team for a post-game drink in the pub and was not amused when he was presented with the match ball. It surprised his team-mates when the shortness of the boundaries at Burrough Green was not an item in his 'Mr Angry' column in yesterday's *Racing Post*. JULY 6, 2005

IT'S a measure of the desperation in the Australian camp that cricket supporters from down under are now taking two Group 1 victories in horseraces – Kerrin McEvoy's win on Warrsan in the Grosser Preis von Baden and Starcraft's in the Prix du Moulin – in Europe over the weekend as evidence of an upturn in Aussie fortunes ahead of the last Test in this enthralling Ashes series.

But I have some horrendous news for them. If the trickle-down effect of England's Test side's form is anything to go by, then Australia are doomed. Ed Dunlop, who can't normally be relied upon to score enough runs to test his five-year-old daughter's maths let alone the scorer's ability to count, knocked up an unbeaten 122 for the Julian Wilson XI (which included Sir Michael Stoute, William Haggas and Walter Swinburn) playing against Burrough Green in the 25th and final Lester Piggott trophy on Sunday. Luckily for Ed, Michael Holding, the retired West Indian fast bowler formerly known as Whispering Death, was umpiring rather than bowling.

"It is the highest individual score in the 25 years," says Wizlon. "It was greeted with considerable admiration, even by Michael Holding, and included nine sixes."

In a small way modest Ed also avenged the six sixes in six balls scored off Wizlon's bowling by Burrough Green earlier this summer. He hit one ball harder than he'd ever hit a ball before. It took a nasty deflection off a bump in the outfield and missed the offending player's 'long barrier' and hit him in the Nutbush City limits. It laid him out for 45 minutes.

Fittingly for the last charity Lester Piggott Trophy the great man was there to present his trophy to the winning side. It has now been won 13 times by Wilson's XI and 11 times by the village. "We've run out of space on the trophy for the result," says Wilson, "and I'm considering retirement – that's why it's finished. I'm struggling in the field. Lester mumbled that it was a shame and I half thought he offered to give us a new trophy but, thinking about it, I must have misheard him."

September 5, 2005

THE TOUR DE FRANCE has been beset by all sorts of problems in the last few years but, for the first time, it faces a problem that isn't dope related on Monday.

Lance Armstrong may have retired and Jan Ullrich may have been sent home, but stand by for Team Lard and James Crispe, an associate director at the International Racing Bureau and a regular commentator at East Anglian point-to-points.

On Monday, with puncture repair kit in pocket, he will wobble across the start line on a saddle that looks like the handle-end of a broom in the amateur leg of the once-great race.

This year's 'Etape' takes place on probably the stiffest leg of the Tour's route, the 120 mountainous miles between Gap and Alpe d'Huez with three alpine peaks to be conquered on the way. Physically and mentally it will be like skiing – without lifts.

Training round the Fens and Newmarket – where alpine villagers would, frankly, laugh at the concept of Warren Hill being considered as such – has been nothing if not an adventure for James, 38, and his padded lycra shorts. Indeed if he travels as fast as he did from Burwell to Addenbrooke's Hospital in April in an ambulance he should be well ahead of the pace.

On that occasion he was assimilating the feed from his new on-board bike computer (speedometer to you and me) when he rode smack into a stationary car. He broke his jaw and didn't wake up until in the comfort of a hospital bed – the best way to do it according to his pointing pals, who have experienced similar situations. That way you feel no pain.

James's figure apart – he's shed a stone and a half in training – it's all in a good cause. He's raising money to fund a quad bike to allow Paul Tiano, who is paralysed following a fall at Horseheath in 2005, unrestricted point-to-point access. Sponsorship details are on www. pointingEA.com. If not money then he'd be mighty grateful for a small phial of steroids. JULY 4, 2006

AFTER a spell in the wilderness, Charlie Brooks' return to competitive riding would appear to be good news for the entertainment industry. Ironically it took him instantly back to, if not a wilderness then the microclimate of the bottom of a hedge and ditch. Were it not for the fact that Brooks' Brook just doesn't have a ring about it, the obstacle would now be named after him in much the same way that Becher's was named after the first man to be dunked in that particular tributary of the Mersey.

Post-Pony Club but before he became a trainer Charlie's finest hours were not, as popularly believed, on the dance floor, but on the back of a horse. He won the Cheltenham Foxhunter on Observe for Fred Winter and once led the field down to Becher's in the Grand National on the aptly named Insure.

Brooks recently invested in a new, chunky, soup plate-footed liver-chestnut hunter named Shane bought from jump jockey Chocolate

Thornton. Shortly afterwards he entered Shane in the Old Berks Hunt Race. A good result and it would have been a prep for the Grand National of such races, the Melton Hunt Ride.

All went smoothly for the first mile. The cruising leader fell at the 12th and by a process not dissimilar to ten green bottles, Shane had, by default, moved into fourth, on the heels of both the new leader and a jockey trying to catch his loose horse.

Unfamiliar with the expression 'time spent in reconnaissance is time seldom wasted' Charlie had only really taken any notice of the last two fences – where he planned to hit the front – on his course walk and he thought he would take the 13th at an acute angle to save yards of ground.

Shane was momentarily ready to help out his jockey in this madcap manoeuvre but, too late, saw reason and decided against it. In the ensuing melee most of the rest of the field behind Charlie came to a standstill, some like Charlie on the take-off side in the ditch, and one who had made such a mess of the fence that the organisers are now seeking retrospective planning permission for hedge clearance.

Up front the two de Giles brothers, Freddie and Felix, sons of Highworth trainer Jonathan and about to impact themselves upon the National Hunt world, had the race to themselves. Meanwhile quick-thinking Charlie, having surveyed the carnage around, still reckoned he might have an each-way chance if he reloaded. Unfortunately running loose with Shane was another liver chestnut and it was that horse who Charlie was trying to catch. It was a good thing, one imagines, that the best horse he trained, Suny Bay, was grey. DECEMBER 6, 2005

DOESN'T the obstinacy of AP McCoy, lying there in an Oxford hospital trying to deny medical opinion about his broken back, remind you of someone? Well, that other famous resident of Nutsville, Arizona and also former champion jockey, Richard Dunwoody, expects to reach the South Pole later this week – in good time for his 44th birthday on Friday.

Yesterday he rang – a facility not available to Shackleton or Scott – to say it was the toughest thing he'd ever done. And to think that when he started leading horseback safaris in Africa and rides from Argentina to Chile over the Andes, I thought he had overdosed on sensible pills; with a horse to do the getting from A to B, animals to look at in Africa, scenery to marvel at in Argentina.

But no, not a bit of it. On the Interchange FX Shackleton Expedition 2007 he is his own packhorse and even when there isn't a whiteout it is, well, white out there. There was huge excitement the other day when they bumped into some scientists who were cock-a-hoop at having discovered a couple of cells of lichen on a rock. The news, when it filters out, may not be quite enough to boost sightseeing tours to the area. "It's 700 miles of nothing," he said – hardly the ringing endorsement the Antarctic Tourist Board were looking for.

Yesterday he and his guide Doug (as opposed to guide dog) Stoup were 46 days into their trip, 64 nautical miles from the geographical South Pole and they are covering 18 miles on a good day. A third member, James Fox, cried off and had to be flown out at Christmas. "He didn't like my cooking," explained Dunwoody, who has lost 2st in weight, which may not be the best advert for it either.

But it is amazing what spurs you on in desperate situations. Yesterday they were planning a 'party' – I presume in Dunwoody's case that means they grunted at each other – when they crossed the 89th degree south latitude, not so much a furlong marker covered in bunting and welcome signs but a notional line in the ice. "It's the last degree we cross before reaching the pole," said Dunwoody, outlining its significance.

A veteran of trips to the North Pole, he was quick to point out that he would not be claiming – one imagines that what we assume to be explorers splitting hairs is taken very seriously by members of the National Geographic Society – that he had now conquered both poles. "That was magnetic north," he said. "Not the same thing."

"Keeping everything together has been hard," he added. "Navigating in a whiteout is difficult and we nearly lost Doug down a crevasse. He went in up to his armpits and if he'd gone any further he'd have dropped 100 metres."

In what one presumes is an Antarctic practical joke, the people supposed to be flying in to pick up the pair when they have finished told Dunwoody it would be much easier if they walked 60 miles back from the pole. "We'll be out of fuel and food by then," he said. "We're not going another yard." JANUARY 14, 2008

PAUL ROY, in the letters page of the *Racing Post* on Sunday, wanted placed on record the BHA's congratulations to Richard Dunwoody for conquering the South Pole. But you were probably wondering what happened to the great explorer's welcome home party.

Well, Dunwoody's Beyond Shackleton expedition has now become beyond a joke – the great explorer is stuck, for the foreseeable future, in Antarctica. Worse still he is stuck at an all-male, alcohol-free (not sure which is worst) Russian base called Novo. It's tipping down with snow, there's only porridge and borscht to eat, the only reading material to supplement porn mags in cyrillic is the Count of Monte Cristo and the flight timetable makes unhappy reading as the next scheduled flight out to Cape Town is on February 6.

He's even started writing – having written two books with him I know that's a first – so the first clinical signs of cabin fever are setting in. But he should be grateful for small mercies – at least he's now in a hut in which to get the fever.

When he planted his flag at the South Pole you may have noticed in the background the huge building behind him. After three days he was, according to his mum, eventually let into it for a shower 'on humanitarian grounds' because of the smell that accompanied him – 48 days being not so much a measure of the time it took Dunwoody and his guide Doug Stoup to complete the 700-mile journey but the time since they had last washed. JANUARY 29, 2008

AS HE has recently retired, you may be of the opinion that jump jockey Ollie McPhail is the past. Far from it, he is likely to have as much bearing on racing's future as his ex-colleague AP McCoy.

His retirement, aged 31 after 130 winners, is to facilitate his promotion to full-time regional education officer for BHEST (the British Horseracing Education and Standards Trust).

While much of this august body's time is taken up with dishing out certificates to workers in the racing industry to comply with health and safety legislation, McPhail is working on the organising of its Racing To School initiative, which aims to get 10,000 schoolchildren to the racecourse annually.

Like all the best jobs he fell into it by accident and he's never looked back. There are now thousands of children out there who've never heard of McCoy but the one live jockey they know and like is Ollie McPhail.

Of course the job is not without incident. As a rule of thumb schools tend to take two views about Racing To School; one is to reward high achievers and the other is to stimulate the dunces and non-triers and naturally it is the lower end that causes the trouble. As teachers aren't allowed to lift a finger to an unruly pupil now let alone cuff one, they once had to have two policemen called out to Newton Abbot to remove a disruptive influence.

But McPhail has ways of getting round it and keeping their attention. A favourite trick is taking a bunch of kids into a racecourse sauna and tipping a bucket of water on the hot coals. Working out the weights on the racecourse scales and handicap ratings are good maths lessons while at the same time racing's hope is that one day these children will return as fully paid-up racegoers or, better, become involved.

It is an interesting point he makes about teachers not being able to whack pupils these days. When McPhail came into racing, as a cocky amateur at David Nicholson's, men were men and employment law was still the figment of some civil servant's imagination.

As a new boy who was adjudged to have been a bit too lippy towards the head lad, he was summoned to a lunchtime meeting in the tack room. It dawned on him, too late, that he was the focus of attention at this kangaroo court. He was tied to the table, the clippers were produced, the fuzzy bits shaved off and he was covered from top to toe in kaolin, a quick-drying clay that is normally used to cool horses' shins.

For good measure another then-unknown amateur 'Choc' Thornton was given the same treatment and, while the rest of the yard headed for the warm hostel and lunch, this unlikely pair had to hose each other down under cold taps.

It was while this was going on that the Duke walked into the yard with two important owners, Bill and Shirley Robins. "This is Viking Flagship," he pointed out before reeling off some of the most famous horses in training at the time.

"This is Relkeel etc," and, in that unflustered, deadpan style of his as they passed the two buck-naked jockeys in the middle of the lawn – who looked like they were scrubbing up after a bout of mud wrestling – he added: "And these are my two stable amateurs." Oh happy days. FEBRUARY 19, 2008

ONE of no doubt many happy outcomes of Jamie Spencer's wedding to Emma Ramsden was the emotional moment that overcame Andrew Balding. The trainer and pretty much confirmed bachelor proposed – not before time – to long-time girlfriend Anna-Lisa Williams.

She is well qualified to become a member of the world's most sporting family. Now working for Johnno Spence Consulting in the world of racing promotions, she is one of the few females to have warranted a mention in the usually male-dominated cricket annual Wisden. In 1994 she scored a century for her school, Charterhouse Girls First XI, in a match against Wellington (boys?).

The wedding is a week before the King George, in which Andrew hopes to run Phoenix Reach. "I've already been told he needs to be back to work the horse on the Wednesday," says Anna-Lisa, who looks like being shortchanged with regard to the honeymoon. MARCH 8, 2005

100 v. Wellington

AFTER years of defying the scales with his 6ft 1in frame to ride in point-to-points and hunter chases Chris Stockton – purveyor of fine marquees to Chester races this week and husband of successful three-day-eventer Polly – has swapped four legs for four wheels.

He is now a part of the British Touring Car Championship, the next most popular type of car racing in Britain after Formula One and bread and butter of ITV Sport these days.

Chris, 38, who rode over the big fences at Aintree four times, finished 11th in the 2004 Le Mans 24-hour, driving for TVR. But he is already earning something of a reputation for his 'assertiveness' in touring cars, a sport where pulling over to let someone overtake is a big no-no.

According to Richard Thomas, chief executive of Chester and a close friend, he has brought to the sport the same competitive principles that he employed in the point-to-point field, ie there's no such thing as an honourable second, it's better to take the leader and yourself out in one manoeuvre and leave it to the man who had settled for third.

As far as I can make out running two www.montysmillions.com-sponsored Lexus – incidentally the preferred make of car for the discerning trainer these days – costs about the same as the gross national product of a small country, per weekend. But Chris is finding cars no more reliable than horses and after finishing a creditable tenth of 26 at Brands Hatch first time out, the car has been afflicted with an engine management problem – sounds like Michael Hourigan's jumpers this winter.

"It's just like a virus in a horse," he says. "The car's straight line speed is 10mph slower than it was at Brands Hatch. There's £14,000 of electrics in each car and no-one seems to be able to put their finger on the problem."

While he, therefore, had a moderate day at Thruxton on Sunday and was last off the grid, wife Polly did not fare much better at Badminton on Saturday. Feeling the firm ground her good horse Tom Quigley refused at the coffin. MAY 8, 2007

NOTHING happens in early August – even Flat trainers go on holiday – in the racing world except golf and cricket. The good news is that racing folk have been enjoying unparalleled success in both spheres.

Charity, they say, begins at home. Cotswolds-based jump jockey Jodie Mogford cleaned up in a two-day charity celeb-am golf tournament at Dartmouth sponsored by Sabre Hind Insurance and in aid of the Injured Jockeys' Fund (ie probably himself).

He not only won both golf competitions but also won the raffle, a motorised golf caddy. If he has that much luck on the racecourse this season we're looking at a Grand National winner at the very least.

The scorecard from a game of cricket at the Oval last Friday reads 'D.Smith (ex-Sussex and England), caught Sir Vivian Richards, bowled Nick Gifford.' The great West Indian captain taking a catch off his bowling – one to tell the grandchildren? "Not really," says the modest Findon trainer of the wicket that I'd have put up there with Walter Swinburn's clean bowling of Sir Garfield Sobers. "It was a shocking ball. It was so wide the batsman did well to reach it." AUGUST 9, 2005

NICK GIFFORD'S ambition to become, by my reckoning, only the second current licensed racehorse trainer to play cricket at Lord's, fell at the last on Sunday.

For the second year in succession his village side, Findon, were beaten in the semi-final of the National Village Knockout, the final of which takes place at the home of cricket. Though he didn't play last year, he was drafted back into the side for his batting. Though he refused to disclose the number of runs he scored – it sounds like it was more than nought but less than two – he was part of a middle-order collapse in the away match against Sully Centurions at Barry in south Wales.

Set a score of 251 Findon looked good at the halfway stage when 120 for 2 but the Sussex village were, despite a quick 50 smashed by Mark Stewart, son of Singapore-based handicapper Martin Stewart, all out for 214.

Nick, who will have 30 horses in the yard for this season including a four-year-old owned by JP McManus and long-range Grand National hope Joly Bey, left his father Josh at home holding the fort. "It's a long way home from Barry when you've been beaten," commented Nick yesterday.

Of course William Haggas is the trainer who has played at Lord's – three times in the Eton-Harrow game when it was a two-day fixture in the late seventies. He is the most competitive of Newmarket trainers – with the possible exception of Michael Bell, who used to turn up for the fathers' race at his son's school sports day with spikes and specialist sports drinks.

"You don't want to know how many runs I got," yawns William before giving a Wisden-style breakdown of his batting figures. The last time, as captain, he did something most un-Harrovian, declaring his side's innings when in sight of a maiden Lord's century on 87 not out. "Would have spoiled the game if I hadn't," says the magnanimous trainer. Sounds like Findon need him. AUGUST 10, 2004

SPARE a thought, while the thermometer is pushing 90 degrees in the shade, for JP McNamara, the jump jockey who broke his neck in two places in a fall at Bangor at the end of April.

It is bad enough having to lie on your back for three months let alone in this weather, which is what JP is doing in Oswestry Hospital while the feeling gradually returns to his limbs. But if positive thoughts count towards recovery then he won't just walk out of there, he'll be jogging.

This weekend the first of several fundraising events for the Injured Jockeys' Fund with a focus on JP will happen on Mont Blanc. Ed Gretton, clerk of the course at Bangor and Chester, Ran Morgan, the Jock jockey, Ed Haynes and Jimmy Saville (not the TV's Jimmy Savile) – four old boys from Ampleforth College – bid to climb to the 15,800ft peak of the mountain the French call La Dame Blanche, the white lady.

While the rest of the team leave today to begin altitude adjustment,

Ed leaves a day later because of racing at Chester tonight. They begin the serious part of the climb at 2am on Friday and hope to be boiling eggs on top of Europe for breakfast.

"It is a bit more technical than walking," says Ed, a novice climber who admits to issues regarding vertigo. "You need crampons, pickaxes and ropes for the last bit. We have two expert French guides and, though it is the done thing on Everest to leave people with altitude sickness to die, we hope not to leave anyone up there, not even Ran."

Ran predicts the worst thing will be the hut they spend the night in before the final push. "Apart from having to share it with hairy Germans there are no lavatories, I'm told, so if nature calls you have go outside and park your backside over a cliff," he says. "There are two ways up to the hut and I just hope we're not going under that cliff."

The team's experience so far is limited to the three peaks 24-hour challenge and a training session on Snowdon. But it is all in a good cause. Besides the Injured Jockeys', they are raising funds for the Charlie Waller Memorial Trust (for depressives) and you can sponsor them by visiting www.justgiving.com and calling up either charity. My helpful advice is that which my mother used to give before every race – don't fall off. JUNE 13, 2006

A FEW weeks ago this column previewed a charity climb up Mont Blanc by Chester's clerk of the course Ed Gretton and three mates and, last week, James Crispe's attempt in the Etape du Tour, the amateur leg of the Tour de France. Both were raising money for jockeys with serious back injuries.

Well, the good news is that rookie climber Ed and co made it to the top after an eight-hour climb. They were allowed two minutes to admire the view over Europe before beginning a six-hour descent.

It was not such good news for James, who covered 110 miles in seven hours 45 minutes to the foot of Alpe d'Huez, only for the road up the infamous mountain to be closed while he refuelled (himself) at the last pit-stop before the climb. "I'm gutted but I'm not," he said as he stood looking up the mountain last night. "I can't believe anyone could bike up there."

By some considerable margin the climbers' biggest achievement of their whole weekend was getting their Swiss guide to laugh.

According to point-to-point jockey Ran Morgan, who also made the climb, much amusement was caused by the unknown quantity among them, Ed 'Desmond' Haynes. He turned up for the climb wearing lightweight Cornish beach rambling shoes and instead of a state-of-the-art climbing rucksack had an M&S suitcase with shoulder straps in which were enough clothes for a three-week holiday.

Due to the difficulty in attaching crampons to his shoes he constantly hit the deck, at which point the rope to the guide would tighten and everyone would have to stop while he got back to his feet. After numerous falls the guides decided no longer to wait for him and he was dragged through the snow, chin first, earning the nickname 'the snowplough'.

There's a time and a place for most things but halfway up an 80ft vertical ice wall is not the most opportune time to quit mountaineering. "Gretton," he called upwards, "this isn't for me." Despite the bad timing of his notice to quit, he made it to the summit with the others. JULY 11, 2006

ON THE first day of Glorious Goodwood, Tuesday August 1, the last race is being run in memory of the late Colin Ingleby-Mackenzie, captain of Hampshire, president of the MCC and Captain of Sunningdale Golf Club.

Dickie Davies once said that when Colin walked into a room it was "like the cork coming out of a bottle of champagne". Colin's advice to his championship-winning Hampshire team was: "By all means have a drink, but I insist you're back before breakfast." JUNE 13, 2006

RACING celebrated the marriage of colourful owner Tony Collins, after whom the late Robert Sangster named his *Racing Post* Trophy winner

Commander Collins, to Lizzie Wrathall last week. Many racegoers might recognise Lizzie as the person who drags off winning connections for a celebratory drink on the house at Newmarket.

Apart from spotting a brother-in-law having his wheel clamped during the 'formal' marriage proceedings in Northampton registry office, and the blades of the helicopter in which the pair left the reception revealing that, contrary to what the papers say, thongs are still popular in that part of the country, all went smoothly.

Lizzie is no mean sportsman herself. She was once playing a golf foursome with her husband, the actor Hugh Grant and one other at Troon. Midway through she hit a tremendous drive. It bisected the fairway and had the perfect trajectory; as she watched it disappear as a speck over the horizon towards the green, the actor complimented her on one of the finest shots he had ever seen a girl hit. Flushed with success Lizzie stepped backwards off the tee and tripped clean over a dustbin. Thus was the moment ruined. SEPTEMBER 13, 2005

LAST WEEK'S Tattersalls Golf Day, held at Woburn, is one of the most eagerly awaited sporting occasions of the British summer. Well, at least to those in receipt of an invitation it is. It's where racing's great and good mix with a few well-known bloodstock agents and sundry Tattersalls debtors for 18 holes of golf followed by a bit of a knees-up in the clubhouse.

Anticipating the event more than most was Johnno Mills, who runs the Rabbah wing of Sheikh Mohammed's bloodstock empire, looking after the horses owned by 'associates' of the boss. Johnno's influence on the competition of late has been like that of Tiger Woods on the British Open and some – he had won it three times on the trot.

Of course such overwhelming success never sits too comfortably on what, after all, is meant to be a fun day out. Having tried and failed to handicap him out of the contest before, Martin Mitchell, a director of Tatts, took it upon himself to have a quiet word with the player before he teed off. While not actually asking him to throw the contest, avuncular arm around shoulder, he pointed out that this year it would be very nice if it proved to be someone else's turn.

That, however, is like asking McCoy to let Richard Johnson win the jockeys' championship for once and Martin's carefully chosen words appeared to act as a spur rather than a deterrent. At the halfway stage Johnno was setting a great gallop.

A short while later, however, organisers had news of a man down on the 13th – unlucky 13th as it happened – and a rapid-response paramedic ambled down there to find the tournament favourite out sparko on the ground, his face covered in blood just like a scene from Midsomer Murders. It wasn't Mitchell – he doesn't do menace – rather Johnno had whacked a ball into a tree and it had rebounded and hit him clean between the eyes.

"What day of the week is it?" asked the ambulance man, administering smelling salts and his own concussion test. Lucky really, when you consider it, that the question wasn't: "Can you name a decent Darley stallion?"

Jimmy George, another director of Tatts, had at first been worried about insurance cover for the tournament. "I thought he must have been hit by a ball," recalls Jimmy, "but I was quite a bit happier when I realised it was self-inflicted. Usually to stop someone winning the tournament they're paired up with me but Johnno has gone to extraordinary lengths."

The man himself, who retired hurt, is now recovered though his forehead looks a bit like it has been used for airgun target practice, with a small cut surrounded by a large bruise. "It looks and feels like I stood up and hit the corner of a kitchen unit," he says.

So who did win this year's tournament? Tattersalls director (and owner of the course) the Duke of Bedford, partnered by Philip Freedman, who was winning it for the, um, fourth time. Expect him to get the arm-round-shoulder treatment next year. MAY 15, 2007

JONATHAN DIMSDALE, the senior racecourse judge, presides over his last meeting before handing over to Alastair Stewart at Haydock on Thursday.

On Friday, wasting no time in joining the massed ranks of OAPs, he will start his first jigsaw puzzle – not a 500-piece copy of Constable's The Hay Wain but the re-assembling of a 1973 Formula 2 racing car, which is currently in bits in several large boxes. It has come without an instruction manual and he hopes to have it ready in time for Silverstone's 'Historic' meeting in July.

Dimsdale's first meeting as a racecourse judge, the man who announces the finishing order of a race, was Market Rasen on Easter Monday 1977 as a 'casual'. He gave up what one assumes was a goldmine – a Toyota dealership in Bradford – and went full time in 1978. In 1993 he took over as senior judge from Michael Hancock and during his time he has announced the winner of countless epics from Desert Orchid's Gold Cup to Ouija Board's Nassau Stakes win. The only race he presided over which he did not have to give a result for was the 1993 'Void' National.

His first solo Derby was Benny The Dip's short-head victory. He remembers 100,000 racegoers on the Downs falling silent as he cleared his throat to announce the winner.

He's never missed a race while on duty but at Stockton once the runners had gone a lap before he realised the race had started. He had to leg it across the course and up a 60ft tower while the runners were on the last circuit. At Cartmel, before a photo-finish was installed, he announced the winning margin of a short head. The trainer of the runner-up demanded to see the photo. He was told he would have to wait – though no-one told him he would have to wait five years.

The car thing goes back to his rebellious youth. His father, John, was killed in a fall at Huntingdon and young Jonathan was discouraged from race-riding. Instead he took up the then lethal sport of motor racing and he once drove in the Macau Grand Prix.

Macau's street circuit was a poor man's Monte Carlo but they had made great progress that year – they'd paved over the cobbled part of the circuit. However, on the last corner there was a large gap in the sea-front wall which meant if you missed it you were in the drink. When he asked why there was no wall he was told it had been knocked down so often it was easier to fish cars out of the water than rebuild it. OCTOBER 17, 2006

IT IS testament to Johnny Ferrand's character that more horses (three) have been named after him than most of the great men, or for that matter women, of history. The landlord of The Pheasant, Lambourn's number one racing pub, is universally known as Johnny the Fish and though the horse with whom he shared that name has been sold, he still has legs in John Le Poisson and Fish Called Johnny.

Last week Nicky Henderson invited Johnny on his annual salmon fishing holiday to the Spey in Scotland. Though something of an inexperienced fisher – most of Johnny's adult life has been spent accompanying fish on the post-Billingsgate part of their long journey from cradle to table – he armed himself with nothing more than boyish enthusiasm and the vital statistic that Scotland's most famous fish, the largest ever landed, was a 64lb salmon caught by Miss Georgina Ballantyne in 1922.

While Tessa Henderson, the trainer's middle daughter, was landing fish like she was casting into a salmon farm, Johnny was having less luck. Pitching his flies on the water like crash-landing Lancaster bombers, he solicited little in the way of interest from below the surface.

Keen for Johnny to catch his first fish, on the last morning his host sent him to the best pool with the ghillie. Surely, Nicky reckoned, that would swing it. With the breeze up, his first few slightly uncontrolled casts impressed the ghillie – by their proximity to his ears.

Sensing that Johnny might indeed be on for Miss Ballantyne's record by catching himself, the ghillie decided to come at the problem from a different angle. He would give Johnny a quick lesson on the rudiments of Spey casting, a lower, albeit slightly more complicated snake-like cast out in front of the fisherman that, theoretically, makes the foul hooking of an ear less a probability and more of an impossibility.

Fast forward an hour. The trainer received a call on his mobile expecting news of a fish. It was, of a kind. It was Johnny – from Elgin Hospital where he was sitting in casualty with a large purple fly stuck through his top lip – looking not unlike a sad attempt to go to a fancy dress party as Charlie Chaplin.

As you know it's sod's law that when you want a doctor there's never one about. Well, when word got out about what was sitting in casualty, namely a bloke called Fish with a hook through his lip, an endless stream of doctors on any old excuse passed through the waiting room hardly able to contain their mirth. Two were so amused they volunteered to unhook him – a painful process that involved pulling the hook through and cutting it off at the barb – and immediately thus he was able to bypass the queue.

Two things have emerged from this unfortunate event: (a) fish do have feelings ("it hurt like hell," says Johnny) and (b) Miss Ballantyne's 84 year-old record has been supplanted by Johnny Ferrand's, which now stands at 186lb. Whether he's stuffed and/or mounted is an altogether different story. JULY 18, 2006

IT WAS, they reflected after it had gone out with a bang, a fitting albeit premature end to the last ever Rotters golf day.

The Rotters has been played annually on the eve of Newmarket's July meeting at nearby Royal Worlington, when 36 long-time mates from racing get together to raise a few quid for charity with two laps of the course and an auction.

Now, with the grim reaper and, slightly less terminally, arthritis catching up with the regulars as well as the indisputable hard fact of modern life that the longer a trainer spends on the fairway the less horses he is likely to have in his stable, the tournament has run its course. It has become increasingly hard to get the players.

At the 'turn' the skies darkened menacingly with cumulonimbi, thunder clapped and forked lightning lit up the Suffolk countryside. Had it been last week's British Open or a tournament of health and safety inspectors then they'd have scurried for cover but not the Rotters midway through their final fling. With the same determination as the band on the Titanic they played on. Somewhat recklessly, some might have said, as each had what for all intents and purposes was a bag of lightning conductors on his back or in the hand.

Teeing off on the tenth, therefore, it will come as no surprise to learn that larger-than-life bloodstock agent David Minton was struck by lightning. It is, in the unlikely event that my geography A-level counts for anything, a new phenomenon in meteorology. Lightning has until now usually struck the tallest object in an area – not the widest.

No-one actually saw the offending bolt but there was no disputing the fact that momentarily Minty's hair took on an 'Afro-perm' look, his arms tingled and he dropped his club like it had just bitten him. It wasn't a million-volter but, equally, it wasn't static from his jumper either. "It wasn't major," he says dismissively, using a trait hitherto unknown among bloodstock agents – modesty. Nevertheless he was lucky not to have left the course as a pile of ashes and scorched earth scooped up into an urn. Thus the tournament ended abruptly.

"Everything stood on end for a moment," says his wife Juliet, before confirming: "It hasn't affected anything." JULY 19, 2005

IS THERE no end in sight to this summer of sporting excellence? You might recall, earlier this summer, that David Minton, the larger-than-life bloodstock agent, was struck by lightning in a golf tournament just before Newmarket's July meeting and survived to tell the tale. Shortly afterwards one wag pointed out that there was more chance of Minty being struck by lightning than there was of him ever scoring a hole-in-one.

Well, funny that. I haven't troubled the odds compilers at Ladbrokes for the chances of it happening – the noughts would run off the page

– but last week at Chipping Norton in a tournament between a ten-man team from Alan King and a team from Rick Allen, an owner of King's, Minton drove the green on the par three 156-yard tenth. I won't bore you with the details (he's so chuffed about it he could give the O.S. map co-ordinates of where the ball plopped and the route it took) but the ball landed six yards to the left of the pin, rolled up a bank and back down again into the hole.

Tradition decrees that anyone hitting a hole-in-one buys everyone a drink in the 19th. Mercifully there were enough people in the bar for it to cost him £75 – it was the Monday of the Oval Test and most were at home – although not before the authorities had concocted a bar bill for £205. "When I went white at the gills they gave me the real bill," recalls Minton of his finest golfing moment. Ironic, really, that the consequences of a hole-in-one and a lightning strike were the same – a hole burned in his pocket.

The feat was witnessed by his playing partner, trainer Henry Daly. "It was extremely painful to watch," says the trainer. "I'm not sure we'll ever hear the end of it. The only good thing was that the bar wasn't completely deserted when we got back." SEPTEMBER 20, 2005

WE'RE in danger of gazumping the *Angling Times* here but, after hapless Johnny the Fish hooked his upper lip on his fishing debut in Scotland earlier this summer, we have news of another altogether more impressive fishy tale from north o' the border.

You'll recall how we reported that Johnny Ferrand, racehorse owner and landlord of The Pheasant, near Lambourn, ended up in Elgin Hospital having a fly surgically removed from his lip after attempting a cast into the breeze. This time our hero is another Lambourn man making his debut with the rod but he, clearly, has a defter touch.

Seven weeks after landing his first Derby with Sir Percy, Marcus Tregoning has landed a Group 1 salmon, an absolute whopper, at the first time of asking. The Derby apart we'll gloss over the rest of the trainer's season but last week, at the invitation of neighbouring Kingwood Stud's owner Fiona Marner and husband Christian, he took off – presumably, one imagines, as the great 19th century Derby-winning trainers might have done in Augusts gone by – to Scotland for three days fishing on the Spey.

Salmon, even small ones, have been in short supply these last few years mainly due to the over-fishing of our oceans, and even experienced fishermen like Nicky Henderson and Kim Bailey have returned south with nothing for the freezer from week-long fishing trips to Scotland.

Marcus, however, who has never had the luxury of a salmon fishing trip before, had no great expectations when, bang, his line ran out to the opposite bank. Three-quarters of an hour later he landed a 23½lb cock salmon.

Just to give this fish the respect it deserves and put its enormity into some sort of perspective, it was the height and weight of an old-fashioned apprentice. Its length, 3ft 8in, is longer than the distance between Sir Percy, first, and Hala Bek, fourth (a short head, head, short head), in this year's Derby.

But instead of making a feast of the beast it's now in the capable hands of an Edinburgh-based taxidermist who, once he's over the indigestion from eating so much salmon at one sitting, will stuff and mount it in a glass cabinet. It is a sporting trophy to match that which Marcus received for the Vodafone Derby.

Eventually it will take pride of place upsides photos of Sir Percy in the study at Kingwood House Stables and just to prove it wasn't beginner's luck the trainer landed another 'handsome' fish the following day. Only now, however, is the form book being questioned. Johnny the Fish, also on this trip, partially redeemed himself with his first fish but experts are putting that down to a suicide among the Spey's salmon population.
AUGUST 22, 2006

ONE horse recently retired and clearly enjoying his new Cheshire home is the Trevor Hemmings-owned Chives, a horse who was good enough to run in a Gold Cup and Grand National.

He has been given to Charles Barnett, the managing director of Aintree, as a hunter. However it may be some time, according to my spies in Cheshire, before he competes with another ex-racehorse, Aghawadda Gold, in the Barnett family affections.

On an autumn morning hunting recently Chives was standing on point in a ploughed field enjoying the view and his new career when he decided the best thing to do to help would be to roll. His new jockey had to take swift avoiding action at the run.

Seconds earlier bystanders had suggested Chives was about to do this but Aintree's MD brushed aside these claims with "Oh, I don't think so. He's just got an itchy knee." OCTOBER 24, 2006

WHILE the England cricket team have catching practice the Australian tourists are today expected at Goodwood. This evening, on the square in front of Goodwood House, the second Cantor Challenge takes place between my colleague Jim McGrath's media XI and a Graham Cowdrey XI. Last year the outcome was a tie.

Both skippers are reluctant to name their respective teams. Graham's reasons are tactical, Jim's are because he's only assembled four players. We can reveal, however, that in the Cowdrey side Giles Bravery has kept his place though he has been sacked from behind the stumps and Nick Gifford replaces Carl Llewellyn as their National Hunt representative. Llewellyn doesn't fancy it after being hit a few times last year.

"I know this sounds a bit bad coming just a week after the Cowdrey lecture on the spirit of cricket – given by Geoffrey Boycott – in memory of my father," warns Graham, "but there will be no charity this year – it could be England's only chance of getting one over an Australian this summer.

"Jim turned up with what was meant to be a media team last year. We were expecting Lord Oaksey to open the batting with John Hanmer and Lydia Hislop coming in at three. Instead he rolled up with semi-

206 Turn Me On Guv

professional players whose only link with the racing media was to have watched Attheraces once. As a consequence I've strengthened my team."
JULY 26, 2005

LAMBOURN is going through a relatively quiet spell in several respects. A few years ago it welcomed home either a National or Gold Cup winner annually, usually with a Classic or two thrown in for good measure. Even its hard-earned reputation for sexual shenanigans has taken a knock lately and, it seems, the tabloids have lost as much interest in the place as its trainers have in other people's wives or vice versa.

However, there is good news on the second front. A sub-committee of the parish council met recently to discuss improving security in the high street and top of the agenda were CCTVs. At £20,000 an installation it is not cheap and if you put up a camera in one place the culprits will just move 100 yards down the road.

It was then pointed out to the rather surprised council of a recent incident in the laundrette, which already has CCTV installed. An unidentified couple, except for the fact that the male had a large backside so probably wasn't a jockey, were caught in flagrante on top of a washing machine during the spin cycle. "It is potentially very em-bare-arsing for the couple involved," says former trainer Peter Walwyn.
SEPTEMBER 27, 2005

IT CAME with the following recommendation from the former Newmarket correspondent of the *Sportsman*. "Listen, mate," he said (he's Australian, of course, and that seems to be how they start a sentence down there these days) "there are some good sorts in this."

The original Calendar Girls, their modesty protected by the assorted produce of an allotment, inspired a charming film. The Newmarket Stablegirls Calendar 2008, which is launched on Saturday, is a bit more raunchy and more likely, one presumes, to inspire a few Group winners. It's less Women's Institute, more Pirelli meets Polly Track

– 'sans' most of her kit and relaxing, as I imagine any decent stable lass does between the hours of lunch and evening stables, in a provocative pose in the hayloft. There's not, for those who like that sort of thing, a jodhpur in sight.

The man behind the project is Newmarket-based photographer Chris Bourchier, who is the man on the spot for many national newspapers. The object of the project is, unashamedly, to make him richer.

Did he have any trouble persuading Newmarket's finest to take their clothes off? It sounds like he had more success than Sam Thomas would have done had he tipped up in a stable girls' hostel looking for action on Sunday night. "They were queuing up wanting to be in it," says Chris.

"One lass, October I think she is, said she didn't think she'd want to take her top off but she was so comfortable with it we had a job persuading her to put it back on at the end of the shoot. She was just wandering round John Ryan's yard with her top off." NOVEMBER 27, 2007

LAST YEAR Johnny Ferrand, better known in racing circles as Johnny the Fish, earned an entry in the Angling Times, this diary and the in-patients register at Elgin Hospital for his exploits on a fishing expedition to Scotland.

In precis, the landlord of Lambourn's number one racing pub, The Pheasant, hooked himself with a salmon fly – the sort of hook on which you hang bridles – on his maiden visit to the Spey and spent an afternoon in A&E having it removed from his upper lip by doctors who were too jovial by half according to the patient.

Well, the first bit of news about this is a new horse. The Pheasant Inn Racing Partnership, which Johnny fronts, has done well in the past with horses named – not that he's a megalomaniac – Johnny The Fish, Fish Called Johnny and Jean Le Poisson. Now, however, they are about to do battle with a two-year-old cleverly named both in honour of that incident and how they expect him to perform, Fly In Johnny.

Apparently also a bit accident-prone, he will have to win a Classic to recoup the vets' fees amassed so far. But Richard Hannon has high hopes for the colt, who is due out in the next fortnight. Tight lines, as they say.

Even better news, though, is that the man with the wayward tackle has just resurfaced after another expedition north o' the border, once again at the behest of Christian Marner whose wife, Fiona, owns the Kingwood Stud. Once again he went full of amateur enthusiasm and without recourse to the bleeding obvious given last year's results, a month's live-in course at fly fishing school.

This year, clearly working towards his eyes and a trip to Moorfields Hospital, it was his nose that bore the brunt of his expert casting. I'm not entirely sure it's the done thing but he clearly needs protecting from himself and perhaps the bailiffs would let him sit there quietly dangling his worm rather than erratically waving about his person what amounts to a dangerous weapon. Otherwise his contact with fish on these trips should be restricted to kippers for breakfast.

This year, though, the fish and the water – it's usually a positive correlation – were plentiful. But the first rise of the week was not from a hungry Atlantic salmon chomping a fly on its epic journey upstream back to the very spot it was born. No, it was from the leading jump trainer Nicky Henderson.

He was wading up to his waist when a flotilla of canoes sailed past, one of which hit him amidships (I've always found canoes hard to steer too). At that moment 'surface tension' was not so much to do with the molecular structure of water as the trainer's temper. Though he caught the lion's share of the fish this random accident clearly unsettled his equilibrium because he also managed to foul-hook Sharpie, Johnny's spaniel. "He howled a lot," says Johnny, without making it clear whether it was the trainer or dog. SEPTEMBER 5, 2007

A COUPLE of years ago we had Johnny the Fish, racehorse owner and publican, foul-hooking himself in the gills when he went salmon fishing on the Spey. But it would appear bloodstock agent Cormac McCormack – "My mother either had a stutter or a sense of humour; it's not quite clear" – has surpassed that.

Cormac, whose past purchases include Never So Bold and Mr Brooks, has recently returned from the self same river as a guest of stud manager Willie Macauley.

For the background to this story we must go back to last year when Cormac made his salmon fishing debut. As a veteran trout fisherman he was inclined to strike too quick when a fish showed interest. There are, I guess, parallels in his own industry. "Sir, sir, sir," Bill, the 75-year-old ghillie, had said, "you'll have to get out of that habit. Count to five before you strike, sir."

There were a couple of other noteworthy incidents from the 2007 trip. The ghillie was criticised by the host for wearing a baseball cap – not the done thing on such a noteworthy salmon river. And having been told he had been "unlucky" not to catch a fish Cormac was of the slightly cynical opinion that ghillies were the equal of Irish bloodstock agents – full of blarney. There had been, he concluded over a glass of Scotch, no fish.

A year on Cormac returned determined to land his first salmon. Again he struck too quick at the first fish and lost it. "Sir, sir, sir," said the ghillie, sporting a brand new Breton cap bought particularly with these (somewhat awkward some might say) clients in mind, "keep your hand off the line. I think what we'll do, sir, is take the boat out."

The boat anchored at the head of the pool, and Cormac cast his fly. "Lovely, sir. A beautiful cast if I may say so," gushed the ghillie. And bang, Cormac was straight into a fish (one, which I might add, varies in size between 9lb and 29lb depending on the hour of evening, drink taken etc, that this tale is told).

And thus began one of nature's great contests; thoroughbred fish versus bloodstock agent. It ran furiously up and down the river.

"Let him run, sir ... reel him, sir ... let him run, sir, not under the boat, sir. Try to get his head up, sir ... I'll just slip into the water, sir."

At this point, belying his age, the agile ghillie eased himself into the water with a net and stood, in his waders, up to his chest in the river. But he must have been slightly off-balance because all it took was the gentlest of nudges from the boat and with that he disappeared under.

It can't be easy trying to land your first fish when the boat is rocking all over the shop and the ghillie drowning, his expensive new cap bought specially for the occasion floating off. In all the excitement, the fish made a last, unexpected, bid for freedom in the direction of the Moray Firth.

Cormac's concentration was not aided by the next beast to break the surface of the pool – the gasping ghillie with a look upon his face that suggested he'd just met Lucifer at the gates of hell. In 65 summers working on the river he'd never been 'in' it.

But full credit to our bloodstock agent; he steadied the boat, landed the fish, rescued the ghillie and caught the cap, not so much an unlikely four-timer, more like Dettori going through the card.

After such a battle, our magnanimous fisherman decided to go with river convention and put the fish back but the ghillie had different ideas. The fish had nearly been the demise of him and Cormac's pacifist tendencies went against the grain. "In your case, sir," he said, "the fish is very shocked."

"No," pointed out Cormac, "you're the one who's shocked. We'll put it back." And so, as the ghillie trudged off home, water still spilling out of his waders, the fish swam off – there, one assumes, to cause mayhem for another day. AUGUST 5, 2008

THESE days, it seems, Nicky Henderson regards pitting his wits against the noble salmon by way of relaxation as mere kids' stuff. Recently he was taken in search of bigger game by an owner, and just precisely who was hunting who still isn't entirely clear.

It all began to go pear-shaped for the trainer when he and his fellow hunters arrived in Zimbabwe while his baggage, containing two brand new safari suits, failed to materialise, courtesy of British Airways (who else?).

So, while the rest of the party blended seamlessly into the scenery, indistinguishable from the African bush, Henderson, who only had what he'd arrived in – a blazer and tie – appeared, from a buffalo's angle, as a slightly bemused but truly outstanding target.

Next stop was the range, where the novice big game hunter is taken to hone his eye and familiarise himself with a surface-to-air missile or whatever calibre of gun it is that's required to stop dead in its tracks something the size, to put it in a British farming context, of a Charolais bull that might be charging at you; pea-shooters need not apply.

As practice goes it was a failure in as much as shooting a static tin can hardly replicate the panic that's likely to set in with a one-tonne beast, and a pissed off one at that, bearing down on you. On top of this the rifle had a kick like a zebra and after firing three rounds Henderson discovered his right shoulder had dropped some three inches.

It is very clear who was most relieved he didn't fire a shot in anger all week – and that is despite my unprofessional failure to interview the buffalo.

But Henderson did make some friends in Africa because he proved irresistible to the tsetse fly, which, for the uninitiated, is like a bluebottle trained in America (that's to say on steroids).

As flies go the tsetse is either optimistic or stupid if it thinks it can infect Henderson, a man who famously kips about ten minutes a night, with sleeping sickness. He's the living antidote and there's more chance that the poor bugs are now paralysed with insomnia.

But he did come up in rashes and welts on his return, which required a trip to the tropical diseases department for tests. "They're just like vets," he says. "They'll get back to me in three weeks and tell me what I've had, and when I've had it." June 3, 2008

Chapter Eight
HEROES AND VILLAINS

ON MONDAY Johnny Harrington, husband of Moscow Flyer's trainer Jessica, received a frantic call from his host for this week, Lambourn trainer Nicky Henderson. In much the same way, one supposes, that you might ask a Flat trainer to bring back authentic Newmarket sausages from Headquarters or Francois Doumen to pack some foie gras in the horsebox when he comes over from France, Barry Hills, who patently hasn't been shopping since he was head lad to John Oxley, asked Nicky to ask Johnny to bring over some of his favourite food, Irish soda bread.

However, by the time he'd got the call, and the all-important bread order, Johnny was already in England. At the same time he was keen not to disappoint Barry so, on the advice of a regular shopper, he acquired two loaves of soda bread from a local Waitrose. "I took the wrappers off and had them delivered them to Barry," says Johnny. "As far as I know he's absolutely delighted." MARCH 14, 2006

RACING'S catering corps has been playing to its strengths again. After the debacle over pink gins at Goodwood – they didn't have Angostura bitters but they did have Worthington's – it was York's turn this week.

Bollinger, which sponsors the amateur riders' series in conjunction with the *Daily Telegraph* that culminated in a final at York last week, had a box for the day, which they generously shared with the Telegraph. Naturally it's thirsty work being a journalist and the first arrivals were members of our racing team.

"Would you like a drink?" asked the old girl in charge.

"Is the Pope Catholic?" came the reply, which is usually accepted as a long-winded, slightly jovial, "yes".

"I dunno," said the old girl. "Is he? What is this? Mastermind? I'm afraid I ain't no good at questions." SEPTEMBER 5, 2005

THE BBC'S new Sunday night family drama Rough Diamond, a sort of Ballykissangel meets Dermot Weld, began on Sunday night.

Although set in Kildare, most of it is filmed in Meath. Just in case you wondered about the locations, the smart yard of fictional millionaire trainer Charlie Carrick is not a racing yard but Dollanstown Stud, a dressage yard belonging to Lars Bjoerk. However, the estate over which the young lad was run away with on an unbroken colt is Rahinston, near Summerhill which belongs to real-life trainer John Fowler and is where Maid Of Money and Opera Hat used to be trained.

According to his son, Harry Fowler, an auctioneer at Tattersalls, there's a sex scene in one of the next episodes which takes place beside the Fowlers' pond – not, apparently, an automatic choice for trysts of a romantic nature, certainly among members of the Fowler family. "You'd have to be very careful not to sit in a cowpat," says Harry. "Nevertheless Dad volunteered to help on that scene but his offer was declined."
FEBRUARY 5, 2007

IT IS tough being a stable lad all your life but it has not done Bill Peel too much harm. On Thursday 'Old Pop' will celebrate his 100th birthday and John Francome will make a special presentation at his Newbury nursing home.

He is one of the few people still around who remembers when the train was the principal method of racehorse transport. He recalls riding horses from East Ilsley to Churn Station where horses would board race trains, on the Newbury-Didcot branch line of the Great Western Railway, and a trip to the races often meant four days away.

Bill, who lost an older brother in the first week of World War I, was apprenticed in the 1920s and later in his life worked for George Beeby. He was also an expert on form, not only of his own horses but the opposition.

In the early 1970s he answered an advert to work for my father, Roddy, and, having been out of racing for a while, arrived a bit out of shape and even then was old enough to be most of the other lads' grandfather. But he ended up looking after Barona who won the 1975 and 1976 Scottish Grand Nationals.

Later on my father suggested that as he was nearing his 70s, perhaps the time had come to retire and he duly left on a Friday. The following Monday he started a new job in the same village, East Ilsley, with Flat trainer Gavin Hunter. He was next seen trotting up the road on a two-year-old. Ease up, seize up – as they say. JANUARY 5, 2009

AN IRISH jockey was in the evening of his career a while ago and he was down to very few rides a year. It had come to the last day of the season and the trainer for whom he worked realised he had not put him up on a horse all year and, as he had half a dozen runners in the two-year-old maiden, he stuck him up on one. One of the horses was to win the race while the other five were to be given "an edu-cashun"; their winning would, as it were, be another day, probably in a handicap, the following season.

The race went roughly to plan and the right one of the sextet won, but the elderly jockey's mount was somewhat better than he had hitherto shown at home. He was keen at the start and even keener at the finish and to prevent him mucking up the plans he came up the straight with the horse's head cocked over the rail to stop him finishing too close.

The fact that the horse had not been unduly busy was noted by the stewards and after the race they demanded to see the old jockey. A stipendiary steward was sent to fetch him. "The stewards," he said, "would like you to see the film."

"What film would that be?" replied the jockey. "Black Beauty?"

At the conclusion of the inquiry the stewards took no action but they did warn him about his future riding. "Do you really t'ink," he asked, "aged 58, dat I have a future riding?" APRIL 3, 2007

EDWARD GILLESPIE, chief executive of Cheltenham racecourse, has just been made a Deputy Lieutenant of Gloucestershire and, as such, is on the reserves bench should the county's Lord Lieutenant, Henry Elwes, the Queen's representative, be indisposed.

One of Edward's duties is to welcome people to the county on behalf of Her Majesty – it's pretty safe to say he has the relevant work experience in that department, each March for the last 20 years.

Another is to be around when immigrants take the plunge – by correctly answering a test on Britishness (what's going on in EastEnders and can you name David Beckham's children?) – and become fully fledged British citizens.

In case you're writing to him in the near future it is also formal to address him as Edward Gillespie DL. A cricketing friend of his mistakenly thought it stood for Duckworth-Lewis, the method for working out a result in limited-overs games after interruption by rain.

"It's a huge honour," says Edward. "And, in the hierarchy of these things, is slightly above the mayor of Cheltenham." Now when the mayor presents the trophy for the Grand Annual, annually, he will have to bow to Edward rather than the other way round.

Explaining the history of the position, he adds: "It's only relatively recently that you couldn't be a Deputy Lieutenant unless you had served in the armed forces. And there was a time when you could raise a small army. Regrettably those days are over." AUGUST 2, 2005

WHEN Hugo Bevan, the immensely popular clerk of the course at seven different tracks – never less than four at a time – retired after 30 years in 2003, we packed him off into the sunset with an easel and some paint and we thought, with some confidence, apart from the odd postcard from Venice, we'd seen the back of him.

But he's returned and, actually, the picture is considerably less blurred than his going descriptions used to be. For although he continues to play a crucial, albeit unseen, role in racing running the visitor scheme for the beneficiaries of the Injured Jockeys' Fund, it is in the footsteps of his famous ancestor that he now treads.

Robert Bevan (1865-1925) was one of the English 'Camden Town Group' of painters – that's to say he just missed the boat on being

an impressionist, which means his pictures sell for a mere six figures rather than seven. An authentic Hugo Bevan (1936-) is more our range, though, and varies from £175 to £500.

After 'retiring' Hugo enrolled on a three-year course at art college in Leamington along with 300 students a quarter of his age. When he started he found himself painting stimulating subjects like dustbin lids and broom handles and, quite frankly, it all seemed a little dull after the trials and tribulations of a winter's afternoon at Huntingdon ... until he stumbled into the wrong classroom one day where eight nubile young girls were painting a nude model in a 'life class'.

He changed courses forthwith and there isn't a nude model in Warwickshire who he hasn't painted since. "One chap was covered from head to toe in body pierces and I had to ask the girls why he had a curtain ring in his old man," he recalls, somewhat less naive now than he was at the time. "It's a psychological thing but they always accused me of over-endowing the male subjects we painted, though one stroke of the brush and I could do enormous damage."

A bit like the furniture-maker Robert Thompson, whose signature was a carved mouse, a fairly sure sign of a Hugo still-life appears to be the presence somewhere on the canvas of a wine glass. "That's just a co-incidence," he says. OCTOBER 2, 2007

THE DUKE of Roxburghe will be in his castle this morning, a happy man. As Royal Ascots go his was a memorable one. His two days 'duty' as a steward did not result in an inquiry worth having except for fining Alec Wildenstein £1,000 for telling his jockey to take off Westerner's earmuffs in the Gold Cup. So, we can assume, mild satisfaction there too.

An extra piper has been employed this week to play 'Flower of Scotland' on the battlements of Floors Castle at seven o'clock in the morning to wake up Kelso in celebration of his great filly Attraction and, such is the duke's current run of good luck, one assumes from where he sits in the dining hall he will, in one direction, be able to see salmon leaping in the Tweed and in the other Attraction's half-sisters (with their legs in corrective leg braces) frolicking in the meadows.

I hope, therefore, this won't upset his equilibrium but, at the risk of having the hall redecorated with porridge, I am going to suggest something for which the punishment is probably eternal damnation. The equine performance of last week was Rule Supreme's in the Grande Course de Haies d'Auteuil (the French Champion Hurdle) on Saturday – a jumper always has a chance with me.

As feats go it is even more extraordinary because trainer Willie Mullins, having contracted food poisoning on his previous visit to Paris three weeks ago, was still too ill to travel and sent jockey David Casey on his own. His only two words of French are 'bonjour' and 'merci'.

"I use bonjour when I arrive at the races and merci when I leave," says David. "And don't say much in between." But having ridden a double on Saturday worth £150,000 it's no wonder he said 'thanks' on leaving rather than 'goodbye'.

In the process Rule Supreme, winner of the Royal & SunAlliance at Cheltenham, beat the best thing in France since the Resistance, Kotkijet, a horse as unpronounceable as it was meant to be unbeatable. "He's been away six times this year," says David. "He's more stamps in his passport than Kofi Annan and he loves the boat. Maybe he should have been a sailor."

At home a very rough Mullins celebrated by keeping a cup of tea down and employing half of his jockey's French vocab: "Mercy". Three weeks on he's just about struggling out of bed to see a couple of lots. "It was definitely the steak tartare," he says. "It was beautiful but I was bad the next day and I haven't been right since." AUGUST 18, 2004

SEDGEFIELD hosted something of a first at its evening meeting a week ago today when it held a beauty contest, Miss Durham 2004. Nothing particularly innovative in that but it was the first time that the Tote pool system had been used for anything other than a horserace.

Carrie-Ann Green, the winner who will now go on to contest Miss UK, paid out £7.20 for a £1 stake, roughly 6-1. At the head of the queue to collect his winnings, once the result was announced, was an old chap of about 90 and with the widest of grins. He had spotted her earlier and backed his judgement with his pension. "I expect he went to bed that night," surmised racecourse manager Jim Allen, "in the firm belief he'd still got it." MAY 31, 2005

WHEN Jockey Club Racecourses announced it would be 'rationalising' its workforce and singled out Carlisle clerk of the course Jonnie Fenwicke-Clennell as a candidate for the order of the boot, they may not have quite reckoned with the Cumbrian Resistance led by Tony Dobbin.

Last night www.backjonniefc.com appeared on the world wide web and the feeling is that there will be no shortage of support for one of the north's most popular clerks.

It is as an amateur jockey in the early 1980s that Fenwicke-Clennell holds an unofficial record – for carrying the most overweight. The first year he rode in the West Percy Members' Race he went to scale at 19st 6lb (2.5 Ryan Moores or 2.0 Timmy Murphys) and a year later, after a crash diet, he weighed out at 18st 6lb.

His steed, which he bartered for 40 South Country Cheviot lambs, was equally massive, an 18.2hh gelding called Willie who must have only just missed out on Horse of the Year. A day after completing the course, both years, he competed in an open team chase.

Since 1971 Fenwicke-Clennell has been a regular fixture as a commentator on the northern point-to-point circuit, remarkable as during his first 'call' he had backed Weymouth Road and spent much of the commentary cheering him on. APRIL 22, 2008

THE story behind Barbaro's trainer, Michael Matz, is up there in the realms of Bob Champion.

Matz, 55, showjumped for America in three Olympics, winning silver at Atlanta in 1996. That year he was also chosen, above athletes Carl Lewis and Michael Johnson, to be his country's flagbearer at the closing ceremony, something he rated even higher than his medal.

However, while hero is an often overused word in sport, it genuinely applies to Matz who, 17 years ago, was by chance – he had missed his connection – a passenger on a plane that crashed. Of the 296 passengers, 111 died when the plane cartwheeled into an Iowa cornfield after an emergency landing at Sioux City airport.

When the plane eventually came to a halt he was upside down in the middle section strapped in by his seatbelt. Having calmly chatted to the three children travelling alone beside him for the three-quarters of an hour while the stricken plane dumped fuel, Matz and his girlfriend (now wife) DD persuaded them to hold on to his belt. He led them through the smoke to safety.

When he and another passenger heard a baby crying they went back in while other passengers were still scrambling to get out. They retrieved an 11-month-old baby girl. The three siblings who had been sitting next to him, all now in the late 20s and 30s, were at Churchill Downs on Saturday.

Much criticised beforehand for not having run Barbaro for 35 days before the Kentucky Derby, Matz argued that if there was one lesson he had learned from his showjumping days it was this: in 1976 six riders had been competing for two places on the US team. When he got to the Olympics he found he had no horse left. He was determined Barbaro should go there fresh. MAY 9, 2006

THERE IS what some might describe as a delicious irony at Ascot Bloodstock Sales today. You'll recall when eight pro-hunt protestors found their way into the Palace of Westminster in September that one of them was Brightwells auctioneer Andrew Elliott.

At today's sale, which includes yearlings and mares, he will, among others, be auctioning the last three lots, Highlander, Gauntlet and Devon. All are property of ... wait for it ... the Metropolitan Police Authority, the very same people to whom he must answer bail on December 17.

When his police-horse contact rang up two days after his overnight incarceration Andrew told him he had met a sergeant colleague of his (not that he'd been handcuffed to him!). The contact asked where, when and why Andrew had met the sergeant and when the penny finally dropped so did the phone. "I shouldn't be talking to you if you're on bail," he said.

"Police horses are usually super buys," says Andrew, ever the professional. "The ones we sell have very slight chinks in their armour. They are 99 per cent bombproof which is fine for everyone else but not for a police horse in central London's heaviest traffic." NOVEMBER 9, 2004

AMONG the horses Tor Sturgis trains in Kingston Lisle is an as yet unnamed three-year-old escape artist. It has proved impossible to contain in a field and, frequently during the summer, she has been called to local villages to collect it. Once it even found its way to the Star Inn in Sparsholt. On another occasion she watched it jump out over a five-foot post and rail.

On its most recent tour it was spotted outside AP McCoy's house by the great jockey. He called and she arrived across the field to retrieve it. Having caught it, she was determined not to let go of it but was on the horns of a dilemma – its head-collar was in her car.

Like a good Brownie she thought she'd use her belt as a lead until she realised she wasn't wearing one. This left one option: her bra but – Hello boys – not just any old bra, her Wonderbra.

"I can't think why I was wearing it," says Tor, having led the horse home on the improvised elastic leash. "I've only got one Wonderbra and it normally only comes out on special occasions – like when I'm trying to persuade an owner of the advantage of having horses with me." OCTOBER 10, 2006

LIKE ALL owners on occasion, the Queen is going through a thin time of it this season. So far she has had just three winners. So unless one or two of her horses start pulling their finger out, she is unlikely to surpass the six winners she had on the Flat last year.

Last Thursday, with her football team out of the World Cup, her cricket team rolling over to Sri Lanka, her rugby team in disarray, no athletes to speak of and with the distinct possibility of the BBC's Sports Personality of the Year having to be cancelled through lack of contenders, she needed some sporting solace so sat down to watch Banknote – who was shortly to become her third winner – run in the 3.50 at Haydock.

It may come as some sort of comfort to those of us who make similar cock-ups at home but when she switched on the television she was greeted with a blank screen. Someone had forgotten to pay Racing UK's £20 monthly subscription and she had been cut off. One imagines that, following an internal inquiry, the television won't be the only thing that's cut off. JULY 11, 2006

THE PHEASANT, the Lambourn pub run by Johnny the Fish, is in the news (yet) again. It seems that the watering hole for some of racing's finest is also quite well known to some of our boys serving in Iraq and Afghanistan.

And, when they're trudging through the dust out there, a spook around every corner, a booby trap in every culvert, one of the things that sustains them is the thought of a pint of real ale in the garden of an English country pub (no matter that it is a stone's throw from Junction

14 of the M4). One imagines the same pleasant thoughts sustained soldiers through both World Wars.

So, The Pheasant, not being a million miles from Brize Norton, where the soldiers fly into and out from is, occasionally, one of their first ports of call. Sometimes they turn up in uniform, sometimes in civvies but you can usually tell them apart from the locals with their short-cropped hair, their lean, haunted looks, their relief at being back in Blighty, their general air of exhaustion and the fact that they dive under the nearest table when a passing car backfires. And Johnny, a true master of his trade, welcomes them in, gives them their pint and then leaves them in peace.

Not long ago a group of young, fit men with the short-cropped hair, haunted looks and dressed in smart casual gear arrived at the bar – you could almost smell the desert dust on these young officers – solemnly ordered their pints and went outside to taste the hops of good ol' England and home.

"We all know where they've been," said the landlord to the bunch of locals propping up the bar with a nudge and a wink. "But," he warned sternly, "they've had a bloody tough time, they've come from somewhere bloody horrible, for God's sake leave 'em alone to have a drink."

Well one customer, probably a graduate of those war mags with the 'Achtung . . . Englander Tommy' stuff we all read as young boys, couldn't resist having a chat and finding out where the boys had been serving, just how bad it had been and what the situation was really like on the ground. On the pretence that he was loo-ward bound, he slipped out into the garden to engage our heroes.

"You look like you've been somewhere bloody 'orrible?" he said, addressing their table as compassionately as he could. "What awful hell-hole have you just come from?"

"Goodwood," they replied collectively, reminding him that first and foremost The Pheasant is a racing pub. SEPTEMBER 11, 2007

A HALF-CENTURY in racing is a long time so let's hear it for Rob Wood, one of racing's unsung heroes who recently clocked up 50 years as a part-time clerk of the scales.

Wood will be retired next year when he reaches 70, the age at which BHA part-timers have to leave the crease. But, ever since he was 19, when Newton Abbot couldn't find anyone else at its Easter Bank Holiday meeting in 1957 and he was roped in without a minute's training, it has been his passion.

In between much has changed. Then, of course, jockeys weighed out on balance scales and the clerk had a helper to put 28lb blocks on one side of the scales while the jockey sat on the other. Before long, the scales will be connected by computer to Weatherbys and all the information will be downloaded to an industrial estate in Wellingborough. But the clerk of the scales is not an endangered species; a machine can't tell if it's raining heavily outside and that's why a jockey has weighed in 3lb heavy.

Of course, just as poachers have tried to put one over gamekeepers for centuries, so have overweight jockeys tried to cheat the scales with varying degrees of ingenuity. Rob can spot a pair of paper-thin cheating boots from 50 yards and usually greets their arrival at his scales with the avuncular but firm inquiry: "You are planning to ride in those boots aren't you?"

"The camaraderie of the changing room has always amazed me," he says. "I remember one jockey, who retired shortly afterwards because of weight problems, who came to weigh out with three colleagues. They were trying to get their feet under the scales and lift it to make him appear lighter. In the end he had to weigh out a stone overweight."

He has only once ever had to object to a 'winner' – when a euphoric jockey walked straight back past the scales into the weighing room at Towcester, thereby committing one of racing's cardinal sins – forgetting to weigh in.

Of course, this was only his part-time job. His day job was flying planes.

After 12 years in the RAF and the rest of his career in commercial flying, he rose to be chief pilot for Monarch Airways flying boisterous holiday-makers to places like Malaga. One day one of his hostesses told him that they had a 'celebrity' on board. "Oh, who's that?" said Rob. "John Francome," said the air hostess.

"Well, send him up," he said. To this day Francome has never really recovered from seeing the clerk of the scales at the helm of the plane flying him to Spain.

"Racing people and aviators are completely different breeds," Rob says. "And there's no comparison with flying a plane these days and riding a novice chaser down to an open ditch – 99 per cent of flying is incident-free."

His aviation career did have its moments. On one occasion he had over-speeding propellers. One imagines Purple Moon must have experienced something similar in the Melbourne Cup, having an Australian jockey on board instead of a British one restricted to half a dozen strokes in a finish.

In America someone once tried to smash his way into the cockpit. Obviously his involvement with racing's best-known passengers Timmy Murphy and Paul Carberry has been restricted to weighing them out.
NOVEMBER 13, 2007

ANTHONY SPEELMAN likes to put a bit of care into naming his horses. Unlike, for example, the effort that went into naming Paddy Power second Vodka Bleu – by Pistolet Bleu out of Viva Vodka – he likes to combine the parent names and some lateral thinking to come up with something clever.

In America, for example, he came up with Your Tent Or Mine for a horse by Forest Camp out of She's Got The Look. It still tickles American racegoers.

Here, though, he has Weatherbys to cope with and he has just received a slightly curt letter from them saying that the organisation "doesn't accept names with a vulgar connotation" after he applied for the name French Oral, a three-year-old by Beneficial out of Lessons Lass.

We all sat French Oral as part of our O-levels and I imagine children still do to this day and it's beneficial. There's only the slightest hint of double entendre (for those who never sat French oral that is a double meaning).

Speelman framed the letter, sent it to his trainer Nicky Henderson and handed the naming over to his children, who have come up with The Polomoche, a character from Babar. NOVEMBER 14, 2006

NAMING horses after people who are still alive requires the permission of the person concerned. The late American actor Gregory Peck was delighted when he received a letter asking if someone could, cleverly, name a horse by Henbit after him. Someone with a mare by Supreme Leader also once wrote to Diana Ross asking for her permission to use her name. He neglected, naturally, to mention that the horse's dam was called Black Nancy.

But there seems to be plenty of scope for owners of young horses by the stallion Presenting. In Ireland the name Jeremy Paxman has, I believe, been reserved for a horse by Presenting out of a mare called Sarcastic.

Thinking along the same lines is Peter Curling, the artist. He 'christened' if that's the right term (and got away with it) a horse now in training with Sue Smith: The Kew Tour, ie The Cute Whore. One of the doyens of clever nomenclature, he also wants to give his Presenting colt out of his mare Ticking Over the name Jeremy Clarkson.

However, before he could fire a letter off to the Top Gear presenter he was vetoed by his wife, Louise. Is it because Clarkson is like the human equivalent of Marmite, you either love him or hate him? "No," says Louise, "I just like nice, pretty names, like the names of places not people." NOVEMBER 15, 2005

ALL his friends agree, it couldn't have happened to a nicer bloke. David Redvers, MFH, bloodstock agent and owner of Tweenhills Stud, is sporting some interesting bruising after being kicked amidships while trying to load a mare in a trailer.

"Oh, no, which of my tosser friends told you that?" he asked when I hit him with the news that he might be in possession of a diary story to tickle the nation of a Tuesday morning. "Andrew Elliott," I replied, always fiercely protective of my sources.

Redvers, one of the 'Westminster Eight' who stormed parliament, was loading a reluctant mare in a trailer (this method is not straight out of the stalls handler's manual) and stuck his shoulder under the mare's backside to help lever her on to the box. She half-kicked out (that's called a warning shot, David) and as he stepped away she lined him up in the wing mirrors, flew backwards and double-barrelled him. Her hind legs connected with his pubic bone. If your eyes are watering, it's nothing compared to his. Let's just say there won't be a drought order in Hartpury this summer.

However, just as is the case when you bruise your forehead, the swelling moved due south. "My wife, who was away at the time, was rather impressed by my large black todger when she returned," boasts Redvers. "But, seriously, a couple of inches lower and I'd have been in real trouble."

He adds: "The reason Elliott [an auctioneer with Brightwells] knows is that I turned up early recently to a hunt meeting and he was on the phone boring someone to tears about some upcoming Brightwells auction so I dropped my trousers to show him. He soon enough put the phone down then."

It's still all quite tender so if anyone sees Redvers, give him a flick from me. APRIL 17, 2007

THERE are several reasons to go to Stratford on Saturday but the most compelling will be to see the performance, not to mention entourage, surrounding Yeoman Sailor, a runner in the Intrum Justitia Cup Champion Hunter Chase. And I'm just talking about the saddling up.

Yeoman Sailor is trained by Grace Muir, hitherto better known for her role in the retraining of racehorses – a process that requires them to be taught to go slower rather than faster. She turns round ex-chasers at a rate of roughly 50 a year.

As the job seems to require, Grace is part armour-plated steel, part cuddly bear with a work ethic that would put even the Chinese to shame. Educated at a girl's public school, the founder may have intended many things of the school but not that troopers in the British army could expand their barrack-room vocabulary by listening to a former pupil. In its defence, though, Grace did subsequently work for Jenny Pitman where the habit may have originated.

In many ways Saturday is her Cup Final and, let's put it like this, if it was Roy Keane's – luckily for him his is at Cardiff – he wouldn't be favourite for any 50-50 balls with our Gracie.

In a training career spanning three months she has sent out two winners and two seconds, neither beaten more than a neck, from four runs with two crocks who had been out of training for an aggregate of seven years. The Gold Cup's there for the taking with the first horse she's sent who hasn't previously broken down six times.

In one respect her success with Yeoman Sailor is due to one of her few failures with retraining. She found placing the old horse more like trying to give away a racing pigeon – he kept coming back. At his first home he refused to go anywhere and at the second he consented to go forward but at such a speed that the only thing his nervous pilot could do at a remotely similar pace was hand him back. After the second time Grace got the message that he had no wish to leave the stud again.

His preparation for the race is being filmed for Racing Country, a BBC documentary for the autumn. "It should be called 'Carnage Comes To Town' when they're filming us," says Grace, who will have at least a dozen helpers to put the saddle on. MAY 18, 2005

JUST occasionally – not often in this column admittedly where the truth is rarely allowed to distort a good story – when a journalist thinks he is in possession of a potential scoop, he has to dutifully check it out and, upon finding it doesn't stand up, is forced to knock it down.

Recently I had it on 'very good authority' that Chris Stickels, now bedding in well as clerk of the course at Ascot, was once engaged to a girl called Tess but she broke it off when the full implications of the name she would emerge from the church with dawned on her.

"Not true," says Stickels. "But Tess was my nickname at school." Neither, it seems, a scoop nor original. DECEMBER 19, 2006

WHILE police involved in the current investigation into race-fixing need degrees in applied mathematics, it seems slightly incongruous that, on the eve of Cheltenham, a good old-fashioned Dick Francis-style attempt to stop a well-fancied – well, Richard Evans tipped it in this paper – runner took (or might have taken) place.

So, Newmarket, hold on to your hat. Could it be that with the 2005 Flat season about to start the nobblers are back in town?

Going into the Festival no trainer was in better form than Lucy Wadham. She had sent out more winners than losers in the immediate build-up and had high hopes for The Dark Lord in the Pertemps Final on Thursday.

On Monday night she checked round her yard, a stone's throw from Godolphin's base at Moulton Paddocks, and all was well. In the middle of the night her husband, Justin, heard a noise and poked his nose out into the yard but saw nothing.

When Lucy got up at 5.30 the yard had been ransacked – by two of her horses. They'd dug up the flower beds and upturned bales of paper bedding (ie this article will not be fish'n chip wrapping paper tomorrow night it'll be racehorse bedding). It looked like the scene of an all-night rave for vandals. They had, it seems, made the most of their freedom.

The question is, though, how did two of her horses get out of boxes that had kick-bolts on the doors? Plenty of trainers have the odd horse who is adept at escape or a yard so old that the doors occasionally fall off their hinges but for two horses to get out is a bit more than a coincidence. And, though one of them wasn't The Dark Lord, it came from the box with his name on it. He had been moved shortly before but Lucy had forgotten to change the label on the door.

The Jockey Club was informed and was concerned enough to take blood samples. Godolphin, who have more security staff than horses there at this time of year, checked through all their CCTV footage from Monday night but it revealed no-one lurking in the shadows. The Dark Lord duly ran, finishing 12th at 12-1.

"It's all a bit strange," says Lucy. "It seemed pretty innocuous but, at the same time, a bit more than a coincidence. The Dark Lord ran well in a slow race which didn't suit him." March 22, 2005

IT IS all there in the pedigree. Brough Scott's most recent book, and the one that gave him most pleasure researching, was *Galloper Jack*, the story of his grandfather General Jack Seely, Secretary of State for War, a friend of Churchill's, brave to a fault and the only Cabinet minister to serve the whole of the First World War on the front line, in his case leading the Canadian cavalry.

Just before Easter, Brough was visiting publisher Raceform/ Highdown's office in Compton when smoke started billowing from the windows of the pub (the Compton Swan) opposite and when I say smoke I mean a little more than would have been generated had the chef merely overdone the sausages. Downstairs the hostelry was ablaze.

With no sign of the fire brigade Brough, temporarily forgetting that someone from the pub had once told him to go forth and multiply for parking his car there while on Raceform business, and 'Mr Books', Jonathon Taylor, broke off from their meeting and legged it to the pub.

There, from a top window, the landlord, Brian Bayliss, awaited rescue. Cue Brough to shin up the drainpipe and give Mr Bayliss a fireman's lift back down to the ground. Well, not quite. The landlord shouted that there was a ladder round the back, which Brough duly fetched, and mine host, after an initial wobble, was able to descend to safety. "Anyone else in there?" inquired Brough. "Mick? Where's Mick?" replied the landlord. And so Brough disappeared round the back again shouting for Mick. Mick duly appeared from a neighbouring cottage and, er, that's it.

Shortly afterwards the *Newbury Weekly News*, with colour photos all over the front page, hailed Brough one of the greatest heroes to have ever set foot within its area. "No," says Brough. "Just put my foot on the bottom rung of the ladder while the landlord climbed down it." And modest with it, too. APRIL 25, 2006

A PART of the furniture will be missing when we all descend on Aintree again this autumn. Unusually for Liverpool, however, this is not a police matter – it hasn't been stolen, it's retiring.

After 31 years as press officer at the racecourse, Nigel Payne, 61, one of the National's great unsung heroes, is to leave the job to allow the new managing director, Julian Thick, an opportunity to build up his own team. He is not retiring as such, though, and will continue to be chief executive of the Horseracing Sponsors Association and administer the Sir Peter O'Sullevan Trust.

It all began in 1976, when Red Rum was in his pomp and when Ladbrokes signed a seven-year deal with the then owner, Bill Davies, to run the race and Nigel was part of a four-man management team. But through different jobs and different MDs, Nigel has, like all good Aintree jockeys, not been easily unseated. If he ever was, he soon remounted.

His highlights have included Red Rum's third win, Aldaniti, the void race of '93, the bomb scare of '97 and, of course, capping it all with his own horse Earth Summit's victory in '98.

But press officer for the National – it's a bit like doing PR for Hans Christian Andersen or being chocolate-liaison officer to a kindergarten isn't it? A fairytale every time. Well, actually, no. Hell hath no fury – actually the analogy with a load of kids hyper from overdosing on Kinder Surprises isn't far off – like a hack without a workstation or the phone which, incidentally, he didn't order, not working.

For the 31 years, starting off in a portable cabin in front of the County stand when wifi was nothing but a pet name for the spouse, through various tents, a double-decker marquee to the new hangar-sized press room, Nigel has smoothed the way to enable great words to flow in a coherent order and, crucially, flow back to Fleet Street after each National.

Of course there's more to the job than meets the eye. After the void National, Charles Barnett, Lord Daresbury, David Hillyard of RHT and Nigel were to meet to discuss how to play the debacle with the press the next day. They wanted to keep their discussions internal but couldn't shake off Roger Buffham, then the Jockey Club head of security, and it fell to Nigel to give him the slip.

Thinking on his feet – and it has to be said with rather more success than the Jockey Club when it fired him – he told Buffham they would convene in the Grosvenor Hotel, Chester for a summit meeting that night. They, of course, buggered off somewhere else.

He has one of the most unusual National mementos too. Before Aldaniti's victory, Josh Gifford had told Nigel he would give up smoking if the horse won. In the winner's enclosure the trainer handed him his half-smoked box of Benson & Hedges. "I smoked the fags but I've still got the packet," says Nigel, who still sports the same distinctive 'soup strainer' that he first grew as a 19-year-old and which, I believe, like Aintree's fences, gets trimmed but twice a year.

There is, of course, no greater honour at Aintree than having a fence named after you – if you can hack the fact that Becher's and Foinavon are both named after minor disasters associated with their namesakes. It strikes me that the first fence, the scene of so much mental anguish and where so many dreams come to a premature end, would be the most appropriate recipient of the title, the Payne. SEPTEMBER 25, 2007

NOT many men are described at their funeral as a "cantankerous old bugger" but that summed up legendary travelling head lad Andy O'Dwyer, who died recently, aged 74.

In 1963, when working for Jeremy Tree, he nearly pulled off a bet that would have set him up for life. Each week during the winter he doubled up Tree's Only For Life with Spree, horses who he looked after, for the 2,000 and 1,000 Guineas respectively. Only For Life won at 33-1 but Spree was beaten a length at 100-8. Both horses were ridden by Jimmy Lindley, but O'Dwyer never forgave the jockey the defeat of Spree, even though it was at the hands of the odds-on future champion Hula Dancer.

After he had retired from racing Andy went into the antique trade. There is, after all, virtually no difference between selling a three-legged horse for ten times its true worth and a three-legged chair for the same.

But Andy took with him to the antique trade some of the same principles that he applied to horses. One day he was having awful trouble fitting a load of antique furniture into his van. Several times he reloaded it in order to get the last piece, a wheel-back chair, to fit. Eventually, unable to squeeze it in, he raised it above his head and smashed the antique chair to smithereens on the pavement. As he stuck all the broken pieces into a small gap he muttered: "You're in now, you little bastard."

When asked why he'd done it he replied: "No chair's getting the better of me."

More recently he was taken shopping. On arrival he took a trolley and filled it with stuffing. "What are you doing?" asked the supermarket manager as Andy wheeled a trolley full of sage and onion round the aisles. "I'm putting it where it should be," he replied, "next to the frozen chicken." JULY 26, 2005

THE NON-RACING highlight of this year's Festival was the stirring recital on Gold Cup day of 'Best Mate' by Cheltenham's 'racing poet', Henry Birtles.

This week Henry, 40, will be concentrating on the day job as a consultant to Sunset & Vine selling the world television rights for Saturday's Dubai World Cup. His verse, initially a hobby to while away the time on aeroplanes, is becoming something of an unlikely hit within the sport that, until now, has only really recognised art if it can be hung on a wall.

He initially approached Edward Gillespie, managing director at Cheltenham, in November to ask if he could flog illustrated copies of his poems in the car park to arriving racegoers. "No," said Gillespie, "the car park is for parking cars. Better still, come into the racecourse and I'll set you up."

To demonstrate how far he has come in such a short time, he delivered verse to the royal box at this year's Festival, a posting that is sure to raise the possibility of him jocking off the current Poet Laureate.

But an artist never loses sight of his roots and, by night during the Festival, he went out to the local pubs to declaim his poetry to the ordinary man – much like a minstrel from the Middle Ages. He went down a treat at Jonjo O'Neill's local, the Plough at Ford, but it was not all plain sailing at The Hollow Bottom.

He'd delivered his epic, 'Desert Orchid', to one bar when the landlord requested that he recite 'Dawn Run' to the whole pub. Calling for silence, he handed Henry a microphone.

Now it just so happened that in the next-door bar a band had been warming up and in there were some young, apparently well-oiled Irishmen who had come, specifically, to listen to music, not poetry.

He was halfway through 'Dawn Run' when he suddenly felt an arm tightening round his neck followed by the immortal if slightly slurred line: "Shing us a shong, you ****."

Not shy of interaction with his audience, Henry challenged his assailant. "No," he said handing him the mic, "you sing us a song, you do your bit." The drunken heckler had the wind taken from his sail and, discovering a new-found shyness, slunk off back to his seat.

Henry completed 'Dawn Run' without further interruption but, at its conclusion, he again returned the mic to his heckler. By this stage he was, alas, already asleep. MARCH 27, 2007

IF THE end of the world was nigh, how would you cope? Vic Strauffer, an American commentator and the self-styled 'goof on the roof', coped rather magnificently I think you'll agree.

He was recently calling a race from Hollywood Park which is, one imagines, one of the courses closest to the notorious San Andreas fault if not actually on it. When the runners were midway down the back 'stretch' during a fillies' race the ground began to rumble, his eyrie on top of the grandstand started, one assumes, to wobble and in the back of his mind he must have reckoned this was the big one, that California was about to be rent asunder and chief among the fatalities would be the 'Goof'.

He first drew attention to the earthquake with a very matter-of-fact statement. "We are in the middle of an earthquake here in southern California," he said before returning to his call. The enormity of that then hit him. "Lady Lucayan tries to slow it down. She leads by two and a half lengths. By the way folks I'd like you to know I love you all and that horseracing was my first love."

He then returned to his call and turning into the home straight Pleasant Thunder began making a move through the six-runner field, an occurrence that only served to remind him of his impending doom. "That wasn't thunder you heard, that was an earthquake. I've got to make this my greatest ever call."

Up front it was ding-dong; Lady Lucayan was being caught in the dying strides by the fast-finishing Pleasant Thunder, who had "come to win in a shaker". By this stage he was clearly warming to his theme and, as they flashed past the post together he reported that it was a photo. "And I don't know or care who won the photo," he concluded his great call. Wouldn't it be good if all commentators were so glad to be alive? JUNE 28, 2005

DAVE MUSTOE, the former jump jockey-turned-jockeys' valet, was working at York last week but had not arranged anywhere to stay so Ryan Moore, who presumably had accommodation elsewhere, offered him the room he'd booked in a hotel.

In the middle of the night – or so he thought – Dave, wearing nothing but a very tatty old pair of pants, went to the loo and, in time-honoured fashion, his bedroom door closed on him. When he arrived at reception it was not as late as he had first thought and the party in the bar was still in full flow.

The presence of a semi-naked man, whose jockey's figure has long since gone, did not go unnoticed and he was duly catcalled and cheered louder than Authorized had been earlier that afternoon. But as he crept, embarrassed, back to bed he had the last laugh as he overheard, one punter to another, in the bar: "That Ryan Moore's a fat bastard."
SEPTEMBER 28, 2007

WHEN Gordon Richards, later the trainer of Hallo Dandy and One Man, weighed out for his first ride as an apprentice jockey there was some confusion because (Sir) Gordon Richards, the multiple champion Flat jockey, was still in his pomp.

The clerk of the scales told young Gordon to pluck an initial out of the air – 'W' in this case – and place it between the Gordon and Richards to avoid confusion with the great jockey; thus he was forever after known as G.W. Richards.

Now, it was only a matter of time before someone confused George Baker, the jockey, with George Baker, the first-season trainer who has sent out five winners in the last fortnight and already surpassed the target he set himself of sitting down to Christmas lunch with ten winners in the bank. Admittedly they are both tall but one weighs about 8st 7lb while the other does more lasting damage to the scales at 14st.

First off trainer Baker received a call from fellow trainer James Given asking him if he was going to Yarmouth later that week. Assuming that

Given was about to invite him to lunch in the Seafood Restaurant, one of the better reasons for patronising the seaside resort, he replied "yes" and mentally he was already going through the numerous fishy possibilities from the A La Carte at his colleague's considerable expense.

"Well," said Given, "would you ride mine in the seller?"

"Technically I suppose I'm available," replied a downhearted Baker, "but I'd struggle a bit with the weight!"

Swift on this episode's heels, however, comes official recognition of the confusion. The trainer recently opened a letter from 151 Shaftesbury Avenue, home of the BHA. "Dear Mr Baker," it began. "I'm writing to inform you that further to the suspension imposed upon you by the stewards at Leicester the BHA has suspended you from riding in any race at any meeting on Wednesday, August 13, 2008."

Baker rang them back and told them he'd be quite happy if they banned him from riding in perpetuity. "I'm thinking of calling a horse George Baker," he says. "It would be George Baker, trained by George Baker and there'd only be one man who could ride it." AUGUST 26, 2008

UNTIL now Charlie Hills, son and assistant of Lambourn trainer Barry, has been more concerned about the fitness of his father's horses but now he is paying some attention to his own – he is running in this year's London Marathon.

Hills is one of a five-man team selected to run for the Countryside Alliance this year. As usual it is an eclectic mixture. The others include David Redvers, who has successfully built up Tweenhills Stud near Hartbury from scratch, and Nick Wood, private chef to Lady Weinstock and a former racehorse owner in his own right.

As you'd expect, his horse, Tour Eiffel, never quite aspired to the lofty heights of those belonging to or bred by his employer and it earned the nickname Tour F-all after a series of disappointing outings over hurdles.

The non-racing members of the team include former England and Kent cricketer Matthew Fleming, a man not unfamiliar with Cheltenham, and a Leeds University student called Edd Burge.

It is an interesting fact that people in racing are far more concerned with and critical of the conformation of their horses than themselves so Hills received something of a shock when he went to be fitted up with a decent pair of running shoes in Swindon recently.

While not quite a shooting job, he was told he was bow-legged but while he may not stop a pig in passage, for running purposes his flat feet would compensate for this 'deformity' – a clear case of two wrongs making a right.

Three weeks into his training Hills knocked off 13 miles in a couple of hours and, like all the great Kenyan runners, being classically ectomorphic (tall and lean) in shape he looks like a stayer rather than a sprinter.

But the smart money is on Redvers, racing's favourite narcoleptic, to be the first of the five home. He did 14 miles in an hour and a half recently and his aim for the marathon – providing he doesn't fall asleep along the way – is a sub-three-hour time and certainly to improve on his PB of 3hr 17min. He had his first prep last weekend in the Forest of Dean – admittedly not the sort of place you want to hang around in given some of the locals – and came home in sixth, just out of the money.

The only event Wood has ever run in is a pancake race and while I have no idea about the youngster Burge, Fleming has never run further than 22 yards without a stop. FEBRUARY 26, 2008

THE KIWI VET is a curious creature. Its wife gives birth to its first child and, barely out of the delivery ward, he sugars off to Argentina for a month, not to play a spot of gentlemanly polo or ride a pony across Patagonia but to take part in the Dakar Rally – on a motorbike. At least those people driving cars into ravines had seatbelts on.

The Dakar – it's the rally that has undertakers along the route pricking their ears in anticipation of work as cars are driven off cliffs, people get lost and broken bones become commonplace. Even the winner of this year's bike section was called Coma. It's like riding the Grand National – for 92 hours without stirrups.

So congratulations to Mike Shepherd, a Newmarket-based vet with Rossdales, firstly for getting the project past his feisty wife and, secondly, for finishing 94th (only 113 of 234 starters completed the course). For an amateur who, on previous form and experience, set off ranked 234 just finishing the course is a stunning achievement.

Behind the scenes in Newmarket, Shepherd is the man who kept the oil levels topped up for Ouija Board and Soldier's Tale. But he is also a danger junkie and closet biker. Put the two together and, really, the Dakar was an entry form waiting to be signed.

On Sunday he was presented with his medal in Buenos Aires. "My goal," he said on a high, "was just to get to halfway but to finish in the top 100 is fantastic. I had a good team behind me so when I came in late at night, once after 18 hours in the saddle, I'd just hand over the bike like I was handing a horse to its groom. They'd take it apart and put it back together again for the morning start, which usually meant getting up at 3.30."

The one thing that nearly drove him mad was a bad smell that seemed to follow the bike about. Eventually his mechanics discovered not his socks but a large bug, which was slow-cooking inside his headlight.

His proud wife Camilla, an eventer, was fine about his early sabbatical from nappy changing. "In fairness," she says, "I've been trying to go to Badminton and Burghley for years and he's not getting any younger. I saw him on Eurosport a few times, stuffing his face and looking very hairy. A bigger worry than keeping safe on the rally was that he'd get injured celebrating in Buenos Aires." JANUARY 20, 2009

DAVID WILSON'S career in racing has been slightly back-end-round in that he trained and then became an assistant – it's more commonly the other way.

But it is fair to say he is slightly accident-prone. Once on the way to Doncaster Sales he and Gary Moore, whom he assists, stopped at a motorway services for a break. While Gary kipped in the car David sat on a concrete flowerpot in the car park reading a form book. When Gary woke up he couldn't find his assistant – until he looked in the pot and found David upside down in there having been knocked in by a reversing lorry.

His most recent injuries are self-inflicted after he took his own horse, Vanadium, for a paddle on Lancing beach to help reduce a haematoma the gelding had picked up.

Jayne Moore, wife of Gary and mother of Ryan, Jamie, Hayley and Joshua, is not stupid by a very long chalk and questioned the wisdom of her youngest accompanying their assistant and his horse to the beach, given he had an important ride in a Bollinger race later that day. "Don't worry, Mum," said Joshua, "it'll be fine." It appears he must have merely been referring to the weather.

David, 67, and so much known for not being a jockey that Jayne didn't realise he still rode, was loaded up on Vanadium. He 'paddled' a bit in the shallows and, emboldened by the success of this, eventually over-reached Vanadium depth-wise.

Horses will swim all day but, like humans, they don't like mouthfuls of sea water and to avoid this and the prospect of being enveloped in the swell, Vanadium stuck his head up sharply as a wave approached. It caught his pilot a shocking blow to the head and knocked him off the horse.

Thus Joshua, who has not long grown out of sandcastles, was suddenly faced with several apparently insurmountable problems: a racehorse loose on Lancing beach and a concussed, drowning assistant trainer who was bleeding so heavily that the prospect of drawing in the nearest great white was not unrealistic.

The remarkable Moore Minimus (size-wise he's actually Moore Maximus) caught the horse, fished the assistant from the English Channel and, to complete the treble, went on to ride a winner at Warwick. He was much relieved that inside one of Wilson's watery pockets jangled the lorry's keys.

For those who have never had concussion, you think you are in control but you are most certainly not. And thus back at the Moore base in Brighton, David stripped off down to his Y-fronts and went to his car, then parked beside the busy main road outside the stables, to get some dry clothes.

But the one set of keys to have washed out of his pocket on Lancing beach were his own. They say that driver distraction is the biggest cause of crashes so it's small wonder that there wasn't a major pile-up on the Brighton-Woodingdean road as the semi-naked, heavily bleeding Wilson tried, in vain, to break into his own car. That there wasn't suggests it's an everyday sight in Brighton.

The consequences were a long morning in A&E, 16 stitches neatly linking his eyebrows plus a couple in the end of his broken nose, and two of the blackest eyes you have ever seen.

The following day Jayne Moore was just sitting down for a meeting with the local health and safety officer when David – it's called timing – walked in reporting for duty. He was off, he explained, beachcombing to see if his keys had been washed up with the flotsam and jetsam on Lancing beach. JULY 8, 2008

YOU can always rely upon friends to keep your feet on the ground. One of the 100 text messages Ralph Beckett received before leaving Epsom on Friday after winning the Oaks with Look Here was from his great pal, Jonny Portman. It read, simply: "How did you run?" JUNE 10, 2008

RON SHEATHER, who died last week, used to recall a story that demonstrates how times have changed. It was about the day he won the 1951 Ayr Gold Cup on Fair Seller as an apprentice for his guv'nor, the Malton trainer Ernie Davey.

Davey couldn't go to the races and, after giving Ron his instructions, he said that if he returned from Ayr with the Gold Cup the following day he'd give him 50 guineas. So off Ron set and the next day he duly returned to the trainer's house with the Ayr Gold Cup tucked under his arm and presented it to the trainer.

As there was no mention of his 'reward' Ron finally plucked up the courage to gently remind the trainer about his promise. "You did say, sir, that if I returned with the Ayr Gold Cup you'd give me 50 guineas."

"Don't be bloody silly, Sheather," replied Davey. "It was a steering job, I could have ridden it. I'm not giving you 50 guineas for that."

The trainer then continued: "I've just got some business to attend to. I'll be back in a minute but in the meantime here's a cigarette."

No sooner had Davey left the room and Ron lit up than Mrs Davey appeared on the scene. "You know it's one of the yard rules that apprentices aren't allowed in the house," she said. "It is also a rule that there'll be no smoking in my house. Get out."

Thus on the happy occasion of his winning the prestigious Ayr Gold Cup his only reward was a flea in the ear. MAY 12, 2009

Chapter Nine
THE PRESS CORPSE

ONE of the golden rules of riding in, say, a novice chase is that you don't follow a horse who has fallen on a couple of previous outings. That way you tend to live longer. The principle of the thing is something that can be carried through everyday life – follow a good lead.

A trip to the Arc for racing journalists, particularly those returning the same day, is fraught with deadlines; getting the copy done, not holding up Horseracing Abroad's coach to the airport for too long after the last, slogging it through the post-race traffic to Charles de Gaulle or Gare du Nord and, finally, catching the plane or train.

So, having extended but effectively beaten all deadlines to get to the airport in time, the *Sportsman*'s two writers Geoff Lester and Mark Jeffreys sat down to wait for their plane in a bar with Tony Lewis, racing correspondent to the *Daily Star* and in good form because he had been given a free upgrade on the flight.

He is a man, however, with some form in the missing transport department, most notably the occasion when on a press trip to Pau, France, he forgot to wind his watch forward to French time.

On reflection, and it was something Mrs Lester pointed out in no uncertain terms when she received the apologetic call from her husband, it was a bad idea to let Lewis volunteer to check the departures board. "Take your time, lads," he said on his return before indulging himself again in his good fortune to be upgraded. "The plane's delayed." And they casually took another 'demi' before strolling up to their gate.

When they arrived there was no-one there – a bad omen – except for one member of Air France staff who, on seeing the three, began shaking her head which, given the complete lack of other passengers, was an even worse omen. Meanwhile, outside, a plane was being unloaded and therefore delayed for a while to be relieved of Lewis's luggage (were you on a flight delayed an hour?).

"He then took us on a tour of the airport but didn't know where he was going – it was like getting lost in Alice Springs," says Jeffreys, a no-nonsense Queenslander, recalling the unfortunate episode after spending the night shacked up in an airport hotel with Lester whom, like Mrs Lester, he partially blames. "Geoff's known the fellow for 30 years – you'd think he'd have learned by now. I'll tell you what, he may work for the Star but he was no ****ing star last night."

A charitable French person on check-in put them on a flight home yesterday morning free of charge but the Japanese, relieved of Yen, may also be relieved to know they weren't the only ones who had a wretched weekend. OCTOBER 3, 2006

THE SAD NEWS from the festive season is that George Ennor, one of the best racing reporters of this or any other generation, finally succumbed after a brave fight against cancer. He was 65.

Two of his greatest friends were the trainers Peter Makin and Charlie Vernon-Miller. Peter recalls a holiday they shared in Tunisia once when a low-budget James Bond-type film was being made in the same location. As they were short of European extras for a swimming scene they hired George because, they said, he looked like Cary Grant.

He took off his glasses and began, as requested, to swim enthusiastically. He did not hear (or see) the director bellow 'cut' however and was still swimming, to the point of drowning, three-quarters of an hour later. When he subsequently saw the film in Guildford cinema he jumped up and announced that the fine figure of a man on the screen was him. Naturally people turned round and told him to shut up.

For more than 25 years he stayed with the Vernon-Millers in Worcestershire for the Cheltenham Festival, never once succeeding to find their short cut to the races. On one evening they or rather George was – Charlie didn't drink the stuff – tucking into some very old Hennessy Cognac, given to the trainer as a memento of his Hennessy winner Big Horn. Quite late on there was a ghastly crash. George was sitting on the floor, quite uncertain of where he was, having taken a purler from his chair. The assembled company then had the racing reporter's age-old problem – determining whether it was unseated or fell. January 3, 2006

BEN CLARKE is, as some of you may know, William Hill's racecourse PR man. That is to say he lounges about the press room for much of the day but springs into action after a race by thrusting a carbon copy of a horse's odds for a future engagement into the hands of racing hacks in the hope that they will stimulate his firm's ante-post market.

Typically, after a two-year-old has just won a minor event, he and his ilk give you the wretched horse's odds for next season's Classics and every autumn they curse one poor beast by making it winter favourite for the Guineas, an honour that as good as guarantees it a slot in an operating theatre at some stage during the winter. What he does on non-race days is anyone's guess.

Anyway, Ben received a bill through the post last week that had its origins in an incident that took place about four years ago when he was between jobs, still a boy-racer, and had yet to register on William Hill's radar. The fateful occasion was preceded by his decision to buy a Renault Clio Sport.

The deal done, he travelled to London by train, paid £50 for the first instalment of insurance on the internet at Paddington, collected the Clio and drove it back home to Bristol – one happy boy.

Two days later he tracked down an original set of wheels – wide, one presumes – and drove to Swindon where they were fitted at a mate's tyre shop and, with another mate in the passenger seat, set off for Salisbury to pick up a "few more bits and bobs" for the vehicle.

Alas, as he was leaving Salisbury "in unhelpful driving conditions", he drove his three-day-old pride and joy into the parapet of a railway bridge. There are, you'll imagine correctly, less consequential walls to knock over than the one that, at that moment, lay strewn over the Salisbury-Waterloo line with the Clio's front-end dangling precariously over the ledge above it.

For starters, it's pretty good going by anyone's standards to have four emergency services – fire engine, police, British Transport Police and ambulance – attend your prang.

Now, though, we come to the crux of this story, the costs. His passenger sued Ben (or more specifically his insurers) to the tune of £4,500 (£2,250 per rib), the highways agency stuck in a bill for £8,000 for the repair of the bridge and, obviously, there was the value of the car to factor into the equation.

This week, however, those figures were made to look piffling when Ben received a letter from Railtrack scheduling the details of delays and disruption to the railway while it was closed for a week for the repairs. It totalled a staggering £2,807,000, the equal to a whole production line of brand new Clios.

He sincerely hopes it's been copied to his insurers and that it was just for his information. In the meantime if he lives to 125 that's the no-claims bonus gone, but he's having a slightly better run in a Honda Civic supplied by William Hill. In betting terms if he had not paid that £50 insurance it would have been something like laying a 56,500-1 winner.
August 7, 2007

YOU may not read too much criticism of Aintree's new facilities in the press – for the very simple reason that the new press room is outstanding. Even after two days it has been rated as the best media facility on any racecourse in the world. The only complaint so far has been that the *Mail on Sunday*'s correspondent couldn't find a coathanger for his coat but he'll get over it.

The jockeys' changing room, though nicely panelled like the old one, looks more like the jockeys' changing room. One of them has likened it to "a prison cell with a shower". The stewards' room is minute, more a shower without a prison cell and good luck to them if they call all the riders in for disobeying the starter. They would have to do it in shifts.

The new paddock, built to give the runners more room, doesn't look a square inch bigger than the old one and the new winner's enclosure lacks atmosphere. The old winner's enclosure is a champagne bar and the old changing room a bistro sort of affair. But, hey, that's progress for you.
April 8, 2006

THE APPOINTMENT of Jim McGrath of Timeform and Channel 4 – as opposed to Jim McGrath of the *Daily Telegraph* and the BBC – to the board of the BHB as an independent director has been highly lauded but the announcement was not without some confusion.

When the news broke the first on the phone to congratulate Timeform Jim rang, instead, our Aussie Jim. It was press-room colleague Colin Mackenzie of the *Daily Mail*. Rather enjoying Colin's eulogistic tribute to himself about his suitability as a candidate for the post Aussie Jim let Colin go on for a couple of minutes before putting him out of his misery. "Thanks Colin," he said, "but you've got the wrong Jim. It's the good-looking one here. Thanks, anyway, for the tip-off about the story."

Let's hope when the BHB sends out top-secret memos to its directors the office doesn't make the same mistake.

Despite the potential, similar mix-ups have been surprisingly few. On one previous occasion Aussie Jim turned up to interview Martin Pipe at 10.30 one Sunday morning to be met by the trainer's late father David, who was unaware that there was a brace of McGraths. "Who are you?" he asked. "Jim McGrath," replied Aussie Jim. "You can't be, Jim McGrath was here at 9.30," said David before shouting into the office: "Hey Martin, there's a fellow here reckons he's Jim McGrath."

"Come in Jim," replied Martin beside his baffled father. Just an hour earlier he had indeed given an interview to Timeform Jim. AUGUST 10, 2004

IN A contracting industry *The Sportsman* was a welcome, albeit brief, addition. Launched in March, its 193rd and last edition appeared last Thursday. Its mere presence did the *Racing Post* a huge favour as its owners were forced to invest. One imagines *The Sportsman*'s demise will be celebrated with a price hike at the Post.

The closure was not good news for the recently married Ed Pownall. Four days after returning from honeymoon the *Sportsman*'s heroic PR man, who even took to the streets – well, Ascot High Street – during the royal meeting to flog the paper (when one of their salesmen whipped round because his mum was selling the *Post* on the next pitch) had to explain to his wife, Charlotte, that it was all over (his job not the marriage). Instead of thankyou letters, he's been updating his CV.

At the wedding, to which a number of high-rolling young bookmaking executives were invited, there was a spread on the combined length of the three speeches, bride's godfather, groom and best man.

The £400 Scoop3 bet was won with 20 minutes by the BBC sport presenter Rishi Persad who – maybe it was foresight – in an act of great altruism handed over all the cash to the newlyweds as spending money for their honeymoon. Had it gone to one of the bookmakers even the grateful Ed reckons it would have ended up going on a hot tip for the 4.30 at Lingfield.

The timing of the closure for editor Charlie Bain isn't ideal either. His wife, Clarissa, gave birth to their first child, Archie, the Sunday before last and now, on extended paternity leave, he has no excuse not to get heavily involved in the finer details of nappy changing.

Archie's timing, half an hour after the Arc, was not ideal either. As Charlie thought the runners for the great race would be circling at the start and believing Clarissa might be otherwise occupied, he surreptitiously reached for the remote controls for the television parked in the corner of the room. "Absolutely no way," sort of got the message through that in 2006, at least, he wouldn't be watching the race live. OCTOBER 10, 2006

THE press room will be a poorer place from Friday onwards when one of its great characters Richard Edmondson, erstwhile racing correspondent for the *Independent,* leaves for pastures new – and, like his sense of humour, dry.

His departure will be a particular disappointment for racecourse caretakers who used to earn good overtime waiting for him to finish his copy before they could switch the lights out and lock up after racing.

After 20 years with the newspaper Edmo is off to India with his family for a two-year stint while his wife, Alex Crawford, takes up the presumably better-paid job of Asia correspondent for Sky News.

Last week Edmo was voted racing journalist of the year and not before time. He had been runner-up four times previously, which earned him the nickname 'The Pilgarlic' after the horse who was constantly placed in the Grand National but never won it.

As he pointed out in his acceptance speech his trip to India – on a week-long recce he found it much as he had expected; big, hot and dusty – could either be regarded as a once-in-a-lifetime opportunity or a desperate attempt to curry the sympathy vote with colleagues and finally land the award.

Hitherto it has been the Yanks who have most appreciated his word-smithery. They have twice lauded him for his coverage of the Breeders' Cup – in 1999 in Miami and this autumn in Belmont.

"People are treating it like I'm moving to the dark side of the moon," he said yesterday as I prepared this 'obit'. "I'll be back in a couple of years' time and no-one will have missed me."

Of all the race meetings he has attended, Aintree 2004 was the most memorable. Ideally I'd like to say it was because he had been extolling the virtues of Amberleigh House to his readers for months before and, indeed, for all I know he may have. However, the meeting was memorable for the wrong reasons and, as he will discover during the monsoon season, it never rains but it pours.

Nearing Liverpool he had a blow-out on the M6 and he tried, in the tipping rain, to mend it himself. His attempt was singularly unsuccessful and didn't get beyond the hubcap, which he couldn't get off. The irony of the situation – taking a wheel (even the steering wheel) off a car is part of the school curriculum in Liverpool – wasn't lost on him and when he finally arrived at his hotel he had to settle his nerves with a drink or two.

When he was woken up in the middle of the night by the call of nature he set off for his room's en suite facilities. In his confusion instead of taking a right turn he took a left. He came to his senses in the corridor at exactly the same time that he heard his room door click locked behind him. His heart sank. He was in his birthday suit.

He tried to raid a sheet cupboard so that at least he could look like he was late back to the hotel from a toga party but, hey, this was Liverpool and every cupboard had six locks on it. His saving grace was that the hotel had hosted Wayne Rooney's engagement party a fortnight before, which had ended in a well-publicised scrap. While slightly nonplussed by the vision that stood before her the receptionist was, we believe, by this stage beyond surprising. DECEMBER 13, 2005

CHARLIE FAWCUS, who spent 31 years as racing correspondent for the *Daily Mirror*, had been chuntering for some time, by all accounts, about how he could possibly get out of his mother's 90th birthday party but no-one appreciated to what lengths he'd go.

Come the day – Sunday – the inclement weather meant that the party, Chez Fawcus in Little Coxwell, had to decamp to the village hall at short notice. First into the Gents was Charlie and as he locked the door behind him there was an unhealthy-sounding clunk. It later transpired the lock had fractured within.

He had some half hour of quiet contemplation – during which time he concluded that escape through the window was not an option on account of its size – before he was rescued by a builder, who had been roused from across the road. His return to the party was greeted with a round of applause. MAY 15, 2007

A LITTLE tardy, a story has just emerged from Ireland concerning Channel 4 Racing presenter Alastair Down and what can only be described as one of life's little triumphs.

Alastair was in Ireland as a guest of Irish trainer Enda Bolger in November. Enda's great friend is one of the biggest names in rock music, Bruce Springsteen, also known as 'The Boss', who was in Dublin for a concert.

I'm pretty sure Alastair doesn't make a habit of trailing celebrities but the next day Enda and he joined the Boss on a trip down memory lane. The Boss wanted to show his children Slane Castle where, 21 years ago, he began the European leg of his Born In The USA tour. Having played to 120,000, one of the biggest concerts to have taken place in Ireland at the time, he had fond memories of the place.

Following a guided tour given by the castle's owner, the party retreated to the local pub for Irish coffees all round. But word got out that Springsteen was in and, one by one, the locals flocked round armed with autograph books.

This had been going on for a good while when a little, wizened old man walked in. One of the Boss's more mature fans, the party assumed as one, and true to form the old fella headed in the direction of the pop star but, completely ignoring him, kept going with his eyes fixed on a far greater trophy autograph: Alastair Down's.

"Mr Down," he said in front of the hushed gathering, "could I ever be having your autograph and would you also be telling me the winner of the Hennessy?" SEPTEMBER 20, 2005

WHAT is it with racing journalists and music at the moment? Last week we had Alastair Down and his NBF (new best friend) Bruce Springsteen in a pub signing – note that's signing not singing – autographs together. This week news has finally reached us from the Shepherds Bush Empire where, during a concert by the band Half Man Half Biscuit, lead singer Nigel Blackwell gave Radio 5 Live's voice of racing, Cornelius Lysaght, a name check.

At first glance Cornelius, three-quarters man, quarter rather nice bottle of Chablis, and Half Man Half Biscuit are a slightly incongruous match and not necessarily one you'd marry together. Put it the opposite way round – it's a bit like the lovely Kylie Minogue breaking off halfway through 'I Should Be So Lucky' to give John Egan a name check.

According to one reviewer the band are as savage as they are whimsical and "an unexpected dessert for British post-punk teenagers who lamented the demise of bands with bite". From Liverpool, Blackwell's first band was called 'Split Gut' which lasted nine minutes and he joined a couple of mates from 'Attempted Moustache' to form Half Man Half Biscuit.

As their best album Back In The DHSS suggests, however, they like sport, are avid listeners of 5 Live and have a satirical sense of humour, all of which brings Cornelius into the equation. Their canon contains songs like All I Want For Christmas Is A Dukla Prague Away Kit, Dickie Davies Eyes and ******' 'Ell It's Fred Titmus. Other titles include The Trumpton Riots, Sealclubbing and I Left My Heart in Papworth General.

As vicious as they sound, however, it transpires that Blackwell is something of a softie – he used to have a picture of the Grand National winner Lucius on his bedroom wall as a boy.

A name check is one thing but not until he's had a mention in a song will Cornelius join such luminaries as Hattie Jacques, Arthur Askey, Brian Moore (the football commentator), Nobby Stiles and Rod Hull. "It's nice to get a mention," he says. "It hints at hidden depths." SEPTEMBER 27, 2005

ONE of the golden rules of tipping – at least I've never seen it done – is not to apologise for a duff tip. Now Saturday's Coral/Racing Post Naps Table, the best bets of 53 of our newspapers' leading tipsters, wasn't exactly heaving with accurate advice for the afternoon's big one.

No-one had – let's remind ourselves of his form – the Welsh National/ Becher Chase winner Silver Birch. Congratulations to Pegasus of the

News of the World and Janus of the *Northern Echo* for selecting the runner-up Mckelvey. No-one had the appropriately named Slim Pickings in third. And the fourth, Philson Run? You're kidding aren't you? Not collectively our greatest moment I think you'll concur.

Now it was, of course, the Grand National, when a hunch, a good story or a nice-sounding name is given equal import to previous form. Even though I gave the followers of my tips – they hold their AGM in a telephone box – a good run for their money with Liberthine in fifth I am kicking myself and here it is – an apology for my tipping. Having never planted a tree in my life I've just stuck a load of silver birch saplings, the equivalent of a small wood, into the ground. I should have known. APRIL 17, 2007

ONE OF the biggest changes in racing journalism has been the amount of ridicule the stewards come in for these days – it's virtually non-existent. Not since a member of York's panel famously told executives from Channel 4 to take their hands out of their pockets when talking to the stewards have they made the back pages.

There are several possible reasons for this. The upper age limit for stewards has been reduced – to 93. They only ever reverse a result once a blue moon now rather than once a day. They have more camera angles than the BBC and they have the redoubtable former cavalry officer Malcolm Wallace to hold their hands. They don't drink, can't bet and there have been major advances in corrective eye surgery. And it's also quite possible, I concede, that they are better trained and actually better at it than some of their forebears. So you get the gist – it's not really the done thing these days.

They may have the very modern name of Urban-i but the builders of the new Doncaster have an old-fashioned sense of humour that harked me back to the good ol' days when steward-baiting was fashionable. For underneath the sign that proclaims the 'stewards' room' is the same notice – in Braille. SEPTEMBER 18, 2007

A JOURNALIST has just returned from a visit to Dubai. Put up at a smart hotel, there was plenty of time before racing, which takes place in the cool of the desert evening, to do his own thing during the day. That ranged from sightseeing to relaxing poolside.

Our intrepid reporter chose the latter option and pulled up a sun lounger for a healthy dose of what the tour operators call winter sun, something that has been singularly lacking from our skies lately.

He was just getting comfortable when a waiter came round asking him if he would like a fresh towel. No, he didn't need a fresh towel. He was just about to nod off again when the waiter asked him if he wanted a cocktail. No, thankyou.

His eyes were just closing again when the waiter, by now becoming something of a pest, asked him if he needed the parasol moving. No, he was fine, thanks. And so it continued ad infinitum. First to our man and then, each in succession, to a long line of sun-seekers lined up alongside the pool. Bowl of peanuts, a drink, an iced coffee, you name it. Nothing too much trouble except, of course, taking a running jump.

Finally the waiter came round with a bowl of freshly sliced and chilled cucumber. "Do you know," said the journalist, cracking at last. "I don't mind if I do." And he helped himself to a good double handful of the succulent fruit and started chomping away.

The waiter looked somewhat surprised but moved on to the next sun lounger where its occupant daintily plucked out two wafer-thin cucumber rings and placed them on her eyes. And this cosmetic consumption of the cucumber continued around the pool. You live and learn in this game. MARCH 21, 2006

NICKY HENDERSON was involved in two cases of mistaken identity at this year's Cheltenham. Having won the race named in memory of his late father, the Johnny Henderson Grand Annual Chase with Greenhope, he was also presented with the Racing Post award for leading trainer at the meeting. But on a recount, like a Belarus election, it went to Paul Nicholls.

Earlier the trainer's family, including his similar-looking but not identical brother Harry, had gathered for a lunch to celebrate the race. While Nicky was absent from his seat, Richard Pitman came up and engaged Harry in conversation in the belief it was Nicky. "It would have been a very interesting interview," says Nicky. "If there was one person at the meeting who knows the square root of nothing about racing it's Harry."

'Pitters', who congratulated Harry on his double the previous day, put his hands up. "I did get one slightly odd answer to a question," he says like the professional he is, "but I put it behind me and moved on." MARCH 21, 2006

ASCOT left some helpful if optimistic guidance lying around the press room last Friday explaining what action should be taken on receipt of a bomb threat. Much of it, like the first question which you should ask the 'bomber' – 'Where is the bomb right now?' – is common sense. Likewise 'when', 'why' and 'what will trigger it?'

It strikes me, however, in the unlikely event that Al Qaeda does give a warning and that you've already engaged them for seven questions that they won't be hanging around long enough to give answers to questions 8, 9, and 10. What is your name, address and telephone number? JULY 26, 2005

SO IT'S possible then. Goodwood's annual Lifetime Achievement Award has gone, this year, to a journalist, mind you no ordinary one. The Duke of Richmond recently presented this year's winner, Peter Willett, with a painting entitled 'Down at The Start, Goodwood' by local artist Paul Maze, who was Churchill's artistic mentor.

Peter, a director at Goodwood for 27 years, was racing and breeding consultant to the *Sporting Chronicle* and *Horse & Hound* for years, has written 12 books and has served on numerous racing committees. As consultant to several studs he was also responsible for the equine liaisons that produced Celtic Swing, Moon Madness, Polygamy and Reference Point.

On receiving the painting from the duke, Peter recalled a story told to him by General Sir Randle 'Gerry' Feilden, who went on to become one of the great post-war racing administrators, to make the point about how much racing had changed since he became involved.

As a young man Feilden was racing at Windsor when he was roped in to act as a steward for someone who hadn't turned up despite knowing little then about the job. After the second race there was an objection by the second to the winner so he went up to the stewards' room, where all the panel except one had assembled for the ensuing inquiry. "Have you seen Major So-And-So," the chairman of the panel asked the man on the door. "Yes," he replied. "He told me to tell you he'd be just a minute. He's gone to have a bet on the objection." JULY 27, 2004

IN THE belief that after a spell on the market Luke Harvey had sold one of racing's most popular pubs, the Blowing Stone, in Kingston Lisle the Radio 5 Live presenter laid on a farewell party a week ago. However, as anyone with any dealings in property will know, nothing is sold until the money is in the bank.

The morning after the most financially lucrative night of his whole tenure Luke received the bad news that the deal had fallen through. "It was one hell of a night," explains Luke, "but not half as good as the reopening party 24 hours later."

It was, happily for Luke, only a temporary glitch and he finally hands over the keys to the 'Blower' tomorrow. "Even I haven't got the nerve for a second farewell party," he adds. FEBRUARY 28, 2006

YOU CANNOT accuse Emily Jones, amateur rider, ATR pundit and now, having bought a small two-horse box, big into the equine transport business, of not working all the hours that God gives. She's been pretty busy at the wheel lately in her purple and orange liveried vehicle.

Last week, though, she received a call from a man, whose own van had broken down, asking her to transport 50 racing pigeons from Winchester to Skegness on Sunday for a championship race. "It's all pretty basic," he said. "If you take the partition out they'll fit in nicely in their cages."

And so he continued, explaining some of the intricacies of pigeon transportation. "But there is one thing," he stressed. "One of these birds is pigeon racing's equivalent of Dawn Run, she's going for her fourth championship but she's a bad traveller; she'd have to sit on the front seat next to you. She also needs 24-hour surveillance so I wouldn't want anyone to know you're moving them."

From the start Emily had harboured a doubt in her mind about whether or not this was a dubious call but she's hungry for work and after he had massaged her ego – "I know you'd do the job well" – and offered her a grand, she pretty much bit his arm off and agreed to it. For "obvious security reasons", he said he'd ring her back on Saturday with a postcode from where she should collect the birds and she awaited the call.

However, there's nothing more dangerous at the moment than a car-full of bored jump jockeys on a long journey back from the races looking for a wind-up. The architect of the fanciful pigeon story was conditional jockey Kevin Tobin who, for his colleagues' amusement, had the phone on loudspeaker. "The bastards," reflected Emily later. AUGUST 26, 2008

AN INCIDENT was narrowly averted at Haydock on Betfair Chase day when a BBC camera crew was moved from the start of the first televised chase before it was trampled by runners eager to get a flyer.

This was similar to an incident at Thirsk one day when the last of 18 runners for a sprint were being loaded. A hundred yards down the course a young man was being filmed with the stalls as the backdrop.

"What the hell are you doing?" asked the starter.

"Oh," said the presenter, "we're nothing to do with the racing. We're students from Leeds University working on a mathematics project."

"Well," said the quick-thinking starter, "you'd better move quick.

Otherwise work out how many 18 x 4 is and that's how many hooves are about to gallop over the top of you." DECEMBER 1, 2008

THE PRACTICE of book burning has been going on since Old Testament times (Jeremiah 36:1-26) but the ceremonial placing of a book upon the fire appears to be a relatively new practice in the genteel world of horseracing.

Never mind, Richard Dunwoody will be pleased to know he still has at least one fan out there, apart from his mum and members of the Royal Geographical Society. News has reached the publishers of Mick Fitzgerald's autobiography *Better Than Sex* that one hardcore female Woody fan burned her copy because she felt it was just too derogatory about her hero.

Although Fitzgerald leaves the reader with the overall impression that he still regards Dunwoody as the greatest jump jockey to have ridden, the problem stems from the chapter entitled 'Woody Woes'.

It describes a fight they had in the changing room following the Mitsubishi Shogun Chase at Ascot – goodness, those were the days when a car manufacturer was going well enough to sponsor a race – which was the result of Dunwoody going for a non-existent gap.

I'm not entirely sure of the year but it must have been about that time when the stewards were picking on Timmy Murphy because, according to the author, he was only a peripheral figure in the incident but the net result was that he was given a ten-day ban for dangerous riding. DECEMBER 16, 2008

THERE were echoes of 1992 for one racing correspondent this weekend. Believing the weekend's bigger racing story might be Big Brown becoming the first horse since Affirmed 30 years ago to win the Triple Crown he went to Belmont, New York. It looked a good call until the great pin-cushion, running without steroids for the first time in the three-race series, trotted over the line in last.

In 1992 a number of racing hacks went to cover 'wonderhorse'

Arazi's run in the Kentucky Derby. While there, they gathered round a crackling radio in the press room at Churchill Downs to hear Lester Piggott, freshly out of jail, steering Rodrigo De Triano to success in the 2,000 Guineas.

The importance of the story was not lost on one local journalist. "You guys," he said on hearing the result, "sound like you're stuck the wrong side of the Pond." To compound their misery Arazi finished down the field behind Lil E Tee. JUNE 10, 2008

Index